Learning and Libraries
in an Information Age

Learning and Libraries in an Information Age: Principles and Practice

Edited by Barbara K. Stripling

1999
Libraries Unlimited, Inc.
and Its Division
Teacher Ideas Press
Englewood, Colorado

Dedication

To Judy M. Pitts
A fine scholar, committed professional,
and true friend

📖

LIBRARIES UNLIMITED, INC.
and Its Division
Teacher Ideas Press
P.O. Box 6633
Englewood, CO 80155-6633
(800) 237-6124
www.lu.com/tip

Library of Congress Cataloging-in-Publication Data
Learning and libraries in an information age : principles and practice / Barbara K. Stripling, editor.
    p. cm. -- (Principles and practice series)
  Includes bibliographical references and index.
  ISBN 1-56308-666-2
    1. Library orientation for school children--United States. 2. Library orientation for high school students--United States. 3. Information retrieval--Study and teaching (Elementary)--United States. 4. Information retrieval--Study and teaching (Secondary)--United States. I. Stripling, Barbara K.

Z711.2 .L42 1999
027.62'6 21--dc21
                                                    99-045329

Contents

Acknowledgments, xv

Introduction, xvii
   Barbara K. Stripling

Contributors, xxi

Part I
Overview, 1

Chapter 1
Literacy and Learning for the Information Age, 3
   Carol C. Kuhlthau

   Introduction, 3
   Technology's Effects on the Learning Environment, 4
   Learning in Information-Rich Environments, 7
         Three Basic Charges of Education, 8
         Restructuring for the Information Age, 9
   An Inquiry Approach to Learning, 11
         Information Search Process, 14
         Information Literacy Competencies, 15
   Conclusion, 19
   References and Additional Resources, 20

Part II
Context of Learning, 23

Chapter 2
How Do We Learn?, 25
Joy H. McGregor

Introduction, 25
Theoretical Approaches, 27
Behaviorism, 27
Cognitive Psychology and Constructivism, 29
Library Applications, 33
Learning Models, 34
Inquiry Learning, 34
Student-Centered Learning, 35
Cooperative Learning, 35
Brain-Based Learning, 36
Authentic, Meaningful Learning, 37
Factors in the Learning Process, 37
Multiple Intelligences, 37
Learning Styles, 38
Motivation, 39
Thinking and Learning, 40
Bloom's Taxonomy, 41
Critical Thinking, 42
Creative Thinking, 43
Metacognition, 44
Mental Models, 45
Tools to Promote Learning, 46
Coaching, 46
Questioning, 47
From Theory to Practice, 48
References and Additional Resources, 51

Chapter 3
Information Literacy Skills Models: Defining the Choices, 54
Greg Byerly and Carolyn S. Brodie

Introduction, 54
Definitions of Information Literacy, 55

Information Literacy Skills Models: Historical
 Background, 57
Current Information Literacy Skills Models, 59
  The Big6 Skills™ Model, 60
  Pathways to Knowledge™ Model
   (Pappas and Tepe), 61
  Essential Skills for Information Literacy
   (WLMA), 64
  INFOhio DIALOGUE Model (Ohio), 64
  Model Information Literacy Guidelines
   (Colorado), 65
  From Library Skills to Information Literacy
   (California School Library Association), 66
  AASL/AECT Information Literacy Standards
   for Student Learning, 67
Six Common Components of Information Literacy
 Skills Models, 69
  Component 1: Need for Information, 69
  Component 2: Information Literacy Skills, 70
  Component 3: Location of Information, 70
  Component 4: Evaluation and Organization
   of Information, 71
  Component 5: Use of Information, 72
  Component 6: Evaluation of Process
   and Product, 72
Conclusion, 73
References, 76
Significant Information Literacy Documents, 78
Information About Information Literacy on the Web, 80
Selected Books Connected to Information Literacy, 81

Chapter 4

Learning in a Technological Context, 83
 Elizabeth K. Goldfarb

Introduction, 83
Greater Access to Information, 85
  What About Safety?, 87
  What About Privacy?, 87

What About Ethical Conduct?, 88
Expanded Information Formats, 88
Telephone, 89
Distance Learning, 90
Computer Software, 90
CD-ROMs, 91
Internet Sites, 93
Changing Schoolwide Structure and Commitment, 94
Changing the Learning, 97
The Nature of Learning with Technology, 97
Information Literacy, 101
From Traditional Research to Inquiry-Based
Learning, 106
Beginning Projects in Inquiry, 108
Assessment and Reflection, 109
Changing the Teaching, 111
A Schoolwide Focus on Inquiry, 111
Requirements for Staff Development, 113
Learning in the Future, 116
Continuously Evolving Technology, 116
New Ways of Promoting Learning, 117
Online Mentors, Experts, and Pen-Pals, 118
Interactive Learning Projects, 118
Changes in Learning from Technology, 119
References, 119
Additional Resources, 124
Books, 124
Periodicals, 126
Internet Resources, 127

Part III

Context of Collaborative Planning and Teaching, 131

Chapter 5

Collaboration in Teaching and Learning, 133

Donna L. Peterson

Introduction, 133
What Is Collaboration?, 134

The Changing Role of the Library Media Specialist, 137
Changing Views of Library Media Programs, 138
Collaboration as a Model for Improving Learning, 142
Barriers That Influence Collaboration, 145
    Norms of Teaching, 146
    Time, 147
    Change, 149
Collaboration Requires Knowledge and Skills, 152
    Knowing How Teachers Plan, 152
    Interpersonal Relations Are Important, 153
    Creating a Collaborative Vision, 155
    Lessons Learned, 157
Summary, 159
References and Additional Resources, 160

Chapter 6

Standards-Based Teaching in the Library Media Center, 163
Sheila Salmon

Introduction, 163
Effort-Based Learning, 165
    Implications for the Library Media
        Center, 166
Clear Expectations, 168
    Implications for the Library Media
        Center, 169
Academic Rigor in the Thinking Curriculum, 170
    Implications for the Library Media
        Center, 171
Accountable Talk, 175
    Implications for the Library Media
        Center, 175
Socializing Intelligence, 176
    Implications for the Library Media
        Center, 176
Learning as Apprenticeship, 177
    Implications for the Library Media Center, 177
Conclusion, 178
References and Additional Resources, 180

Chapter 7

Creating Meaningful Assignments for Student Learning, 181
Denise Rehmke

Purpose, 182
Content Objectives, 183
Information Literacy Objectives, 186
Summary, 195
Suggested Additional Resources, 195

Chapter 8

**Making Sense of a Changing World: Digitized
Primary Source Documents in Schools, 196**
Mark W. Gordon

Archives on the Web, 196
Collaboration: Archives in the Classroom, 198
Seizing the Opportunities, 201
New Roles and Possibilities, 202
Notes, 205
Reference, 205

Chapter 9

Assessment: A Tool for Developing Lifelong Learners, 206
Jean Donham and Barbara Barnard Stein

School Library Media Specialists' Interest
    in Assessment, 207
        Authenticity, 207
        Process, 208
        Integration of Curriculum, 209
        Complex Thinking and Complex Tasks, 210
        Independent Learning, 211
The Purposes and Audiences for Assessment, 211
Match Between Assessment Technique and Purpose, 212
        Improve Student Growth, 213
        Improve Instruction, 220
        Recognize Accomplishment, 221
        Improve a Program, 221

Relationship Between Assessment and
Information Literacy, 224
Conclusion, 226
Notes, 227
References and Additional Resources, 227

Part IV
Context of Library Media Programs, 229

Chapter 10
Developing a Collaborative Access Environment: Meeting the Resource Needs of the Learning Community, 231
Sandra M. Hughes and Jacqueline C. Mancall

The Environment of Information Services, 231
The Paradigm Shift and Its Effect on the
Teaching/Learning Environment, 233
Implications for the Collector, 236
Traditional Collection Development, 236
Constructivist Collection Development, 238
The Collaborative Access Environment Emerges, 240
Learner Characteristics, 241
Teaching and Learning Context, 242
Knowledge Base, 242
Partnerships, 242
The Process of Developing a Collaborative Access
Environment: An Example, 244
Collector Behaviors in the Learning
Community, 245
Becoming a Change Agent, Resource Guide,
Leader, and Learner: An Example, 250
Prescription for Positive Change, 252
Matching the Access Environment to the Requirements
of the Learning Community: Strategies, 254
Challenges Central to the Success of the
Collaborative Access Environment, 255
The Challenges, 257
Notes, 258
References and Additional Resources, 258

Chapter 11

Designing Library Media Programs for Student Learning, 260
Barbara K. Stripling

Introduction, 260
Guidelines for Effective Programs, 264
Using the Rubric to Guide Program Development, 266
Program Development Process, 269
    Step One: Meet with Administrator(s), 269
    Step Two: Form Library Advisory Committee, 270
    Step Three: Develop Shared Vision, 270
    Step Four: Select Areas for Improvement, 271
    Step Five: Develop Action Plan, 271
    Step Six: Share with Entire Faculty, 272
    Step Seven: Implement Action Plan, 272
Driving School Change, 273
Notes, 274
Reference, 274

Part V

Connecting to the Community, 297

Chapter 12

A Community of Learning for the Information Age, 299
Dianne Oberg

The Information Age and Schools, 299
A Community of Learning, 301
    School as a Community of Learning, 302
    Creating a Community of Learning Within
      and Beyond the School, 304
    Obstacles to Building a Community
      of Learning, 306
Building a Community of Learning, 309
    The Principal, 310
    The Teachers, 311
    The Students, 311
    The Parents, 312
    The Library Media Specialists, 312

Library Media Specialists and the Development
of the Community of Learning, 313
Working with Principals, 313
Working with Teachers, 314
Working with Students, 315
Working with Parents, 317
Working with the Community, 318
From Student Learning in an Information
Age to Communities of Learning in an
Information Age, 319
Whole-School Approach, 319
Implications for the Library Media Program, 320
References, 322

Part VI

Connecting to Research, 325

Chapter 13

Student Learning: Linking Research and Practice, 327
A. James Jones and Carrie Gardner

Introduction, 327
Focus on Learning, 328
AASL Task Force on Learning Through
the Library, 330
Organization of Chapter, 330
Section 1: Students and Learning in an
Electronic Age, 332
The Children We Serve, 332
Technology and Information—Emerging Trends,
333
Section 2: Standards—Content and Performance, 335
Overview of Standards, 335
Web Tips, 339
Literacy Standards—Developing Capable
Readers, 340
Section 3: Instructional Strategies, 345
Leadership, 345
Collaboration—Integrating the Curricula, 348

Section 4: Assessment, 350
General, 351
Web Tips, 354
Portfolios, 355
Section 5: Role of the Library Media Program in the
Electronic Age, 356
Technology and Copyright, 356
Library Media Program and the
Curriculum—Making a Connection, 357
Next Steps, 359
References, 359

Index, 361

Acknowledgments

I would like to thank Libraries Unlimited for initiating the Principles and Practice series and supporting my efforts to crystallize its vision and format. That support by everyone in the organization reflects strong commitment to the school library media field.

In the early stages of development, I called upon an informal advisory board to offer ideas, direction, and advice. These professionals provided much of the early brainstorming from which the focus of the first volume emerged. My special thanks to Debbie Abilock, Debby Coleman, Jean Donham, Ken Haycock, Sheila Salmon, and Jane Bandy Smith.

The authors of this volume's chapters deserve high praise for their enthusiastic willingness to dig deep into their own knowledge, to extend their own thinking, to branch out to new connections, and to maintain a focus on implementation for practicing school library media specialists. All of them were committed to creating useful, practical pieces that will actually make a difference in school library media programs. I feel very privileged to have worked with this fine group of authors.

My commitment to the integration of theory and practice in the school library media field has been nurtured over the years by a number of special friends and colleagues. I will mention a few here, but I am indebted to many more. Colleagues in Arkansas have been my long-standing collaborative partners: Judy Pitts, Don Deweese, David Loertscher, Jody Charter, Retta Patrick, Margaret Crank, and my fellow library media specialists, as well as teachers Thelma Tarver, Susie Stewart, Judy Gregson Schwab, Becky Cox, Laura Underwood, and other outstanding educators at Fayetteville High School.

My experience as part of the Library Power network has had a profound impact on my ideas and abilities. I am especially indebted to the DeWitt Wallace–Reader's Digest Fund; to the Library Power directors in nineteen sites across the country; to Suzanne Fraley, Steve Prigohzy, Sandra Blankenship, Janice Neal, and Kristina Montague at the Public Education Foundation in Chattanooga, Tennessee; and to the wonderful school library media specialists and principals in Chattanooga, from whom I learned so much.

Much of my library vision has been formed through my participation in the American Association of School Librarians. I continue to be supported and challenged by my AASL friends across the country, including Pam Berger, Sharon Coatney, Violet Harada, Ken Haycock, Carol Kroll, Jackie Mancall, Joy McGregor, Marjorie Pappas, Donna Peterson, Sheila Salmon, Trixie Schmidt, and Julie Walker.

Finally, I want to thank my two sons, Thomas and Ryan, who have always allowed me to steal time from them to pursue my professional dreams.

Introduction

This volume inaugurates a new series for Libraries Unlimited. Principles and Practice replaces a previous series, School Library Media Annual, and it differs in significant ways.

Principles and Practice is intended to provide practicing library media professionals with research and theory that are grounded in effective practice. Each volume in this biannual series will probe essential principles and avenues for implementation in areas that relate to our bottom line: student achievement.

Another attribute of the Principles and Practice series is that every volume will focus on a theme, in order to provide an in-depth look at a major idea. The theme for this volume is learning in an information age.

A primary emphasis on learning in school libraries represents a paradigm shift for our field, one that is not yet universally understood or effectively implemented. School library media specialists must step forward as instructional leaders in their schools to design library media programs that help students learn important ideas in the curriculum and learn how to learn in this information age. We must prepare our students to *know* and to be able to *do* (to solve problems, draw conclusions, make decisions, and construct their own understandings). No longer is it acceptable for any teacher to say, "Well, I taught it"—the questions now must be, "Did the students learn it?" and "Can they use it?"

The library is in a prime position to lead the focus on learning in a school. By offering access to a world of information and by teaching information literacy, or learning-how-to-learn, skills, school library media specialists collaborate with classroom teachers to prepare students to learn in any situation.

To create learning-centered libraries, we must understand fundamental principles about learning, information literacy, instructional design, collaboration, teaching, collection development, assessment, and building communities of learning. This volume is organized into six sections to provide both background information and practical implementation strategies.

In Part One, "Overview," Carol Kuhlthau provides an overall context for our examination of literacy and learning in an information age.

The next section, "Context of Learning," features three chapters that provide essential background on learning. Joy McGregor delineates major learning theories, shows how they interrelate, and outlines strategies for incorporating those theories into library media practice. Two authors, Greg Byerly and Carolyn Brodie, analyze and compare several information literacy skills models, laying out six essential components of any such model. In the third chapter in this section, Elizabeth Goldfarb provides an in-depth look at the effect of technology on learning and teaching. She includes an extensive list of Internet sites and other references that will help any educator design programs that use technology for learning.

Because no library media program or library media specialist can be effective if isolated from learning throughout the school, the next section focuses on the "Context of Collaborative Planning and Teaching." Donna Peterson shares principles that underlie good collaboration, including an understanding of some of the barriers that affect its implementation. Sheila Salmon offers specific and effective teaching strategies for a standards-based approach to learning through the library media center. In Chapter 7, a practicing school library media specialist, Denise Rehmke, shares her approach for creating meaningful assignments. Mark Gordon, a retired library media specialist and consultant, describes an effective way for teachers and library media specialists to use primary source documents, which are becoming more readily available through the Internet. The final element in the collaborative instruction section is assessment of student learning. Two professionals, Jean Donham and Barbara Barnard Stein, have developed both a comprehensive overview of assessment techniques and very specific implementation examples.

The fourth part, "Context of Library Media Programs," brings the learning focus to the library media program itself. Sandra Hughes and Jacqueline Mancall have combined their expertise to offer seminal insight into collection development in an age of constructivist learning, collaboration, and technology. The editor of this volume, Barbara Stripling, shares a rubric and strategies for designing library media programs based on learning.

The last two sections extend the learning focus beyond the library walls into the community and the world of information and research. In Part Five, "Connecting to the Community," Dianne Oberg lays out strategies for building a community of learning by connecting to principals, teachers, students, parents, and the community at large.

The final part, "Connecting to Research," leads us to our own continued learning. A. James Jones and Carrie

Gardner have provided an extensive annotated bibliography of sources about learning and libraries. The bibliography is part of the Web site of the Learning Through the Library Task Force of the American Association of School Librarians.

Changing practice is never easy. Nevertheless, the evolution of school library programs toward the goal of becoming centers of learning for students, teachers, administrators, parents, and communities is underway. The authors of this volume offer both principles and practice to support and provoke this evolutionary process. As we succeed in building library programs based on learning, so will we enhance the success of our most priceless asset, our students.

Contributors

Carolyn S. Brodie
Associate Professor
School of Library and Information Science
Kent State University
Kent, Ohio

Greg Byerly
Associate Professor
School of Library and Information Science
Kent State University
Kent, Ohio

Jean Donham
Assistant Professor
School of Library and Information Science
The University of Iowa
Iowa City, Iowa

Carrie Gardner
Library Media Specialist
Milton Hershey School
Hershey, Pennsylvania

Elizabeth K. Goldfarb
Program Officer
Library, Literacy, and Technology Unit
New Visions for Public Schools
New York, New York

Mark W. Gordon
Library Consultant
Santa Cruz, California

Sandra M. Hughes
Assistant Professor
College of Information Science and Technology
Drexel University
Philadelphia, Pennsylvania

A. James Jones
National Director of Programs
one2one Learning Foundation
Dallas, Texas

Carol C. Kuhlthau
Professor of Library and Information Science
School of Communication, Information and Library
    Studies
Rutgers, The State University of New Jersey
New Brunswick, New Jersey

Jacqueline C. Mancall
Professor of Information Studies
College of Information Science and Technology
Drexel University
Philadelphia, Pennsylvania

Joy H. McGregor
Associate Professor
School of Library and Information Studies
Texas Woman's University
Denton, Texas

Dianne Oberg
Associate Professor
School of Library and Information Studies
University of Alberta
Edmonton, Alberta, Canada

Donna L. Peterson
Director of Library Media Services
Lincoln Public Schools
Lincoln, Nebraska

Denise Rehmke
Library Media Specialist
West High School
Iowa City, Iowa

Sheila Salmon
Senior Vice-President
New Visions for Public Schools
New York, New York

Barbara Barnard Stein
Library Media Specialist
Weber Elementary School
Iowa City Community School District
Iowa City, Iowa

Barbara K. Stripling
Director of Instructional Services
Fayetteville Public Schools
Fayetteville, Arkansas

Part I

Overview

1

Literacy and Learning for the Information Age

Carol C. Kuhlthau*

INTRODUCTION

The theme of this volume is student learning in the information age. This introductory chapter addresses some of the issues related to the broad conceptual view of information literacy and its importance for education in the information age. A number of critical questions are discussed in this section. How is learning in the information age different from learning before computer technology was introduced? What is literacy in the information age? What is information literacy? Why is information literacy so essential to learning in the information age? How does information literacy relate to restructuring schools? What role and responsibility do the library and the library media specialist have in the information-age school?

*Portions of this chapter were presented in keynote addresses at the Conference on the Future of School Libraries of the New Jersey School Development Council and at the 25th Anniversary Conference of the Pennsylvania School Librarians Association.

TECHNOLOGY'S EFFECTS ON
THE LEARNING ENVIRONMENT

When we think about learning in the information age, what comes to mind first is the presence of technology. Computer technology has significantly changed learning environments in schools in the past ten years. In a similar way, of course, technology has had a substantial impact on the way people conduct their daily lives in the world outside of schools. An important characteristic of technology is that it is in a continuous state of innovation and development. The computer technology of today will be as outdated in the not-too-distant future as the typewriter and filmstrip have become. This climate of instability and uncertainty is the fundamental nature of the information age.

The influence of technology on learning is evident in every school across the country, to a greater or lesser extent. The goal of having every school connected to the Internet is fast becoming a reality. These connections make available vast amounts of information, in many cases directly into the classroom. For the first time, schools have immediate access to a wide variety of unfiltered, unselected, unauthorized information. In addition, computer resources on CD-ROM and computer-assisted instruction (CAI) are commonplace in K-12 education, with new software products flooding the market daily. The economic profit in this market ensures continued production of more, if not always better, instructional materials.

Views of how to regard the infiltration of technology into schooling and learning differ widely. At the extreme ends of the spectrum are two opposing positions, one I call utopian advocacy and the other, cautious warning. The utopian advocacy view is represented by Papert (1994) and Negroponte (1995) from the Media Lab at MIT. Papert, of

LOGO fame, makes a strong case for computers as enabling devices that allow children to perform tasks far beyond what they would be able to do on their own. In his book, *The Children's Machine: Rethinking School in the Age of the Computer*, Papert advocates new approaches to learning to read, write, and calculate for young elementary school students using computer technologies (Papert 1994). Negroponte, in his book *Being Digital*, states that a radical new form of thinking is emerging as a result of using computer technologies; the technologies are changing the way people learn, communicate, and create in the information age (Negroponte 1995). These two authors see technology as enhancing people's lives and are advocates for approaching the information age as a time of utopian promise.

At the other end of the spectrum is the cautious-warning view represented by Stoll and many others. Typical of this view is an article in *Atlantic Monthly* in July 1997 in which Oppenheimer warns that "just hooking up doesn't ensure learning." He cautions that there is more to learning than just making more resources available through new technologies (Oppenheimer 1997). Along this same line, Stoll (1995), in his book *Silicon Snake Oil*, makes an impassioned plea for acknowledging that virtual reality does not replace real experience. He presents a compelling, often humorous, case that students need to draw from real-life experiences to gain a depth of understanding. He supports his position with vivid, commonsense examples (such as: when one is studying astronomy, nothing takes the place of going out at night to look at the sky).

We need to listen to both views. What they tell us is that the learning environment is changing and we need to be cognizant of what it means to be human within this new environment. How do students learn in the technological environments of the information age? How do students learn to live meaningfully in the world around them? Here we are getting close to a definition of *information literacy*. Being literate in the information age involves the ability to find meaning in the vast barrage of diverse messages that form our learning environment. Information literacy involves being able not only to locate information, but also to interpret it within the context of our real-life experience. Information literacy is the ability to use information meaningfully in all aspects of our daily lives.

One of the most important characteristics of technology is that it changes the learning environment from a scarcity of resources to an abundance of resources (McClintock 1996). The impact of this extremely important change, on the learning environment within schools as well as in the world outside the school, cannot be overemphasized. The textbook was an excellent resource for solving the problem of a shortage of resources. One textbook contained sufficient information to conduct an entire course. The textbook presented predigested information in a logical sequence designed for students at a specific level. In an environment of scarcity of resources, the textbook was an ideal tool for learning.

However, the environment of abundant resources makes the textbook approach to teaching and learning inadequate and out-of-date. To prepare students for the world outside of the school, we need to develop ways for them to learn from information as they will encounter it in real-life situations, information that is not predigested, carefully selected, or logically organized. In pretechnology days, the library addressed the shortage of resources by providing a carefully selected and classified collection of resources that targeted the needs of particular groups of students. We have moved rapidly from dependence on the contained collection to direct access to a vast range of networked information on the Internet and to a variety of digital libraries. Some people go so far as to say that now, because we have information coming into schools and classrooms from the Internet, we may not need the library. So what is the role of the library in the information-rich environment?

Just as information can no longer be managed and delivered, so the act of teaching has moved away from controlled delivery or didacticism. The role of the teacher in an information-age school changes from transmitter of knowledge to facilitator and coach in the process of learning. What are the implications for the role of the library media specialist in the information-age school?

LEARNING IN INFORMATION-RICH ENVIRONMENTS

Before we address the important role of teachers and librarians, let us consider a bit further the critical issues of how learning is different in the information age and what it means to be literate in this time of abundant resources. Today's students are not only engaged in learning in information-rich environments, but also in learning how to learn in these new environments. This involves the ability to learn in dynamic situations where information is constantly changing. It involves the ability to manage information overload, where determining what is enough information is as significant as locating and selecting relevant information. Most importantly, it involves the ability to find meaning by making sense of numerous and diverse messages that do not fit together neatly in a predigested, prepared text. Students must learn to construct personal understanding from incompatible and inconsistent information.

Literacy, then, is the ability to construct one's own meaning from an information-rich environment. The challenge for the information-age school is to educate children for living and learning in an information-rich environment. Teachers cannot do this alone. The library media specialist plays a central role in meeting this challenge.

Three Basic Charges of Education

The three basic charges of education in a free society are to prepare students for the workplace, citizenship, and daily living. Let us briefly consider how these three charges must be interpreted in the information age. First, in preparing students for the workplace, consideration must be given to the ways that technology changes the nature of work and raises new questions about how we contribute and innovate productively in the global economy. Second, in preparing students for citizenship, consideration must be given to the ways that technology changes our sense of community and raises pressing questions about how we participate as an informed electorate in a democratic society. Third, in preparing students for daily living, consideration must be given to the ways that technology increases the complexity of everyday life and raises troubling questions about how we gain a sense of self in relation to others and experience creativity and joy in our personal lives. Basic to meeting these three charges is developing student competence in learning and making sense of a variety of sources of information. All three charges involve an inquiry approach to information seeking and information use; inquiry underlies information literacy.

Thus, we return to the question of what it means to be literate in the information age. The basic skills of reading, writing, and calculating must be applied and adapted to information-rich environments and to new technologies. Teaching to the test, memorizing simple right answers, and reproducing texts are not enough to prepare students to lead fulfilled lives in the information age (Newmann,

Secada, and Wehlage 1995). Students need to develop the ability to learn in changing situations without becoming overwhelmed and discouraged. Students need to develop the ability to learn from abundant information without becoming frustrated, distracted, or bored. Students need to develop the ability to go beyond finding facts to constructing their own understanding at a deep level.

Restructuring for the Information Age

Information-age schools have to be restructured around an inquiry approach to learning rather than a transmission approach to teaching (Brown 1991). Students must be actively involved in the process of constructing meaning in an information-rich environment. Students must be engaged in problems and projects that involve them in raising questions, seeking information from a wide variety of resources, changing their questions as they learn more, identifying what they need to know more about, demonstrating what they have learned, and sharing their new understandings with a community of learners. Students must be creating what Bruner calls "products of mind" (Bruner 1990). This is a far cry from the "reproducing texts" and "repackaging information" that have been the focus of schools in too many cases. The library media center provides the means for an inquiry approach to learning.

The old practice of having twenty-five or more students locked in a classroom with one teacher and a textbook is out-of-date. The old school library as the resource room down the hall where students go once a week for library lessons or to check out a book is a model of the past. In the information-age school, the library is an extension of the classroom, integrated into the curriculum, providing opportunities and resources for students to pursue their lines of inquiry and construct their own meanings. The teacher and the library media specialist collaborate as an instructional team. The library media specialist provides essential expertise in (1) access to the network of resources, (2) selection of resources from the network, and (3) teaching the use of resources and information in the learning process. Connecting to the network of resources on the Internet is only the beginning of restructuring for the information age. The larger task involves accessing, selecting, and using these resources for learning across the curriculum. The expertise of the library media specialist as the information specialist is critical in the information-age school.

The trend toward national and state curriculum standards is viewed by many as the solution to the restructuring problem. Standards can indeed provide a good foundation for recommending the content and context of learning within K-12 schools. However, standards will not improve learning in schools where the teachers, administrators, and library media specialists are not fully committed to providing standards-based education. Underlying standards is the philosophy of creating enabling learning environments that authentically relate to real-world situations in which students can actively construct their own deep understandings. Standards without a strong philosophical base result in teaching to the test and shallow learning that does not transfer to real-world application. Standards with a strong base lead students beyond the test to developing abilities for living and working.

During the past ten years, we have come a long way toward building the philosophical base for learning in the information age. Considerable progress has been made in developing programs that incorporate problem-based learning, authentic assessment, and process approaches to basic skills. Standards can provide the content of learning, but an inquiry approach provides the *way* of learning in the information age. The combination of standards and information literacy prepares students for the information age.

AN INQUIRY APPROACH TO LEARNING

Inquiry requires information literacy skills. When library media specialists and teachers collaborate to create an inquiry approach to learning, students develop dual competencies in subject content and information literacy. The concept of information literacy has evolved from library skills to information skills and on to information literacy. Library skills stressed location of sources (for example, how to use the Dewey Decimal System or a periodical index to find specific sources). The information-skills approach stressed strategies for using information (for example, techniques for selecting and evaluating information related to a topic).

Information literacy incorporates both library skills and information skills, but adds the critical component of understanding the process of learning in information-rich environments. Information literacy extends library skills beyond the use of discrete skills and strategies to the ability to use complex information from a variety of sources to develop meaning or solve problems. Because information literacy is the ability to use information meaningfully in the workplace, for citizenship, and for daily living, it adapts the three charges of education in a free society to the information age.

Collaboration between teachers and library media specialists is essential for an inquiry approach to learning. The role of the library media specialist in the information-age school, therefore, has changed from providing resources and teaching library and information skills to enabling an inquiry approach to learning, from a variety of resources in each area of the curriculum, and thereby developing information literacy along with content learning.

The National Library Power Project, funded by the Dewitt Wallace-Reader's Digest Fund, has had considerable impact on the development of school libraries in more than 500 schools across the country (Hopkins and Zweizig 1998). Many lessons can be learned from this project about restructuring schools for the information age. As a research consultant in the evaluation of this project, I was involved in studying the impact on opportunities for student learning. Findings of the evaluation study reveal that the basic elements of a library in the information-age school are:

1. Adequate funding for resources and technology
2. A full-time library media specialist with competence in the use of resources and technology
3. Flexible scheduling, so that classes can work on projects for extended periods of time without being restricted to a rigid schedule with no connection to classroom work
4. Collaborative planning and teaching involving extensive professional development for teachers and library media specialists to design curriculum units supported by the expectation of administrators that this will happen.

Although these elements were found to be essential for improving the impact of the library in the school, having all of this in place did not guarantee a significant improvement in student learning. There was one critical element that was necessary for changing the learning environment of the school: an underlying philosophy of learning shared by the library media specialist, teachers, and principal with a mutual commitment to work together to create an environment based on this philosophy. The underlying commitment to an inquiry approach to learning in all areas of the curriculum was the essential element that challenged faculty and administrators to change their instructional approaches.

The case study of one school describes an instructional program based on an inquiry approach to learning where using library resources was not an additional, occasional activity but at the very center of the instructional program. Inquiry was a way to learn; the resources in the library and the research process were essential components in the learning process (Kuhlthau 1998). In schools where this philosophy was not present, restructuring was difficult to sustain. Collaboration with the library media specialist was viewed as just one more task in an already loaded curriculum. When research projects were considered add-ons rather than a way to learn, some change may have taken place initially, but the overall, long-range impact on student learning was minimal.

A clear understanding of how students learn in the information age, grounded in a commitment to creating inquiry-based learning, allows us to implement real change. When, as professional educators, we clearly understand the underlying principles of learning, we are able to distinguish useful from ephemeral innovation and are able to implement it without disruption and disillusionment. Library media specialists have the responsibility to align the change process in our schools with a philosophical center that is grounded in a clear understanding of student learning and the commitment to provide education that prepares students for living fulfilled lives in the information age.

Information Search Process

In my study of the research process, I have developed a deep respect for the process of learning that students experience when they encounter new ideas (Kuhlthau 1993a and b). My recent studies of information literacy in the workplace reveal that although workers do need a high level of skill in reading, writing, and calculating, they also need competence in the process of learning that leads them to innovate and create (Kuhlthau 1999). No longer does the workplace provide a lifelong job on the assembly line or in the office of the industrial age. Information-age workers need to be learning constantly as the environment around them changes. Novice and experienced workers alike are confronted with complex tasks that require learning something completely new as the world around them demands that they go beyond the routine. Information-age work requires people to be able to go beyond merely locating information; now they must add value by making sense of information in the context of the tasks to be accomplished. Preparation for this very sophisticated use of information must be at the center of K-12 education.

My work on the Information Search Process (ISP) has revealed that the research process is experienced by students in seven stages: Initiation, Selection, Exploration, Formulation, Collection, Presentation, Assessment (Kuhlthau 1994). One of the most important findings of this research is that the stages of Exploration and Formulation are critical to learning within the process. If students are to go beyond fact finding to learning something new, they need to engage in considerable exploration and formulation in the process of locating, gathering, and collecting information.

Exploration in learning is not necessarily linear. Nor are students simply solving an information problem as they formulate new ideas and construct their own understandings. A student in one of my studies captured it best when he said, "I have learned to accept that this is the way it works. Tomorrow I'll read this over and some parts will fall into place and some still won't...The mind doesn't take everything and put it into order automatically and that's it. Understanding that is the biggest help."

The inquiry approach develops skills that are fundamental to learning in an information-rich environment. Students develop competence beyond location and use strategies in their ability to interpret, understand, and learn from information—and *that* is information literacy. They learn to incorporate reading strategies, such as using prior knowledge, asking questions, drawing inferences. They learn that the research process is not an end in itself, but an avenue of discovery as they are building a knowledge base.

Information Literacy Competencies

In an important recent study, Limberg (1998) found that students approached information in three ways, with very different results. The first way was simple fact finding, in which students reported on information related to the topic being researched. The second way was looking for a right answer, in which students reported on information that they judged was right and left out what they judged was wrong. The third way was what Limberg called scrutinizing and analyzing. Students who approached information by scrutinizing and analyzing came up with their own perspectives of the topic. Although all three ways of using information are helpful for students to know, the third way is essential for information literacy.

An inquiry approach to learning should begin in the earliest grades and continue through high school (Kuhlthau 1997). Basic information literacy competencies in recalling, summarizing, paraphrasing, and extending can be developed with very young children. Recall what the story is about; summarize by telling the most interesting and important parts; paraphrase by telling in your own words; and extend by telling what else you know and what questions you have. These fundamentals of information literacy are central to the inquiry approach to learning for young children.

In the middle grades through high school, six strategies for learning from information can be introduced and applied across the curriculum: collaborating, conversing, continuing, choosing, charting, and composing. These strategies are useful in all stages of the learning process, but are particularly helpful during exploration and for formulating a focus in the search process.

Collaborating

Collaborating involves students working together to try out ideas and develop questions. Consulting with peers, in pairs or in small groups, at various stages in the research process enables students to learn from each other. Students need not be working on the same project to benefit from peer learning; they may be involved in completely different topics or on different aspects of the same project. Collaboration takes away from the common experience of isolation in research projects and enables students to help one another in the process of learning.

Conversing

Conversing is an important strategy for constructing new understandings and is the basis of collaborating.

Talking with someone helps students to think through their ideas by requiring them to apply the competencies of recalling, summarizing, paraphrasing, and extending for articulating their thinking. Conversation fosters making connections between ideas and leads to forming a focused perspective. Peer conversation groups may be organized with the teacher and library media specialist setting the task, monitoring and guiding progress, and calling for a summary statement at the end of the session.

Continuing

Continuing involves understanding that learning is a process that requires time. When students become aware of the stages in their research process, they begin to see that inquiry involves more than selecting a topic, collecting information, and reporting. Learning through inquiry involves not only gathering information, but also reading, reflecting, raising new questions, and exploring over an extended period of time to construct a new understanding. Library media specialists and teachers can help students to think about where they are in the process and offer guidance in the particular tasks of whatever stage they are currently experiencing. Continuing is an essential concept for learning how to learn in information-rich environments.

Choosing

Choosing is the strategy that gives students a sense of control over their own learning process. Inquiry is a process of making choices: choosing a topic and questions for research, choosing resources, choosing information within those resources, choosing what to pursue, choosing what to leave out, and finally choosing what is enough. These decisions in each stage of the search process are essential for moving along to culmination. An inquiry approach requires students to be actively involved in making choices for themselves, rather than just copying and reproducing texts that reflect other people's choices.

Charting

Charting is the strategy of depicting ideas in the form of a drawing, graph, or table (sometimes called graphic organizers). Opportunities for charting offer alternatives to the written word for presenting ideas. Charts enhance written communication by illustrating, summarizing, and elaborating ideas. Charting also enables students to visualize emerging ideas and to discover connections between ideas. In short, charting enables thinking.

Composing

Composing is formulating thoughts in written language. Writing is not just an activity to culminate a project, but a helpful technique throughout the process of constructing understanding. By keeping journals in the early stages of a project, students keep track of developing ideas and questions. In the later stages, the journal becomes more of a notebook for collecting and preparing a presentation of the new learning. Short pieces of writing at various points in the process require students to articulate the main ideas they are finding and forming; they also reveal questions that remain and are emerging. Students may find that writing the title of their project at various points is a useful exercise for monitoring change and progress in formulating a focus. When writing is used to foster thinking throughout the entire learning process, students are less likely to experience writing blocks at the close of a project.

All of these strategies aid students in each stage of the information search process, but they are particularly helpful in the critical stages of exploration and formulation. Four competencies (recalling, summarizing, paraphrasing, and extending) and six strategies (collaborating, conversing, continuing, choosing, charting, and composing) enable students to finding meaning in an information-rich environment and are critical components of information literacy.

CONCLUSION

To restructure schools for the information age, we need to keep our attention on the central task of enabling student learning. A study that I conducted, comparing schools that were successful in implementing an inquiry approach to learning with schools that were struggling but unable to develop a sustained program, illustrates the importance of keeping student learning as the central goal (Kuhlthau 1993a). The library media specialists in each school were asked the question, "What problem are you having?" The responses of those in successful programs stressed *learning* problems of students, such as, "Students had trouble getting started" and "Students had difficulty focusing in on a particular theme or aspect of the problem."

The responses of those in struggling programs, however, stressed *logistical* problems, such as, "We didn't have enough time," "We were confused about our roles," and "The assignments didn't allow for real inquiry." In a roundtable discussion with the instructional team (the library media specialist, teachers, curriculum supervisor, principal, reading/study skills specialist) at one of the schools that had implemented and sustained a successful program, all agreed on total commitment to the inquiry process approach to learning. The curriculum supervisor summed it up in his remark that they had a goal of teaching students proficiency in reading and writing and the inquiry approach was their way of accomplishing this goal.

The information-age school requires a new configuration to prepare students for work, citizenship, and daily living. An inquiry approach prepares students for real-life demands. The library in the information-age school is an inquiry center that provides the means for an integrated inquiry approach to learning. The library media specialist in the information-age school is more than a resource provider. The library media specialist is a partner on the instructional team and an expert in the process that leads to information literacy. The library media specialist and teachers collaboratively plan and teach, with the library media specialist as the resource and process expert of the school, the teacher as the content and context expert, and the principal as the facilitator. Together they form a team for providing inquiry-based learning for the information-age school.

REFERENCES AND ADDITIONAL RESOURCES

Brown, Rexford. 1991. *Schools of Thought*. San Francisco: Jossey-Bass.

Bruner, Jerome. 1990. *Acts of Meaning*. Cambridge, Mass.: Harvard University Press.

Hopkins, Dianne, and Douglas Zweizig. 1998. *National Library Power Program Evaluation*. Unpublished report of DeWitt Wallace-Reader's Digest Fund, School of Library and Information Studies, University of Wisconsin-Madison.

Kuhlthau, Carol C. 1993a. "Implementing a Process Approach to Information Skills: A Study Identifying Indicators of Success in Library Media Programs." *School Library Media Quarterly* 21, no. 1: 11–18.

———. 1993b. *Seeking Meaning: A Process Approach to Library and Information Services*. Norwood, N.J.: Ablex.

———. 1994. *Teaching the Library Research Process*. 2d ed. Metuchen, N.J.: Scarecrow Press.

———. 1997. "Learning in Digital Libraries." *Library Trends* 45, no. 5: 708–24.

———. 1998. *Student Learning Opportunities Through the Library*. National Library Power Evaluation Report. New York: DeWitt Wallace-Reader's Digest Fund.

———. 1999. "The Role of Experience in the Information Search Process of an Early Career Information Worker: Perceptions of Uncertainty, Complexity, Construction, and Sources." *Journal of the American Society for Information Science (JASIS)*, 50, no. 5: 399–412.

Limberg, Louise. 1998. "Experiencing Information Seeking and Learning: A Study of the Interaction Between Two Phenomena." Ph.D. diss., Department of Library and Information Studies, Gothenburg University, Gothenburg, Sweden.

McClintock, Robert. 1996. *Renewing the Progressive Contact with Posterity: On the Social Construction of Digital Learning Communities.* Unpublished manuscript. The Institute of Learning Technologies, Teachers College, Columbia University.

Negroponte, Nicholas. 1995. *Being Digital.* New York: Knopf.

Newmann, Fred, Walter Secada, and Gary Wehlage. 1995. *A Guide to Authentic Instruction and Assessment: Vision, Standards and Scoring.* Madison, Wis.: Wisconsin Center for Education Research.

Oppenheimer, Todd. 1997. "The Computer Delusion." *Atlantic Monthly* (July): 45–62.

Papert, Seymour A. 1994. *The Children's Machine: Rethinking School in the Age of the Computer.* New York: Basic Books.

Stoll, Clifford. 1995. *Silicon Snake Oil: Second Thoughts on the Information Highway.* New York: Doubleday.

Part II
Context of Learning

2

How Do We Learn?

Joy H. McGregor

INTRODUCTION

What do we know about learning? How does that knowledge apply specifically to what school library media specialists do? Much of the study of learning has been done in the fields of cognitive psychology and educational research. Just as the academic disciplines apply that knowledge to their disciplines, so must we apply those principles and theories to resource-based learning and information literacy.

Information Power: Building Partnerships for Learning (AASL and AECT 1998), the standards and guidelines document published by the American Association of School Librarians and the Association for Educational Communications and Technology, focuses on student learning. These standards demand an understanding of how children learn and an ability to incorporate effective teaching techniques to guide learning. Many states have also created standards documents that emphasize the role of the library media program by integrating information access and use directly into the learning curriculum. Organizations in all curriculum areas have developed national standards, within which are embedded information literacy skills applied to the particular subject area. The library media specialist who understands learning theory can enrich collaboration in planning curriculum-related activities with teachers in all subject areas, and can work as a partner to meet standards. Learning theory can also improve the teaching of media specialists.

In applying learning theories, we must be careful not to make unfounded assumptions. This chapter discusses many concepts very briefly. It might suggest or imply connections between some theoretical ideas that purists could claim are inappropriate. Those who believe firmly in a particular approach or theory might regard adaptation of pieces from multiple theories as unacceptable. In addition, space limits a discussion of the theories to highlights only, which could lead to superficial understanding and application. I strongly encourage readers to pursue further information on any of the theories, theorists, or concepts that they find intriguing. Theories can become meaningful and useful only if they are explored, understood, experimented with, and tested in a variety of circumstances. The practitioner can then decide whether they are of value or are wanting.

The chapter discusses two major theoretical approaches, one of which dramatically affected the world of education for many decades and the second of which has only recently begun to have a significant impact on educational practice. Several learning models based on this second approach are described, and then some factors that affect learning are considered. The chapter explores the link between thinking and learning and then discusses a few tools for promoting learning. Finally, some suggestions for putting theory into practice are provided.

THEORETICAL APPROACHES

Educational psychology has given rise to two major theoretical approaches to learning in this century. The behaviorist view is based on a belief that reality is external and absolute. Reality is measurable, and cause and effect can be determined and standardized. The constructivist view, in contrast, looks at reality as something that is socially constructed by individuals who determine their reality based on their unique prior knowledge and experiences. These two views of reality affect how learning is perceived and studied.

Behaviorism

As we think about our own learning experiences, we remember some commonly used strategies which arose from the learning theories that were in favor at the time of our schooling. For example, we may remember practices, many of which are still in place, that derived from behavioral psychology, such as standardized testing and behaviorist discipline practices.

Conditioning

Behaviorists interpret learning according to observable behavior. Only that which can be observed can extend learning. Behaviorists study what people do, rather than what they think or feel, believing that we cannot know what goes on in the mind and the emotions. In the 1920s, Pavlov studied *conditioning*, or using a stimulus to cause a particular behavior consistently. His well-known research with dogs showed that they could be made to salivate (an observable behavior) when a buzzer sounded, if food were offered at the same time. Eventually the dogs salivated at the buzzer alone, having been conditioned by associating the buzzer with food. Behaviorists concluded that providing the appropriate stimulus would then create the desired behavior.

Reinforcement

Reinforcement, or stimulus provided after an act is performed, was studied by B. F. Skinner as a way to encourage or discourage repetition of a particular behavior. Reinforcement resulted in strengthening a desired response, and both positive and negative reinforcement were found to play a role in changing behavior. In the field of education, teachers used reinforcement to stimulate positive classroom behavior. Using extrinsic rewards as motivational strategies for student learning is an obvious application of behaviorist research on both conditioning and reinforcement. Behaviorists such as Skinner believed that learners can be "programmed" to learn systematically through appropriate reinforcement—an idea that led to programmed instruction and learning through positive feedback. Even today, librarians use negative reinforcement by installing security systems that sound an alarm when someone tries to remove a book that has not been desensitized. Such negative reinforcement attempts to encourage the appropriate behavior of checking the book out.

Observational Learning

Another behaviorist concept, *observational learning*, was supported by Albert Bandura's research on learning that occurs through watching and then imitating behavior. A child who learns to mistreat animals by watching others do so is learning through observation, or *modeling*. In a more positive sense, teachers model the behavior they want children to imitate, from reading and writing techniques to practicing the scientific method. Librarians reward the children who are sitting quietly at their table and following instructions by allowing them to line up first, partially as a reward, or positive reinforcement, and partly to encourage other children to learn the desired behavior by observing it.

The behaviorist endorses setting measurable behavioral objectives for teaching activities. Because behavior change is the desired effect of learning, the expected changes are described and measured, producing evaluation instruments that are standard for all learners. Because the behaviorist sees reality as objective, standardized objective tests are assumed to be capable of effectively assessing learning for all children.

Cognitive Psychology and Constructivism

Many elements of behaviorist psychology remain part of education today, but cognitive psychologists have looked in another direction to find out more about how we learn. Believing that it is possible to examine what is not observable, cognitive psychology attempts to understand what happens in the mind when we learn.

Current thinking about learning is strongly influenced by constructivist theory and research. Constructivists view learning as a process by which learners construct understanding themselves, rather than simply taking in ideas and memorizing them. Meaning might be constructed individually or socially, in groups. The constructivist believes that rather than being taught an objective reality or a logical organization that exists externally, learners need to explore sensory data for themselves and construct their own meaning from those data. A picture of an active learner emerges.

Practical Problem-Solving Activity

Although constructivism has recently reached new levels of acceptance in educational circles, not all constructivist thinking is new. John Dewey, in 1916, wrote about active learners grounding ideas and knowledge in their own experiences; the social context of the classroom could aid learning by providing a community of learners. He believed that thinking meant *practical problem-solving activity*. He promoted the idea of reflective thinking to solve problems through analysis of lifelike problems and potential alternative solutions. Dewey advocated students' working in committees to solve problems important to the learners, while teachers act as guides rather than dispensers of information (Ediger 1997). Authentic information problem solving through cooperative learning activities, then, would be a way of developing mental processes and thinking.

Cognitive Developmental Stages

Jean Piaget studied mental processes through his own children's learning development and found that children actively increased their understanding of ideas by building on previous understanding, even though the previous ideas might be inaccurate. He linked learning with *cognitive developmental stages* through which learners move. Piaget suggested that these stages can be roughly linked to ages at which children are likely to be cognitively capable of moving from one stage to the next. During the Sensorimotor stage (ages 0–2), learning is related to development of motor activities, such as learning to sit, stand, and walk. Children explore and conduct experiments, using all their senses and developing motor skills. The Pre-operational stage (from 2–7 years) involves intuitive mental activity rather than logical reasoning. From ages 7 to 11, children are likely to think more logically, but must learn through concrete objects to understand, a stage called the Concrete Operational stage. The stage of Formal Operations (age 11 through adulthood) is the time when children begin to think in abstract terms, no longer requiring the concreteness of the former stage.

Piaget believed that children must move through each of these stages and cannot progress from one stage to the next until certain criteria have been met; that is, until specific learning has been mastered. The teacher's role is to guide students to discover for themselves the things appropriate to their level of development (Leahey and Harris 1989). The developmental view recognizes what children can do, rather than just what they cannot do. Piaget's concept of developmental stages supports the teaching of skills at appropriate levels, with instruction at each stage matching the children's skills and reinforcing what they can learn, without criticizing them for what they cannot yet do. Young children, therefore, need concrete, hands-on experiences, whereas older ones can deal better with more abstract ideas.

Zone of Proximal Development

Although some cognitive psychologists disagree with the hierarchical nature of Piaget's theories, considerable research supports his ideas. Other psychologists, though supporting the concept of developmental stages, argue that children can be led through instruction to the next stage, rather than the progression depending entirely on development. Lev Vygotsky, a Russian cognitive psychologist, is one of those.

In the 1930s, Vygotsky discovered that children learn by connecting ideas to previously learned concepts. They must make the ideas their own by weaving the new elements into the old. He also found that children can learn, with the assistance of an expert (an adult or a more knowledgeable peer), things that they could not learn alone. He called the point at which this best occurs a *"zone of proximal development."* This concept deals with potential—that which is possible if the child interacts with an expert. Vygotsky believed that children learn first on a social level and then on an individual level (Lipman 1991) and that development of language and cognitive growth are closely related. He argued that as children grow, meanings of words change, which leads to development of their thinking. This theory underscores the importance of conversations about understandings, of children and teachers talking about what they are learning.

Building on Prior Knowledge

A contemporary cognitive psychologist, Jerome Bruner, endorses the idea that learners build on their prior knowledge to reach more advanced levels of understanding. Learning is an active process of discovery and categorization. Learners actively seek to organize ideas and events into their personal classification framework, with the ideas becoming more complex as they build on prior knowledge. Students can go beyond the information provided by applying ideas in new ways to fill in gaps. Instruction should sequence concepts and help students create a cognitive structure that allows them to organize information and develop more complex understanding. Bruner prescribed a "spiral" curriculum to provide ever-increasing complexity to learning concepts.

Jerome Bruner decried the movement of cognitive psychology away from understanding how the mind makes meaning, toward an emphasis on information processing/computation which assumes that all information can be broken into discrete bits of data that can be dealt with systematically, the way a computer does. He theorized that the mind deals with ideas and concepts in a less predictable manner and that making sense is based on connections to language and culture. The use of language allows children to make meaning that is shared by their culture (Bruner 1990).

Library Applications

What might these theorists say about what goes on in the library? Although the areas of application are virtually endless, here are a few ideas. A behaviorist would support using extrinsic motivation to reinforce reading activity and would endorse standardized testing of information skills. Constructivists would favor the active learning that often takes place in a library. Dewey would stress the value of students' reflecting on their activities and their learning at all stages of the research process. Piaget would support providing realia in elementary media centers, so children could learn in a concrete manner, and teaching information literacy skills when developmentally appropriate for all students. Vygotsky would support having children discuss stories, words, and information with other children and with library media specialists. The stereotyped quiet library atmosphere where conversation does not take place would interfere with development of language and thinking. Bruner would advocate teaching increasingly advanced information literacy skills and strategies, allowing students to develop more complex abilities, but would be alarmed when information processing was encouraged without emphasis on making meaning, the heart of understanding.

LEARNING MODELS

Educators in the various subject disciplines have described and endorsed a number of learning models, although not all agree on definitions of them. Although we hear about models such as inquiry learning, student-centered learning, cooperative learning, brain-based learning, and authentic, meaningful learning, these are not necessarily mutually exclusive or discrete models of learning. Many characteristics of these draw on cognitive psychology and are based on concepts integral to constructivist thinking. Sometimes the differences among these models are unclear and confusing. This segment of the chapter briefly defines these models; the next deals with various aspects of these learning models and of learning in general. This discussion does not deal with all possible learning models, only a few that can be directly related to constructivist theory.

Inquiry Learning

In *inquiry learning*, teachers provide problems for students to solve and the resources with which to solve them. Inquiry learning is also known as *discovery learning*. The problems might be closed (having definite answers), open (having many possible answers or conclusions), or active (requiring action to determine an answer or answers). Inquiry learning is typically student-centered, with teachers acting as guides and coaches rather than as knowledge providers, and with students discovering solutions for themselves. "Insofar as possible, a method of instruction should have the objective of leading the child to discover for himself" (Bruner 1962). Science and mathematics have been natural homes for inquiry teaching, where students conduct experiments and tests to find solutions to problems. Other techniques might be case studies, simulations, or role playing (hydi Educational New Media Centre 1996). Because inquiry learning requires multiple resources for students to use for problem solving, the school library media program should be a natural and important component of the model.

Student-Centered Learning

Student needs are the basis of *student-centered learning*. Students are seen as individuals who should have a say in what and how they learn. They are provided with whatever support they need at their particular stage of development. Active learning is important, and students are encouraged to be self-directed, taking responsibility for their own learning (Science Applications International Corporation 1996). Inquiry learning is a kind of student-centered learning.

Cooperative Learning

Cooperative learning provides opportunity for children to learn from one another and together in groups. Interaction among students promotes achievement of learning goals more successfully than learning alone. Constructivists who emphasize the social aspect of learning would agree with this model. Although there are several perspectives on and definitions of what cooperative learning actually means, the North American focus has been on a highly structured setting, in which purposes, organization, tasks, group goals, individual accountability, and assessment are carefully regulated and directed by the teacher (Slavin 1995). In the strictest sense, cooperative learning requires students to help and cooperate with one another to ensure their own and their group's learning

(Stahl 1994). Cooperative learning provides a group setting for carrying out inquiry or discovery learning tasks.

Brain-Based Learning

Cognitive psychologists and educational researchers have watched neuroscience with great interest in recent years, as brain research has opened up new vistas for understanding how we learn. Some educators have made unfounded assumptions about what the findings of neuroscience mean to education, making connections that the research does not yet support. By bridging from the physical discoveries of neuroscience through the mental research of cognitive psychology, however, some implications for learning can be determined. The concept of *brain-based learning* links to some constructivist theories in a logical manner. Although a number of concepts are considered important to the idea of brain-based learning, only a few are addressed here.

First, the brain operates by organizing input and making meaning from it. This fact supports the idea that learning is the result of making meaning and that making sense of ideas should be emphasized. Second, the brain functions by searching for patterns, which means that educators should guide students to recognize patterns in their world. Third, the brain can do more than one thing at a time, and it processes wholes and parts simultaneously. This fact supports the constructivist idea of providing a meaningful, complex context for the details to be learned. Isolated details taught without being related to a larger whole will not be learned effectively. Fourth, emotions play an important role in learning: learning will be inhibited when the learner feels threatened, but a certain level of cognitive tension and challenge promotes learning. Educators therefore must remove unnecessary anxiety from learning situations, providing experiences that are nonthreatening but challenging. Fifth, each brain is individual and different from every other brain. This fact supports the logic of the idea that each person constructs his or her own knowledge (Brain-Based Learning 1998).

Authentic, Meaningful Learning

Authentic, meaningful learning sums up many of these ideas. When students are engaged in meaningful, challenging tasks or in solving real-world problems, their learning is considered authentic. They are able to construct their own understanding when they are interested in what they are learning, know how to control and regulate that learning to suit their own needs, can set their own learning goals, are aware of and able to choose their own learning strategies, and are able to work together with other learners. They are engaged learners.

FACTORS IN THE LEARNING PROCESS

Learning models provide us with ways to organize instruction to promote effective learning. But other factors have an impact on learning, affecting whether and how learning occurs. Some factors are the multiple intelligences of learners, their learning styles, and their motivations.

Multiple Intelligences

Howard Gardner conducted research into cognition as a part of Harvard Project Zero, through which he developed a theory that intelligence is a multifaceted concept; that in fact people simultaneously have *multiple intelligences*, or ways in which they analyze their worlds (Gardner 1983). He found that, in each individual, some intelligences are stronger while others are weaker; ability varies in each area, but everyone possesses some level of intelligence in each area. Originally he identified seven "intelligences," but since then he has determined that there is at least one more, and perhaps others not yet identified. Currently, Gardner's research has identified eight intelligences: linguistic, logical-mathematical, spatial, bodily kinesthetic, musical, interpersonal, intrapersonal, and naturalist. (Many books and Web sites exist that describe these intelligences, so further detail is not provided here.)

In an interview, Gardner expressed concern that teachers might use the multiple intelligences theory to label students, rather than to see them as unique individuals. He sees the most important application of the theory as a way to individualize teaching and assessment (Durrie 1997). Typically, our school systems have rewarded students who show strong linguistic and logical-mathematical intelligence, but have tended to ignore the other strengths. Attention to the other kinds of intelligence and provision of various ways of enriching these intelligences will allow students to build on their strengths and be recognized for talents previously disregarded, while strengthening other intelligences.

Learning Styles

Many educators assume that the theory of multiple intelligences is really talking about a set of learning or cognitive styles. Gardner explains the difference by stating that a *learning style* is a general preference that can be applied to any kind of content, whereas an *intelligence* is a capacity for dealing with specific subject content (Gardner 1995). Learning style is another factor that affects learning.

Many approaches to learning-style theory exist, with some writers emphasizing preferences for physical and environmental elements, some focusing on cognitive style, and some on ways of working. Various inventories assess personality types (e.g., Myers-Briggs Type Indicator); sensory preferences such as visual, auditory, or kinesthetic (e.g., Barch); environmental preferences (e.g., Dunn and Dunn); or thinking styles (e.g., Gregorc). Many other assessment tools exist to determine learners' preferences and styles. The value to the educator in understanding learning styles lies in awareness of how individual students are most likely to respond to various teaching and learning styles. Being aware of styles—both the students' and their own—makes it possible for educators to teach consciously to a variety of learning styles and to allow all students to have an opportunity to work in their optimum environment at some point, while also gaining practice in using other styles at times. A teaching goal should be to help students strengthen their ability to learn in multiple ways, providing coping skills for learning with a wide variety of teachers and other learners.

Motivation

A third factor in learning is the motivation of the student. *Motivation* is defined as "the process of initiating, sustaining, and directing activity" (Wittrock 1986). All people, then, are motivated, because they constantly initiate, sustain, and direct their own activity—but they are not necessarily motivated to do what we hope they will do. Students who misbehave are motivated to do so by some personal factor or factors, just as students who are excited about learning are that way for their own particular reasons. Educators do not motivate people, people motivate themselves.

Motivation enters into learning because children are not always motivated to learn—for many different reasons. Attempts to motivate are usually attempts to convince students to behave in a way they would not behave otherwise.

Often motivational programs based on behaviorist theory provide extrinsic rewards (positive reinforcement). A desire to induce children to read, for example, has given rise to many motivational programs based on extrinsic rewards such as fast food, entertainment tickets, points, grades. The unfortunate result, however, is that students tend to focus on obtaining the reward, rather than on reading as an activity of intrinsic worth. Motivational programs of this nature are seen by some researchers essentially as attempts to manipulate and control behavior (Marcum 1998) instead of promoting a deeper learning or meaning-making.

Educators can, however, provide an environment that engages learners and encourages them to want to learn. Research shows that students who believe it is possible to achieve a particular goal through greater effort are more likely to be successful than those who believe their success depends on ability, luck, or the difficulty level of the task (Wittrock 1986). Therefore, providing tasks at the appropriate level of difficulty, with enough challenge to require some effort but not enough to cause fear, will be more likely to interest learners than tasks they believe they cannot accomplish. Appropriate scaffolding, or support from an expert (such as a teacher or a library media specialist), might be the element that makes the difference, with the learning taking place in the child's zone of proximal development. A learning environment that stimulates curiosity, allows for self-direction and choice, and builds on prior knowledge to help students make links to something they already know should help to create engaged learners.

THINKING AND LEARNING

An important element of learning is the way people think and the kinds of thinking they do. Many educators have advocated teaching thinking skills as a separate subject, and others advocate incorporating thinking into all areas of the curriculum. Some thinking skills seem to be generally useful in many areas and are transferable from one area to another; others are more discipline-related and more appropriately taught within the context of that discipline. To talk about particular thinking skills, though, we need to look at a structure or framework for examining skills.

Bloom's Taxonomy

Bloom (1956) devised a taxonomy for classifying learning objectives in the cognitive domain. This taxonomy listed thinking skills in a hierarchical order, which he suggested were the skills that teaching should promote. Although the taxonomy has been both praised and criticized, it offers a useful organizational scheme for discussing thinking. The skills, from simplest to most complex, are knowledge, comprehension, application, analysis, synthesis, and evaluation. These skills are often portrayed as a ladder, with knowledge as the bottom rung and the first step in thinking. *Knowledge* is basic recall, as when a toddler can recite the alphabet or count, but has no understanding of what the letters or numbers mean. Rote memory activities take place at the knowledge level. *Comprehension* requires understanding the basic meaning of an idea. *Application* involves using the idea in a different context or using it to solve a problem.

The levels of analysis, synthesis, and evaluation are generally considered higher-order thinking skills. *Analysis* is the ability to break information or ideas down into basic elements or components and then perform such operations as comparing, contrasting, or categorizing. *Synthesis* creates a new or unique product by combining the pieces in a different way into a new whole. *Evaluation* requires judging ideas based on a set of criteria, whether self-generated or externally generated. It is important to remember, when using the terminology associated with Bloom's taxonomy, that the terms he defined very carefully must be applied according to his definitions. Knowledge, for example, has different meanings in different worlds. Knowledge to librarians is often interpreted as referring to a high level of complexity, more complex than data or information; in Bloom's taxonomy, by contrast, it holds the simplest, most basic spot.

An educator who is interested in students' sense- or meaning-making would probably look for elements of at least application and analysis, as well as the basic knowledge and comprehension levels. Evaluation could even enter into the operation of making complex meaning. Learning activities that require the higher-order thinking skills are more likely to generate interest and engagement than a lot of activities conducted at the lower levels—these invite boredom. Research shows, unfortunately, that most teaching occurs at the knowledge and comprehension levels.

Critical Thinking

Higher-order thinking is often confused with critical thinking. Although critical thinking employs higher-order thinking skills, the two concepts are not the same. It is possible to use one or another higher-order thinking skill without thinking critically. What, then, is *critical thinking*? Actually, no agreement exists on a single definition of critical thinking, but recent definitions have included components of decision making and improvement of thinking. In 1985, Ennis defined *critical thinking* as "reasonable, reflective thinking that is focused on deciding what to believe or do" (Ennis 1985, 54). In 1996, Richard Paul described critical thinking as "thinking about your thinking while you're thinking in order to make your thinking better.... [I]t is self-improvement (in thinking) through standards (that assess thinking)" (Paul and Elder 1996a, 1). He also described it as "the art of taking charge of your own mind" (Paul and Elder 1996b, 1).

Michael Scriven and Richard Paul formally defined *critical thinking* as "the intellectually disciplined process of actively and skillfully conceptualizing, applying, analyzing, synthesizing, and/or evaluating information gathered from, or generated by, observation, experience, reflection, reasoning, or communication, as a guide to belief and action" (Scriven and Paul, accessed 1998). Attempting to improve that thinking takes the concepts of logic, reasoning, analysis, evaluation, problem solving, and decision making to a higher level of self-awareness.

Creative Thinking

Another kind of thinking is valuable in many problem-solving situations: *creative thinking*. Creative thinking, too, has many definitions and interpretations, but can be considered as the ability to look at things in a different way from the obvious or the traditional. It involves generating new ideas and putting existing ideas together in new ways. The term "thinking outside the box" refers to creative thinking or lateral thinking. Creative thinking has two components: divergent and convergent thinking. "Divergent thinking is the intellectual ability to think of many original, diverse, and elaborate ideas. Convergent thinking [is] the intellectual ability to evaluate logically, critique and choose the best idea from a selection of ideas" (Cave 1996). Both the novel ideas and the selection of the most appropriate idea are necessary. A creative thinker is able to employ both kinds of thinking at the appropriate time. Notice that convergent thinking (in this definition) involves some aspects of critical thinking.

An important precursor to creativity is curiosity, something that little children have in abundance. All too often, however, the educational experience stifles that curiosity and limits creative thinking. If we want children to be active, engaged learners, we need to stimulate their curiosity and awaken their creativity. Encouraging them to imagine, explore, and play with ideas and then engaging them in their zone of proximal development to select the most appropriate idea for the situation can help to activate their creative side. Guiding them to ask questions and discover new ideas is an important role that library media specialists and teachers can—and should—play. Encouraging them to read frequently and broadly will stimulate their imaginations and build their experiential background, providing them with sources of ideas and diverse vicarious experiences.

Metacognition

Many people are unaware of their own thinking. Thinking about thinking is known as *metacognition*, an important element of both critical and creative thinking. Students who learn to be aware of what and how they are thinking can improve that thinking. They are able to apply strategies to deal with new situations or consciously move their thinking to new and different planes. Metacognitive thinkers are able to connect the new information with what they already know, select appropriate thinking strategies, and monitor and evaluate their own thinking (Blakey and Spence 1990). Being aware of their own thinking allows students to apply metacognitive strategies to the research process as they find, evaluate, and use information.

A technique useful in developing metacognitive thinking is keeping a journal. Recording their thoughts allows students to revisit and analyze them. A research technique known as an I-Search, first developed by Ken Macrorie, requires journaling throughout the process (Macrorie 1988; Joyce and Tallman 1997). Keeping a journal for an I-Search paper provides a record of thinking that can be useful in talking about metacognition and promoting thinking about thinking. Keeping a thinking journal during other projects allows reflection on whether the kind of thinking used was effective or not.

Mental Models

Thinking of any kind involves developing mental models. We perceive concepts through mental representations that help us understand. *Mental models* are "incomplete and constantly evolving; they are usually not accurate representations of a phenomena [sic]; they typically contain errors and contradictions; they are parsimonous [sic] and provide simplified explanations of complex phenomena; [and] they often contain measures of uncertainty about their validity that allow them to be used even if incorrect" (Mental Models 1996).

Not only are mental models often inaccurate and simplified, but they are also robust, meaning that they are resistant to change. Mental models are held firmly until the learner comes across a contradiction that is too persistent, too unavoidable to ignore. When the learner incorporates the modification or the elaboration into the original mental model, learning occurs. Shawn Glynn said, "Students' initial mental models are simple representations of a concept, but as students learn more, their mental models evolve and become more sophisticated" (Glynn 1997, 30).

Mental models are the framework in constructing new understandings, a principle supported by Vygotsky's and Piaget's theories. These models stress the importance of prior knowledge, as prior knowledge is held within mental models and learning is built on those models. Guiding learners using the concept of mental models requires an awareness of students' mental models, which in turn requires dialogue with and observation of students. Finding out what they already know, or whether they know something in a related area, enables that knowledge to be accessed for building a similar, but new, mental model.

Observing students' strategies for accessing information gives the media specialist an idea of students' mental models for accessing information (Pitts 1995). By determining where students make errors, the wise educator can figure out where the mental model is inaccurate and help students make useful modifications. If a student consistently looks in a table of contents of a book but never turns to the index in the back, the media specialist might assume that the student's mental model of finding information in a book does not include looking in an index. This assumption can be checked very easily through a quick question, and the usefulness of the index can be demonstrated, providing a contradiction to the mental model that would be difficult to ignore if the index made the task much easier.

TOOLS TO PROMOTE LEARNING

Many tools and techniques to encourage learning are available to educators. Some are used by the educators, some by students. Some extend thinking, some organize it, others provide opportunities for practicing skills. The journaling mentioned earlier is an example of a tool that can both extend and organize learning. Two other tools to be discussed are coaching and questioning.

Coaching

Coaching is a technique used by teachers to guide students through a task or train of thought. Rather than being directive, coaching is supportive and facilitative. A coach helps students determine what they need to know or practice and encourages them to develop skills for themselves. Coaching helps students to be actively involved in their own learning instead of being passive receptors. All the learning models discussed at the beginning of this chapter require the teacher to be a coach rather than a lecturer.

Coaching requires special skills. Whether the coach wants to provide practice for skills, help a student generate ideas, promote critical thinking, or develop metacognitive abilities, the coach must be able to listen. Dialogue between learner and coach is an important element, which means listening to learners as well as talking to them. Listening without judging helps coaches develop mental models of the students' mental models, thereby enabling them to determine what each student needs to develop a more sophisticated mental model.

A good coach can adjust advice to the individual and is flexible enough to aid each learner in whatever way will best benefit that particular learner. The coach asks the right questions at the right time, probing for greater understanding and encouraging the learner to ask questions, too. A good coach knows when to allow students to make errors and learn from those mistakes and when to intervene with a guiding suggestion or a hint. Cognitive coaching, in particular, helps students become independent thinkers through learning metacognitive strategies (Cognitive Coaching 1998).

Questioning

Educators and students can use *questioning* to access prior knowledge or extend thinking. A well-timed, open-ended question can do more than elicit a right-or-wrong answer. It can encourage divergent thinking, higher-order thinking, and critical thinking. A teacher or media specialist's question can meet the student in the zone of proximal development and stimulate movement to a higher level of thinking. Questions aimed higher than knowledge and comprehension levels will require more than a yes-or-no answer and will not channel the student into providing the answer wanted by the teacher.

Allowing time for students to think about their answers before replying will also encourage deeper thinking. Research shows that many teachers allow less than two seconds before requiring an answer, but at least four seconds are needed for a student to think through a question and formulate an answer. Calling on a student for an answer before that time cuts off any thinking that students might be doing.

Students also need to learn to ask appropriate questions. If students understand the various levels of thinking, they can become aware of the kinds of questions that require each particular kind of thinking. They can then frame questions for themselves to answer as they explore information and ideas. They can consciously work on developing their own thinking. They can learn to ask more "why" and "what if" questions and fewer "what" and "who" questions. Designing questions to use in an interview can help to make the questioning process realistic (McKenzie 1997).

FROM THEORY TO PRACTICE

How do we translate these theories into effective practice in school library media centers? Of what use is learning theory to the library media specialist? What elements of learning can have an impact on developing information literacy?

Knowing how children learn enables media specialists to move their programs beyond the access level. Though access is vital, affecting what children are able to do with the materials is just as important, if not more so. Many media specialists give lip service to a role involving more than providing materials, but their daily activities typically do not include a substantial amount of time spent directly on learning-related activities. Being aware of how children learn provides the opportunity to move beyond a focus limited to things; media specialists can move conversations with teachers from, "Come see the new books," to "Let's get together and plan how your children can best use our new books for learning." Media specialists will be able to talk about a learning process and about helping students to make meaning.

1. To apply learning theory to developing information literacy in your school, first **emphasize such things as thinking skills, cooperative learning, brain-based learning, questioning, and meaning-making** in your planning sessions with teachers. When media specialists and teachers share teaching and learning goals that go beyond the immediate content-based goals, learning activities will have more meaning and application. The media specialist who not only understands the learning process but also wants to collaborate to address larger learning goals can inspire teachers to revisit their plans with new, overarching goals in mind.

2. Next, **reject any activities that are carried out for activity's sake or are isolated from meaningful connections**. These are not learning activities; they are busywork. Plan authentic activities that engage learners as they get excited about reading, as they search for and strive to make meaning of intriguing information, and as they apply ideas

and concepts to solving real-world problems and making important decisions. Provide opportunities for students to use creative thinking and generate many ideas through brainstorming and group discussions. Consciously include analytical tasks that require students to do more than simply find information and reproduce it. Allow time for exploration, reading, asking questions, talking about ideas, and finding patterns, to guide students to modify their mental models.

3. **Plan to teach with the teachers**. Share the teaching role with large and small groups and with individuals, always being aware of integrating the concepts of learning into any lessons and modeling thoughtful teaching, coaching, questioning, and guiding activities for teachers. Teachers who are uncomfortable with any of these teaching methods can learn from seeing them demonstrated. Teaching alongside the teacher gives students access to more experts, more individual attention, and more opportunity to learn in their zones of proximal development.

4. **Make learning goals obvious to both teachers and students**. Make everyone aware of "why are we doing this?" as well as "what are we supposed to do?" Talk about learning goals to trigger metacognitive activity. Children do not intuitively understand why they are asked to do many of the things that are important to learning. Having that knowledge helps them learn to take more personal responsibility for their own learning.

5. Finally, **talk to students as they learn**. Carry on conversations that help them make sense of the information they find or the books they read.

Establish a dialogue that lets them know that their learning is important, their ideas are interesting, and their questions are of consequence. Give them a chance to explore ideas that are new or difficult to understand by talking about them and asking questions to make sense of them. Encourage them to talk to each other about concepts and ideas they encounter in what they read and view, thereby exposing them to other people's ways of thinking and testing the accuracy of their own mental models. Show them that doubt and uncertainty, though uncomfortable, are often necessary precursors to learning, and that with support, they can move beyond doubt and uncertainty. Meet them in their zone of proximal development. Help them revise their inaccurate models or incorporate their new learning into their existing mental models.

REFERENCES AND ADDITIONAL RESOURCES

American Association of School Librarians and Association for Educational Communications and Technology. 1998. *Information Power: Building Partnerships for Learning.* Chicago: American Library Association.

Blakey, Elaine, and Sheila Spence. 1990. "Thinking for the Future." *Emergency Librarian* 18 (May–June): 11–14.

Bloom, Benjamin S. 1956. *Taxonomy of Educational Objectives: Classification of Educational Goals. Handbook 1: Cognitive Domain.* New York: Longman, Green & Co.

"Brain-Based Learning." 1998. Funderstanding. <http://www.funderstanding.com/learning_theory_how5.html> (accessed November 5, 1998).

Bruner, Jerome. 1962. *On Knowing: Essays for the Left Hand.* Cambridge, Mass.: Belknap Press.

———. 1990. *Acts of Meaning.* Cambridge, Mass.: Harvard University Press.

Cave, Charles. 1996. "The Creativity Web." <http://www.
ozemail.com.au/~caveman/Creative/> (accessed November
5, 1998).

"Cognitive Coaching." 1998. Funderstanding. <http://
7-12educators.miningco.com/msub76learnstyles.htm>
(accessed November 5, 1998).

Durrie, Ronnie. 1997. Interview with Howard Gardner.
<http://www.newhorizons.org/trm_duriemi.html>
(accessed November 5, 1998).

Ediger, Marlow. 1997. "Influence of Ten Leading Educators on
American Education." *Education* 118 (Winter): 267–76.

Ennis, Robert. 1985. "Goals for a Critical Thinking Curriculum."
In *Developing Minds: A Resource Book for Teaching Thinking*,
ed. Arthur L. Costa. Alexandria, Va.: Association for
Supervision and Curriculum Development.

Gardner, Howard. 1983. *Frames of Mind: The Theory of Multiple
Intelligences*. New York: Basic Books.

———. 1995. "Reflections on Multiple Intelligences: Myths and
Messages." *Phi Delta Kappan* 77 (November): 200–209.

Glynn, Shawn. 1997. "Drawing Mental Models." *Science Teacher*
61 (January): 30–32.

hydi Educational New Media Centre. 1996. "Inquiry Learning."
Wellington, New Zealand: Wellington Polytechnic.
<http://webnz.com/wnp/onlinec/introcer/chunk1/inquiry/inq0
.htm> (accessed November 5, 1998).

Joyce, Marilyn Z., and Julie Tallman. 1997. *Making the Writing
and Research Connection with the I-Search Process*.
Englewood, Colo.: Libraries Unlimited.

Leahey, Thomas H., and Richard J. Harris. 1989. *Human
Learning*. 2d ed. Englewood Cliffs, N.J.: Prentice Hall.

Lipman, Matthew. 1991. "Squaring Soviet Theory with American
Practice." *Educational Leadership* 48 (May): 72–79.

Macrorie, Ken. 1988. *The I-Search Paper*. Portsmouth, N.H.:
Heinemann.

Marcum, Jim. 1998. "Engaging Knowledge Workers."
<http://pblib.utpb.edu/marcum/index.htm>
(accessed November 5, 1998).

McKenzie, Jamie. 1997. "Filling the Tool Box: Classroom
Strategies to Engender Student Questioning."
<http://fromnowon.org/toolbox.html#Class>
(accessed November 5, 1998).

"Mental Models." 1996. <http://www.uqac.uquebec.ca/dse/3psy 206/glossair/models.html> (accessed November 5, 1998).

"Multiple Intelligences." 1998. Math Matters. <http://www. mathmatters.net/mupintel.htm> (accessed November 5, 1998).

"Neuroscience." 1998. Funderstanding. <http://www. funderstanding.com/learning_theory_how4.html> (accessed November 5, 1998).

Paul, Richard, and Linda Elder. 1996a. "Critical Thinking: Basic Questions and Answers." The Critical Thinking Community. <http://www.sonoma.edu/cthink/K12/k12library/ questions.nclk> (accessed November 5, 1998).

———. 1996b. "Our Concept of Critical Thinking." The Critical Thinking Community. <http://www.sonoma.edu/cthink/ K12/k12class/Oconcept.nclk> (accessed November 5, 1998).

Pitts, Judy M.; edited by Joy H. McGregor and Barbara K. Stripling. 1995. "Mental Models of Information: The 1993-94 AASL/Highsmith Research Award Study." *School Library Media Quarterly* (Spring): 177–84.

Science Applications International Corporation. 1996. "What Is Student Centered Learning?" <http://inspire.ospi.wednet. edu:8001/curric/weather/adptcty/stcntr.html> (accessed November 5, 1998).

Scriven, Michael, and Richard Paul. N.d. "Defining Critical Thinking." <http://www.sonoma.edu/cthink/University/ univclass/Defining.nclk> (accessed December 24, 1998).

Slavin, Robert E. 1995. "Cooperative Learning Among Students: Theory, Research, and Implications for Active Learning." Center for Research on the Education of Students Placed at Risk, Johns Hopkins University. <http://www.successforall. com/cooplearn.htm> (accessed November 5, 1998).

Stahl, Robert J. 1994. *The Essential Elements of Cooperative Learning in the Classroom*. ERIC Digest, ERIC Document Reproduction Services No. ED370881 (March).

Wittrock, Merlin C. 1986. *Students' Thought Processes*. New York: Macmillan.

3

Information Literacy Skills Models: Defining the Choices

Greg Byerly and Carolyn S. Brodie

INTRODUCTION

Information literacy has always been an integral, if undocumented, component of school library media services. However, not until the introduction of computers into schools and school library media centers did the term gain the urgency and significance now commonly associated with it. Whereas librarians once worried about reading literacy, now the rallying cry is for universal information literacy.

Since the late 1980s, various information literacy skills models have been developed by individual educators, state organizations, and national associations. Teachers are expected to include information literacy skills in their classes. It is assumed that school library media specialists are information-literate and can provide leadership as schools turn to resource-based and student-designed curricula. Also, an increasing amount of technology must be installed, operated, maintained, and incorporated into the overall learning experience.

Information literacy is essential, but certain basic questions still remain:

- What is information literacy?
- How do/did I become information-literate?
- How do I teach information literacy?
- What are the various models? How do they differ? Is one better than the others?
- How do the nine "Information Literacy Standards for Student Learning" in *Information Power* (AASL and AECT 1998) relate to these models?

DEFINITIONS OF INFORMATION LITERACY

Information literacy is the term most commonly used to describe the organized process of information-seeking that students must assimilate to become effective learners. Most definitions of information literacy minimally include three abilities: (1) to access information; (2) to evaluate information; and (3) to use information. However, many attempts have been made to define further the various nuances of the term, especially as the use of technology has proliferated in schools.

One of the earliest definitions of information literacy was from the American Library Association Presidential Committee on Information Literacy, in 1989 (ALA Presidential Committee 1989, 1):

> To be information literate, a person must be able to recognize when information is needed and have the ability to locate, evaluate, and use effectively the needed information.... Ultimately information literate people are those

who have learned how to learn. They know how to learn because they know how knowledge is organized, how to find information, and how to use information in such a way that others can learn from them.

The *Position Statement on Information Literacy* from the American Association of School Librarians (AASL) states that *information literacy* is the term applied to information problem-solving skills that are essential (ALA and AASL 1996):

> To be prepared for a future characterized by change, students must learn to think rationally and creatively, solve problems, manage and retrieve information, and communicate effectively. By mastering information problem-solving skills students will be ready for an information-based society and a technological workplace.

The 1998 *Progress Report on Information Literacy* (Breivik, Hancock, and Senn 1998) reaffirmed the characteristics of information literacy outlined in the 1989 report and concluded that:

> The information literate person, therefore, is empowered for effective decision-making, freedom of choice, and full participation in a democratic society.

Given these definitions, it is easy to see why educators are clamoring for schools to incorporate information literacy skills training into the K-12 curriculum. These definitions emphasize that there is a difference between learning to find information and learning to use it effectively. Locating and accessing the information, whether in a book, on a CD-ROM, or on the Web, is not the same as knowing how to evaluate, interpret, and use the information. Such a switch in instructional emphasis has major ramifications for the teaching of "library" skills in school library media centers, as well as for classroom instruction.

Many changes in instructional methods and educational theories have influenced school library media centers and information literacy instruction. In the past, many school library media centers were collection-oriented and instruction-based. Emphasis was on the size of the local collection and the number of library lectures presented. Now the emphasis is on lifelong learning. The behaviorist teaching philosophy has been replaced or modified to incorporate a constructivist approach, in which students construct their own understanding by active investigation and thought, instead of memorizing facts presented in a class lecture. This has resulted in the concepts of resource-based learning, discovered information, and inquiry-based instruction.

Students explore beyond the textbook and use primary materials and other resources that can be made available. The teacher as lecturer is replaced by the teacher as facilitator. The teacher remains the expert, but serves more as a guide than an omnipotent sage. Questions replace facts and rote memorization. Class content is more student-designed than teacher-imposed. In other words, tedious is replaced with engaging. But how is this being accomplished? How do the information literacy skills models fit into the process? What effect does this have on instruction in school library media centers?

INFORMATION LITERACY SKILLS MODELS: HISTORICAL BACKGROUND

Before these questions can be answered in the context of the various information literacy skills models, some historical background is required. Obviously, school library media centers have always been in the information literacy business. Even years before the term *information literacy* was first used, the 1960 *Standards for School Library Programs* (ALA and AASL 1960, 18) included language that seems to be the precursor of the definitions outlined earlier. The *Standards* stated that the goal of library skills instruction was:

> synthesis of information, the extension of knowledge, the analysis and solution of problems, thinking, reflection, the satisfaction of curiosity, the development of trust, or the derivation of pleasure.

In the late 1980s, several separate publications did a great deal to further the development and refinement of the information literacy skills models that have gained prominence in the 1990s. In 1987, Carol Kuhlthau published a short, but very influential, document through the ERIC Clearinghouse on Information Resources, entitled *Information Skills for an Information Society: A Review of the Research* (Kuhlthau 1987). This was a challenge to all school library media specialists to take responsibility for this new instructional concept and to become information literacy experts. In 1989, she introduced the Search Process Model in an article in *School Library Media Quarterly* (Kuhlthau 1989).

In 1987, the Washington Library Media Association (WLMA) published one of the first step-by-step outlines of the research process and the skills required by students (WLMA 1987). Another early model was *Brainstorms and Blueprints*, also known as the Stripling and Pitts Research Process Model, authored by Barbara K. Stripling and Judy M. Pitts in 1988 (Stripling and Pitts 1988). It was one of the most influential and thought-provoking early models. Significantly, this model actually required students to *think* and reflect as each step in the suggested process was completed.

National publications in 1988 and 1989 set the direction for the development and implementation of information literacy skills models in the 1990s. In 1988, *Information Power: Guidelines for School Library Media Programs* was published by the American Library Association (AASL and AECT 1988). A joint effort of AASL and AECT, *Information Power* outlined three major roles for school library media specialists: (1) information specialist; (2) teacher; and (3) instructional consultant. Instead of setting quantitative standards to assess a school library media center, *Information Power* stressed the need to think in terms of service and qualitative assessment.

Finally, the American Library Association Presidential Committee on Information Literacy released a statement on information literacy, known only as the *Final Report*, in 1989 (ALA Presidential Committee 1989). This document called for an increased emphasis on information literacy and resource-based learning and included a K-12 model in a section entitled "An Information Age School."

CURRENT INFORMATION LITERACY SKILLS MODELS

There are literally dozens of information literacy skills models. Individual educators have developed some, but many states have begun to create their own models. Some are commercially available, whereas others are readily available on the Web. This is by no means an exhaustive study or comparison of the various models; rather, the intent is to identify and briefly present some of the more prominent and well-known models. It will become evident that most of the current models are very similar and that in many cases the terms each uses to describe specific activities, though different, are in fact synonymous (see figure 3.1). After presenting and comparing the models, an attempt is made to answer two questions: Which one is best? Which one should I use?

The following are representative or well-known models of information literacy skills.

The Big6 Skills™ Model

One of the best-known models, the Big6 Skills™ Information Problem-Solving Approach to Library and Information Skills Instruction, has been widely accepted and implemented by many schools. It was developed by Michael B. Eisenberg and Robert Berkowitz and is probably one of the most utilized of the information literacy skills models. It was originally published in their book, *Information-Problem-Solving: The Big Six Skills Approach to Library and Information Skills Instruction* (Eisenberg and Berkowitz 1990). The Big6 Skills™ are:

1. Task Definition
2. Information Seeking Skills
3. Location and Access
4. Use of Information
5. Synthesis
6. Evaluation.

The Big6 Skills™ Web site (<http://big6.com>) promotes use of the model, includes various instructional examples for each of the steps, and offers different categories of Big6 Skills™ TIPS (Teaching Information Problem Solving). Equal emphasis is put on all six of the steps, from defining the project to evaluating the results. Eisenberg and

Berkowitz have also published a book, *Helping with Homework: A Parent's Guide to Information Problem-Solving* (Eisenberg and Berkowitz 1996), which helps parents apply the Big6 Skills™ when working with their children.

Pathways to Knowledge™ Model (Pappas and Tepe)

Developed by Marjorie Pappas and Ann Tepe (1997), Follett's Pathways to Knowledge™ model is available in three print notebooks that cover grades K–5, 6–8, and 9–12 (Angle et al. 1997). The model is designed to be used both as an information literacy skills model for students searching for information and as a broader outline for teachers and school library media specialists developing a plan to integrate information literacy into the curriculum. There is an elaborate diagram of expanding rings that outline the "pathways to knowledge." The notebooks include detailed examples of actual teaching units and outline how to incorporate information literacy skills into various K-12 curricula.

This basic information literacy model has the following general steps:

1. Appreciation and enjoyment
2. Preresearch
3. Search
4. Interpretation
5. Communication
6. Evaluation.

Pappas and Tepe emphasized the initial actions that are required to make the overall information-seeking experience a success. Specifically, they stressed the importance of students understanding and appreciating the reason for the assignment and the necessity of conducting some presearch activities before the search is actually conducted.

Figure 3.1. Information literacy models comparison

Big6 Skills™	Follett	Washington
Task definition	Appreciation and enjoyment	Recognizes need
	Presearch	
Info seeking skills		
		Constructs strategies
Location and access	Search	Locates and accesses
	Interpretation	
		Evaluates and extracts
		Organizes
Use	Communication	Applies
Synthesis		
Evaluation	Evaluation	Evaluates

AASL/AECT	California	Colorado
Recognizes need	Explore and identify need	Determines information need
Need for accurate and comprehensive information		
Formulates question	Formulate central question	
Identifies potential sources	Relate to previous knowledge Identify potential resources	Develops information-seeking skills
Develops and uses strategies	Develop search strategies	
		Locates
	Locate and explore	
	Select most useful and do specific search	
Evaluates information —Accuracy —Relevance —Facts versus opinions	Identify relevant information	Analyzes
Selects information	Evaluate, select, and organize	Organizes
Organizes information	Analyze/Infer	Processes
Integrates information Applies information	Use/Present/Communicate	Acts
Produces and communicates		
[Assessment]	Evaluate	Evaluates

The Follett Web site (<www.fsc.follett.com>) includes information on how to order these materials, but it does not provide much additional information about the Pathways to Knowledge™.

Essential Skills for Information Literacy (WLMA)

Developed initially in 1987, the 1996 revised version by the Washington Library Media Association (WLMA 1996) not only identifies six essential skills for students, but also provides a set of benchmarks for each skill; the benchmarks further explain the skill and provide criteria for measuring the skill. These statements of what a student must be able to do to meet each standard further explain the model. The specific skills include:

1. Recognizing a need for information
2. Constructing strategies for locating information
3. Locating and assessing information
4. Evaluating and extracting information
5. Organizing and applying information
6. Evaluating the process and product.

The model, including the essential skills and benchmarks, is available on the WLMA's Web site (<http://www.wlma. org/literacy/eslintro.htm>).

INFOhio DIALOGUE Model (Ohio)

In 1998, INFOhio, the statewide library automation and information network for Ohio's K-12 schools, developed the INFOhio DIALOGUE Model for Information Literacy (INFOhio 1998). A series of more than twenty workshops introduced the model statewide, and a 230-page *INFOhio Information Literacy Skills Notebook* was widely distributed to Ohio school library media specialists and educators. The DIALOGUE Model has the following components:

1. Define
2. Initiate
3. Assess
4. Locate
5. Organize
6. Guide
7. Use
8. Evaluate.

One unique feature of this model is the explicit inclusion of a school library media specialist and/or teacher to "guide" the entire process. INFOhio provides access to the DIALOGUE Model on its Web site (<http://www.infohio.org>).

Model Information Literacy Guidelines (Colorado)

One of the pioneering state models, these guidelines offer specific and in-depth suggestions and recommendations in five categories:

1. Students as Knowledge Seekers
2. Students as Quality Producers
3. Students as Self-Directed Learners
4. Students as Group Contributors
5. Students as Responsible Information Users
   (Colorado Educational Media Association 1994).

The rationale for the guidelines is particularly well stated. Under the first category, "Students as Knowledge Seekers," nine information-seeking activities are listed: (1) Determine information need, (2) Develop information-seeking strategies, (3) Locate information, (4) Acquire information, (5) Analyze information relative to need, (6)

Organize information, (7) Process information, (8) Act on information, and (9) Evaluate process and product.

The emphasis is on what is done after the search has been conducted and information has been located. Although searching and locating remain essential steps in the process, methods of analyzing, extracting, listening, critically evaluating, creating outlines, assembling materials, and drawing conclusions are stressed.

The Colorado Department of Education provides access to these guidelines on its Web site (<http://cde. state.co.us/infolitg.htm>).

From Library Skills to Information Literacy (California School Library Association)

The California School Library Association has developed and published a handbook for teachers and school library media specialists which demonstrates how to incorporate information literacy into the curriculum (California School Library Association 1997). *From Library Skills to Information Literacy: A Handbook for the 21st Century* outlines an information literacy model with three interrelated components:

1. Searcher's Thinking
2. Search Process
3. Instructional Strategies.

The activities identified in the Search Process are comparable to those in the other information literacy skills models (see figure 3.1). *From Library Skills to Information Literacy* includes many examples of instructional plans, curriculum-based examples, classroom scenarios, and suggestions for implementing and assessing an information literacy skills program.

AASL/AECT Information Literacy Standards for Student Learning

Information Power: Building Partnerships for Learning presents nine information literacy standards for student learning (AASL and AECT 1998). These standards—actually guidelines jointly produced by the American Association of School Librarians and the Association for Educational Communications and Technology—are divided into three categories:

1. Information Literacy
2. Independent Learning
3. Social Responsibility.

Although all three categories incorporate information literacy, the standards in the latter two categories deal with more general attributes of student learning. However, the three standards listed under "Information Literacy" complement the steps included in other information literacy skills models (AASL and AECT 1998, 8):

- Standard 1: *The student who is information literate accesses information efficiently and effectively.*

- Standard 2: *The student who is information literate evaluates information critically and competently.*

- Standard 3: *The student who is information literate uses information accurately and creatively.*

The importance of *Information Power* as a model and framework for incorporating information literacy into all aspects of a school's curriculum cannot be overemphasized. *Information Power* begins by noting that "Information literacy—the ability to find and use information—is the keystone of lifelong learning" (AASL and AECT 1998, 1); it then proceeds to outline, in a concise and highly effective manner, information literacy standards for student learning. Three basic, interrelated themes (Collaboration, Leadership, and Technology) are shown as directly affecting the primary responsibilities of a library media center (Learning and Teaching, Information Access and Delivery, Program Administration, and Connections to the Learning Community).

Information Power is, however, much more than a statement of standards for information literacy. Each of the standards is followed by a series of "indicators" that further delineate the standard. For each of the indicators, three levels of proficiency (basic, proficient, and exemplary) are included, which can be used to assess a student's mastery of the required skill. What truly sets *Information Power* apart from many of the information literacy skills models is its inclusion of two types of real-world applications under each standard. First, "Standards in Action" provide examples of information-seeking situations in four grade-level groups (K–2, 3–5, 6–8, and 9–12) involving various subject areas. Second, "Examples of Content-Area Standards," developed by various national professional organizations in a wide variety of subject areas, are included. These examples of practical applications demonstrate that the AASL/AECT standards can be implemented in any curriculum, at any grade level, and in any subject area.

Information Power will drive and direct the efforts of library media specialists for years to come. The goal, as proclaimed in *Information Power*, is to create a "dynamic, effective, student-centered library media program" in every school (AASL and AECT 1998, xiii). All information literacy skills models must now be judged against the standards and examples presented in *Information Power*. Excerpts from each chapter are available at the

ALA/AASL Web site (<http://www.ala.org/aasl/>), but all library media centers should have, and use, the printed publication.

SIX COMMON COMPONENTS OF
INFORMATION LITERACY SKILLS MODELS

Even a cursory comparison of the seven major information literacy models summarized here reveals many similarities. Each of the models was independently developed, but, as demonstrated in figure 3.1, some truly universal components of a literacy skills model can be identified. Figure 3.1 provides a point-by-point comparison of the models, and the activities are divided into six components.

Component 1: Need for Information

Most of the models begin by either "defining" or "recognizing" the need for information. As noted earlier, the Follett's Pathways to Knowledge™ model emphasizes the importance of convincing students to "appreciate" the need for information, but this also requires definition of the problem or project. The INFOhio DIALOGUE Model is the only model to state explicitly that the next step is actually to "initiate" the search process, but it is clear that all the other models presuppose that students will initiate some action after defining the information need.

Research into information-seeking behavior inevitably concludes that the hardest step for most individuals is actually deciding to do something to find the information they want. The phrase typically given to this is "distressing ignorance": no information retrieval will actually occur until an individual is distressed enough about his or her ignorance to take some action. Students demonstrate this by not starting the paper until the day before it is due or ignoring a project until they realize that it will "affect my grade." Consequently, it is wise to "define" and then formally "initiate" any project.

Component 2: Information Literacy Skills

Models typically call for some sort of assessment of students' information literacy skills and abilities and, as necessary, the provision of initial or remedial instruction. Students often leap directly to the "locate" part of a project and are unprepared to use effectively the resources of the library media center or other sources of information. The library media specialist has an obvious role in ensuring that this skills assessment is completed before the searching part of the process is begun. Also, the library media specialist has the expertise to provide instruction, whether it is on how to develop search strategies or how to retrieve information effectively from a new CD-ROM.

In addition to conducting an assessment of information-seeking skills, this component then calls for the development of questions, the identification of key words, and the location of relevant sources. Significantly, it is during this component that the library media specialist reaffirms the roles of information consultant and teacher.

Component 3: Location of Information

An essential component of any information literacy skills model is actually to "locate" the information. All of the models include the action of locating and accessing the needed information. Increasingly, information is available in full text from various electronic sources; the trick is finding it. However, it is important to emphasize that merely finding the needed item is not enough; the format of that item must also be accessible to the student (through locally available technology, materials, or services).

In the past, the beginning and ending of library instruction has been the task of "locating": how to identify and locate materials—typically materials available in the local library media center—on a specific topic. As curricula have changed to be more resource-based, and as technology has made it possible to go beyond the walls of the library media center to find information, the "locate" part of the process has become more complicated and complex. Library media specialists must take the lead in helping students identify and evaluate potential sources of information, regardless of format or location, and in teaching students how to develop and use appropriate search strategies. Finally, the library media center must ensure that the information located can actually be retrieved and made available to students.

Component 4: Evaluation and Organization of Information

The models follow "locating" with activities related to "organizing" the retrieved information. Other words used to describe this organizing activity include: *analyzing, arranging, categorizing, evaluating, examining, extracting, generalizing, grouping, interpreting, selecting,* and *synthesizing*. This crucial step is often neglected by students writing reports or completing projects. After finding some materials on the assigned topic, many students simply begin writing the paper or undertaking the project. The models correctly emphasize that it is necessary to organize the information retrieved to determine which is the best and most useful.

It is not enough simply to organize the information retrieved. The models also typically note that it is necessary to evaluate the accuracy and relevance of the retrieved information. Critical evaluation as part of the organizing component is increasingly important given the use of the

World Wide Web by students to retrieve information. The library media specialist must demonstrate to students why it is necessary to assess with a critical eye *all* information found, and to organize the best and most relevant materials for inclusion in the report or project. In many ways, this means convincing the students simply to stop and *think* before starting to write or use the information.

Component 5: Use of Information

The information must be used in some fashion. The traditional ten-page, double-spaced paper, with a ten-item bibliography that includes books, magazines, newspapers, and other print sources, is no longer (if it ever was) the optimal final product of an information-seeking project. New methods for presenting results, communicating the information, and using the lessons learned must be incorporated into any information literacy assignment. Consequently, all of the models identify other ways to communicate, present, or use the information. Other critical aspects of using information, as noted by the models, are applying it, learning from it, synthesizing it, or internalizing it as personal knowledge.

Component 6: Evaluation of Process and Product

Finally, all of the models conclude with an "evaluation" component. Evaluation is an ongoing activity that should begin when a project is first defined and continue through each of the phases of the information skills project. The evaluation process must involve all participants in the project. It is recognized that both the project and the process must be evaluated.

Different strategies or methods can be used to evaluate projects. For example, assessment of project logs or presentations may involve both peer review and teacher evaluations. Similarly, evaluation of the process might ask questions such as:

1. What worked? What didn't? What should be done differently next time?
2. Was the topic interesting, timely, engaging, etc.?
3. Were there timing problems or scheduling conflicts?
4. What skills (e.g., using key words or Boolean operators) should have been better explained?
5. What resources were difficult to use? Were there problems with search strategies? What good tricks can be shared?
6. Was more or different help needed? What types of assistance were especially appreciated?
7. Were the expectations clear?
8. Were the presentation methods appropriate? Interesting?
9. What was the quality of the information product produced? Should a different type of final product/presentation have been used?

The models agree that an evaluation that considers both the product and process will result in an assessment of both learning and teaching.

CONCLUSION

Given the number of different information literacy skills models available to choose from, and with publication of the 1998 edition of *Information Power*, is it possible or appropriate to identify which of the models is best? If so, what is required to implement it successfully in a school? If there is no one best model, what can be done? Also, if these models have been around for a decade, why have so few schools actually used them?

It should be obvious that the seven models reviewed are remarkably similar. The different models should be viewed as complementary, not as competing or contradictory. Although there are procedural advantages to simply adopting one of the models and implementing it in a school, a library media specialist may be able to design a unique model to meet local needs and requirements by combining parts of several models. WLMA's Essential Skills model notes, "It is important to realize that it is not necessarily a linear process, and that a researcher may move backward and forward in the process, many times even skipping steps or proceeding in a different order" (WLMA 1996). The same can be said for finding and adapting a literacy skills model that will work in a particular local school.

California's *From Library Skills to Information Literacy* points out that it is "just one of many possible models" and advises (California School Library Association 1997, 15):

> If a program of information literacy is to succeed in a school, then an information literacy model must be "owned" by the library media specialist and the teachers in the building. This means that educators need to develop their own mental model from which a school-wide plan for information literacy will emerge.

Information Power concluded that "[s]chool library media specialists must determine how to interpret these themes and incorporate them into the functions of their individual school media programs. The dynamics of each situation— local politics, personnel, budgets, and communities—and the individual school library media specialist's own style are factors to be considered" (AASL and AECT 1998, 47).

The selection of an information literacy model, or the combination of various components from different models to meet local requirements, is a local decision. The library media specialist should use *Information Power* as a framework to initiate a process to "build partnerships for learning" that meet the school's information literacy needs. A collaborative review of the various information literacy models, involving teachers, library media specialists, administrators, technology coordinators, curriculum planners, and other educators, should then either lead to a determination of which model to use or collaborative work to develop a customized approach.

There may also be obstacles. Some administrators might react negatively to a "movement" initiated by the library media specialist to revise or reform the school's curriculum or teaching methods. Some teachers may have no interest in changing either the content of their units or the manner in which those units are presented and evaluated. Funds may not be available for the support materials and training necessary to launch an information literacy skills program.

Library media specialists must use their skills with technology to lead collaborative efforts throughout the school to meet these obstacles and resolve them. As stressed in *Information Power*, "The school library media specialist can use the information literacy standards for student learning to create and maintain a program for a broad learning community—students, teachers, administrators, parents, and the neighborhood—that will support lifelong learning" (AASL and AECT 1998, 1).

There is no perfect model. There is only the recognition that something must be done to ensure that information literacy is effectively incorporated into a school's curriculum. What works for one library media specialist will not necessarily work for another. It is not a straightforward, linear process. However, a collaborative effort, led by the library media specialist, to develop a process for including information literacy skills in all levels of the curriculum will ensure that the library media center is the center of "information power" in the school.

REFERENCES

American Association of School Librarians and Association for Educational Communications and Technology. 1988. *Information Power: Guidelines for School Library Media Programs*. Chicago: American Library Association.

————. 1998. *Information Power: Building Partnerships for Learning*. Chicago: American Library Association.

American Library Association and American Association of School Librarians. 1960. *Standards for School Library Programs*. Chicago: American Library Association.

————. 1996. *Position Statement on Information Literacy: A Position Paper on Information Problem Solving*. Copyrighted by the Wisconsin Educational Library Media Association, 1993. Reprinted with permission by AASL with additional scenarios by Paula Montgomery. Available at: <www.ala.org/aasl/positions/PS_infolit.html>. Last revised August 1996 (accessed October 5, 1998).

American Library Association Presidential Committee on Information Literacy. 1989. *Final Report*. Chicago: American Library Association. Also available at <gopher://ala1.ala.org: 70/00/alagophiv/50417007.document>.

Angle, Melanie J., et al. 1997. *Teaching Electronic Information Skills: A Resource Guide for Grades 1–5* and *Teaching Electronic Information Skills: A Resource Guide for Grades 6–8* and *Teaching Electronic Information Skills: A Resource Guide for Grades 9–12*. McHenry, Ill.: Follett Software.

Breivik, Patricia Senn, Vicki Hancock, and J. A. Senn (on behalf of the National Forum on Information Literacy). 1998. "A Progress Report on Information Literacy: An Update on the American Library Association Presidential Committee on Information Literacy: Final Report" (March). <http://www.ala.org/acrl/nili/nili.html> (accessed October 5, 1998).

California School Library Association. 1997. *From Library Skills to Information Literacy: A Handbook for the 21st Century*. 2d ed. San Jose, Calif.: Hi Willow Research & Publishing.

Colorado Educational Media Association. 1994. *Model Information Literacy Guidelines*. Denver, Colo.: Colorado Department of Education. <http://cde.state.co.us/infolitg.htm>.

Eisenberg, Michael B., and Robert E. Berkowitz. 1990. *Information Problem-Solving: The Big Six Skills Approach to Library and Information Skills Instruction*. Norwood, N.J.: Ablex.

————. 1996. *Helping with Homework: A Parent's Guide to Information Problem-Solving*. Syracuse, N.Y.: ERIC Clearinghouse of Information and Technology.

INFOhio. 1998. "DIALOGUE Information Literacy Skills Model." *INFOhio Record* 2, no. 3: 1. <http://www.infohio. org/about/id.htm> (accessed June 3, 1999).*

Kuhlthau, Carol. 1987. *Information Skills for an Information Society: A Review of the Research*. Syracuse, N.Y.: ERIC Clearinghouse on Information Resources.

————. 1989. "Information Search Process: A Summary of Research and Implications for School Library Media Programs." *School Library Media Quarterly* 18 (Fall): 19–25.

Pappas, Marjorie L., and Ann E. Tepe. 1997. *Pathways to Knowledge™: Follett's Information Skills Model*. McHenry, Ill.: Follett Software. <http://www.pathwaysmodel.com>.

Stripling, Barbara K., and Judy M. Pitts. 1988. *Brainstorms and Blueprints: Teaching Library Research as a Thinking Process*. Englewood, Colo.: Libraries Unlimited.

Washington Library Media Association. 1987. *Information Skills Curriculum Guide: Process, Scope, and Sequence*. Olympia, Wash.: Washington State Department of Education. Also published as an ERIC document (ED 288 554).

————. 1996. "Essential Skills for Information Literacy." Online. <http://www.wlma.org/literacy/eslintro.htm> (accessed October 5, 1998).

---

*Further information about the INFOhio DIALOGUE Model and the *INFOhio Information Literacy Skills Notebook* is available from TIP Associates, 2881 Bellaire Road, Silver Lake, OH 44224.

SIGNIFICANT INFORMATION LITERACY DOCUMENTS

American Association of School Librarians and Association for Educational Communications and Technology. *Information Literacy Standards for Student Learning.* Chicago: American Library Association, 1998.

> This is a companion publication to *Information Power: Building Partnerships for Learning.* It contains only Chapter 1, "The Vision," and Chapter 2, "Information Literacy Standards for Student Learning," from *Information Power.* It is designed to be distributed to teachers and administrators to introduce them to the standards and other concepts presented in *Information Power.*

American Association of School Librarians and Association for Educational Communications and Technology. *Information Power: Building Partnerships for Learning.* Chicago: American Library Association, 1998.

> This book presents the current national guidelines for school library media programs and information literacy standards for student learning. This document defines the mission and goals of the school library media program and is divided into two parts. Part One defines the first ever nationally published "Information Literacy Standards for Student Learning." Part Two is titled "Building Partnerships for Learning" and includes chapters on "Collaboration, Leadership, and Technology"; "Learning and Teaching"; "Information Access and Delivery"; "Program Administration"; and "Connections to the Learning Community." Appendices include a number of ALA and AECT statements and policies important for library media centers, such as the ALA Library Bill of Rights; ALA's "Access to Electronic Information, Services and Networks"; and AECT's Code of Ethics.

American Library Association and American Association of School Librarians. *Position Statement on Information Literacy: A Position Paper on Information Problem Solving.* Revised 1996. <http://www.ala.org/aasl/positions/PS_infolit.html>.

> This position paper identifies information-seeking skills that must be part of an information literacy curriculum. These skills include:
>
> 1. Defining the need for information
> 2. Initiating the search strategy
> 3. Locating the resources
> 4. Assessing and comprehending the information

5. Interpreting the information
6. Communicating the information
7. Evaluating the product and process.

Eight scenarios are also provided to demonstrate the effectiveness of cooperative instructional programs.

American Library Association Presidential Committee on Information Literacy. *Final Report*. Chicago: American Library Association, 1989. <gopher://ala1.ala.org:70/00/alagophiv/50417007.document>.

> One of the earliest documents on information literacy, this report calls for an increased emphasis on information literacy and resource-based learning. It includes a K-12 model in a section titled "An Information Age School." Those who are "information literate" are defined as:
>
> > those who have learned how to learn. They know how to learn because they know how knowledge is organized, how to find information, and how to use information in such a way that others can learn from them. They are people prepared for lifelong learning, because they can always find the information needed for any task at hand.
>
> This document was developed by an American Library Association Presidential Committee appointed by ALA President Margaret Chisholm.

Breivik, Patricia Senn, Vicki Hancock, and J. A. Senn (on behalf of the National Forum on Information Literacy). "A Progress Report on Information Literacy: An Update on the American Library Association Presidential Committee on Information Literacy: Final Report." March 1998. <http://www.ala.org/acrl/nili/nili.html>.

> This 1998 report refers to the ALA Presidential Committee's *Final Report* and highlights the progress that has been made. Six areas are "presented within the context of the outstanding work still needing to be addressed." Re-addressing those areas of need resulted in five recommendations for priority action in the new millennium from the National Forum on Information Literacy:
>
> 1. Forum members should encourage and champion the growth of support of accrediting agencies.
> 2. Teacher education and performance expectations should include information literacy skills.

3. Librarian education and performance expectations should include information literacy.
4. Forum members need to identify ways to illustrate to business leaders the benefits of fostering an information-literate workforce.
5. More research and demonstration projects should be related to information literacy and its use.

The document includes a useful bibliography.

INFORMATION ABOUT INFORMATION LITERACY ON THE WEB

"Bibliography on Evaluating Internet Resources."
<http://refserver.lib.vt.edu/libinst/critTHINK.htm>

Created and maintained by Nicole Auer, Library Instruction Coordinator at Virginia Polytechnic Institute and State University, this bibliography includes both Web resources and print publications. A good source for materials on how to evaluate Web materials and incorporate them into the learning process.

"Curriculum Connections."
<http://www.ala.org/ICONN/curricu2.html>

Created and maintained by the ICONnect Task Force of the American Association of School Librarians, this site is a good general resource for information literacy.

"Developing Educational Standards: An Annotated List of Internet Sites with K-12 Educational Standards and Curriculum Frameworks Documents."
<http://www.putwest.boces.org/Standards.html>

Created and maintained by Putnam Valley Central Schools (New York), this site lists standards by state and by subject area. It also has a very complete listing of state education departments and other educational clearinghouses, centers, and organizations.

"Information Competency Sites on the Web."
<http://multiweb.lib.calpoly.edu/infocomp/related.html>

Links to Web sites dealing with "Information Competence" and includes reports, projects, and online tutorials and courses.

"Information Literacy Group—Internet Resources."
<http://www.ucalgary.ca/library/ILG/internet.html>

A good source of links to information literacy Web sites. It also provides links to various articles and documents on the Web related to information literacy.

"Kathy Schrock's Guide for Educators: Critical Evaluation Surveys."
<http://www.capecod.net/schrockguide/eval.htm>

A good general resource for information literacy.

National Information Literacy Institute (NILI).
<http://www.ala.org/acrl/nili/nilihp.html>

The Association of College and Research Libraries (ACRL), a division of the American Library Association (ALA), is developing the National Information Literacy Institute (NILI). Although much of NILI's emphasis will be on information literacy and higher education, it will be "dedicated to training and educating instruction librarians at every educational level." This Web site is a source of ongoing research and information about the creation of the NILI.

SELECTED BOOKS CONNECTED
TO INFORMATION LITERACY

American Association of School Librarians and Association for Educational Communications and Technology. *Information Power: Building Partnerships for Learning*. Chicago: ALA, 1998.

Anderson, Mary Alice, ed. *Teaching Information Literacy Using Electronic Resources for Grades 6–12*. Columbus, Ohio: Linworth Publishing, 1996.

Barclay, Donald A., ed. *Teaching Electronic Information Literacy: A How-To-Do-It Manual* (How-To-Do-It Manuals for Librarians, No. 53). New York: Neal Schuman, 1995.

Bleakley, Ann, and Jackie Carrigan. *Resource-Based Learning Activities: Information Literacy for High School Students*. Chicago: American Library Association, 1994.

Breivik, Patricia Senn. *Student Learning in the Information Age*. Phoenix, Ariz.: Oryx Press, 1997.

Breivik, Patricia Senn, and J. A. Senn. *Information Literacy: Educating Children for the 21st Century*. 2d ed. Washington, D.C.: NEA Professional Library, 1998.

California School Library Association. *From Library Skills to Information Literacy: A Handbook for the 21st Century*. 2d ed. San Jose, Calif.: Hi Willow Research & Publishing, 1997.

Colorado Educational Media Association. *Model Information Literacy Guidelines*. Denver, Colo.: Colorado Department of Education, 1994.

Craver, Kathleen W. *Teaching Electronic Literacy: A Concepts-Based Approach for School Library Media Specialists*. Westport, Conn.: Greenwood Press, 1997.

Eisenberg, Michael B., and Robert E. Berkowitz. *Information Problem-Solving: The Big Six Skills Approach to Library and Information Skills Instruction*. Norwood, N.J.: Ablex, 1990.

Everhart, Nancy. *Evaluating the School Library Media Center: Analysis Techniques and Research Practices*. Englewood, Colo.: Libraries Unlimited, 1998.

Stripling, Barbara K., and Judy M. Pitts. *Brainstorms and Blueprints: Teaching Library Research as a Thinking Process*. Englewood, Colo.: Libraries Unlimited, 1988.

Sykes, Judith A. *Library Centers: Teaching Information Literacy, Skills, and Processes, K–6*. Englewood, Colo.: Libraries Unlimited, 1997.

4

Learning in a Technological Context

Elizabeth K. Goldfarb

INTRODUCTION

Imagine a technology that can zap the entire contents of the Library of Congress across the country in half a minute, or a protocol for sending e-mail to the moon or Mars. A recent issue of *Newsweek* magazine offered both not as science fiction but as nearly-here technologies. How can teachers and library media specialists prepare children for a world where wave-division multiplexing technology alters all previous expectations and intragalactic e-mail is coming soon?

Research studies indicate some cautious optimism that incorporating technology in learning results in greater student motivation, greater sustained participation by less able students, and higher student achievement in some project-based learning. However, there is little consensus about what works and why. Ronald Owston suggested that the World Wide Web is a viable means to increase access to education, but noted that "after 50 years of research on instructional media, no consistent significant effects from any medium on learning have been demonstrated" (Owston 1997, 4).

Some researchers suggest that technology in general and computers in particular may actually be harmful for the developing child. Valdemar W. Setzer urged that computers be banned until twelfth grade, stating that computer use is damaging to younger children because it restricts young children to an artificial formal language that is antithetical to their natural thinking; reduces problem solving to mere data analysis; fosters a mechanical view of nature; discourages well-structured, disciplined thinking; and creates emotional and psychological stress that harms development and shrinks childhood (Setzer and Monke 1998).

Though some may be quick to dismiss Setzer (and others who write for the Confronting Technology Home Page) as neo-Luddites or alarmists, it is helpful to read and examine the arguments they offer. An annotated list of readings can be found at <http://www.public.iastate.edu/~lmonke/homepage.html>. Too often, the hype declaring "If it's technology it's got to be good" and "If it's *new* technology it must be better" influences budget decisions in ways that negatively affect planning for teaching and learning.

At the same time experts caution that additional research is necessary on the use of technology for learning, tremendous pressure is building from students, parents, teachers, administrators, educational experts, business leaders, elected officials, and the community to acquire more technology for schools. Tremendous anxiety is also developing that schools are failing children, or falling behind in providing sufficient, state-of-the-art access to technology and in providing instruction on how to use technology effectively. Even when schools do not provide access to videos, cable television, computer software, or the Internet, students frequently have these technologies at home or available in the community, and thus need assistance in learning to use them safely and effectively.

GREATER ACCESS TO INFORMATION

In theory, technology provides greater access to information. For example, the automated library catalog is supposed to provide greater access to existing resources. As more school libraries become automated, library media specialists need to reflect on how well the systems support the promise. Consider:

- How is the catalog maintained? By the librarian? By the paraprofessional? By relying on vendor-produced records?
- How good are the records? Are they up to date? Accurate? Reflective of local practice?
- Does the catalog reflect the entire universe of resources in the library, school, or network?
- Does the catalog include books, videos, periodical holdings, online services, Web sites of interest, a file of experts, teacher- and student-produced resources, community resources, and database links to hardware and specialized equipment?
- Are there reader guidance modules, help, or information?
- Where are the access points: the library, each classroom, online from home?

In addition to providing better access to existing resources, technology also provides new information resources. Testimonials from teachers, students, and parents celebrate the success of new technologies in making information accessible as never before. CD-ROMs, videos, and the Internet provide students with home library resources unimaginable in the past. Students acquire an avalanche of data in a variety of formats with a quick click. However, the information received may be inaccurate, biased, or dated. In the past, subject specialists, editors, and publishers filtered the flow of information. Reviewing media helped the library media specialist make informed judgments. Library media specialists further filtered materials by making selections for a unique collection and audience. Although library media specialists discussed accuracy and authority of resources with users, for the most part inclusion in the collection indicated an acceptable level of both. The user or reader relied on the expertise of the publisher, the reviewer, and the library media specialist.

Some new media, however, come without the old-time safeguards. A CD-ROM, video, or Internet Web site can be produced at home, inexpensively, by almost anyone with basic equipment. Many familiar, reputable publishers have failed or been folded into larger concerns; hundreds of new small companies have sprung up. There are individual author-producers marketing their work or selling their work to others. For many items, it is difficult to determine the source of information, the bias of producers or developers, or the accuracy of content.

Many materials are not reviewed in professional journals, are not reviewed in a timely manner, or are not reviewed for the school library market. "Entertainment" reviews may focus less on the quality and accuracy of the content and more on viewer appeal, ease of use, home purchase availability, desirability, or glitzy special effects. When new media are reviewed, the depth of the review may not be sufficient for the school library media center. For example, a single CD-ROM can hold 350,000 pages of text. How does a reviewer evaluate or read that much text?

Many items are not reviewed at all. How does a user evaluate an Internet site that can be accessed by almost anyone? Where does it come from? Who is the author? What is the bias? Agenda? Purpose? Is it safe?

Many libraries are currently tackling the thorny issue of filtering access to Internet sites. Congress has wrestled with the issue of requiring all school and public libraries to use a filtering program. Vigilant library media specialists and others interested in free speech can follow the debate by accessing the Web site of the Center for Democracy and Technology (1998). The problem is complex: Should the school library filter at all? How well do filters work? What should be filtered? Who decides?

What About Safety?

With or without filters in place, the school community needs to establish an acceptable use policy (AUP). Parents and students should be aware of what constitutes appropriate use of the Internet for educational purposes and the consequences of using the Internet improperly. Many acceptable use policies can be accessed on the Internet. Some useful sites include Odile Heisel's "Internet Acceptable Use Policies. K-12" (Heisel 1997) and AT&T Resources for Educators: Acceptable Use Policies (AT&T 1998). As with any issue of censorship, it is useful to have a clearly defined and agreed-upon policy in place *before* a problem arises.

What About Privacy?

Parents worry both that students will access pornography, hate literature, and other objectionable sites and that the Internet will provide dangerous predators and pedophiles with access to unsuspecting children. For this reason, many schools limit access to chat rooms, restrict and monitor e-mail, and adopt privacy policies establishing guidelines for Internet use and for posting information by and about students on Web pages. Andrew Trotter noted that administrators and parents are sometimes concerned that a story about or photo of a student appearing in a school Web page will violate the Federal Family Educational Rights and Privacy Act or more restrictive state and local laws (Trotter 1998). Some school districts ask permission before posting a student's picture on the school Web site. Others ask how the Web site is different from putting the student's picture in the school newspaper. More information on privacy may be obtained on the Internet at the Electronic Privacy Information Center (1998), the Privacy Rights Clearinghouse (1998), and the Electronic Frontier Foundation database (<http://www.eff.org/>).

What About Ethical Conduct?

Administrators and teachers may worry that student hackers will alter student records, trash systems, incur charges, create viruses, send lurid messages, or "flame" and "spam" others. School districts and school board members are concerned that they may be sued. Doug Johnson presented a thorough discussion of many ethical issues surrounding student use of the Internet, entitled "Ethical Issues Surrounding Technology Use in Elementary Schools," in his Web page (Johnson 1998a). The ease with which students can access, alter, post, and download information makes it important for teachers to discuss and explicitly teach issues of fair use, plagiarism, and intellectual property.

EXPANDED INFORMATION FORMATS

Technology expands possibilities. It makes information available to more learners and different learners. Bilingual children can hear and view a Spanish-language CD-ROM, chat online in Urdu, or visit a virtual museum with exhibits explained in French and English. Less able children can click and have a section of text from a CD-ROM read aloud; mobility-impaired students can use verbal commands to activate a computer or link to a related Web site. A class or small group can get background information on rain forests or ecology through video, cable, or an interactive computer simulation. Students can interview an expert over the telephone or through live chat, e-mail, or a satellite connection. Students can create and share art, stories, hypermedia presentations, research, and data with others around the world.

Sometimes students use familiar technologies in new or different ways: for example, the telephone for an interview, a camera to document observations, a VCR to create an interactive report, or a computer to design a persuasive multimedia presentation. Whether teachers introduce familiar technologies for new purposes or new technologies, some explicit instruction is necessary. As diverse media become a part of teaching and learning, teachers must provide additional instruction in media literacy. *Mediacy*, the Ontario Association for Media Literacy Newsletter Web site (1998), provides an excellent introduction to the key concepts and principles of media literacy.

Telephone

The telephone is hardly a new technology, but it is an important tool that students need to use more productively. Students should be guided in locating an expert, developing questions, preparing a phone introduction, structuring follow-up questions, asking for clarification, practicing oral language skills, taking notes, and expressing thanks.

Distance Learning

Cable television, interactive Internet, teleconferencing, satellite, wide area network—each method for distance learning comes with its own special features and problems. At present, most distance learning permits delivery of an established content to a distant location with some interaction with students; however, developing technologies are expanding the possibilities and reducing the costs. The Distance Education Clearinghouse Web site (n.d.) provides a detailed overview of distance learning possibilities. Information from Engineering Outreach of the University of Idaho, College of Engineering (1995), on evaluating distance learning programs can be found at <http://www.uidaho.edu/evo/dist4.html>.

Computer Software

Computer software may be used throughout the inquiry process. Some software contains content in, for example, encyclopedic, pictorial, or narrative form. Software tools, such as ClarisWorks, Excel, KidPIX, Print Shop, Front Page, and others, provide ways to gather, store, and transform information though text, graphics, and databases. Still other programs, such as "Oregon Trail," are interactive games or simulations in which skills and content are combined. Newer software allows students to manipulate variables and conduct virtual experiments. Both simulation activities and the newer interactive environments raise issues for library media specialists because the tools require expensive hardware and software and access for long periods of time by small groups of students. Consider:

- Who should identify, evaluate, and select the tools?

- Where is the appropriate place to use these tools? Classroom? Lab? Library? Home?
- How can scarce or expensive equipment or software best be scheduled to maximize access?
- Who should train students to use these tools?
- How well does this tool support the learning objectives of the course of study?
- How can the programs be used for assessment and independent learning?

Other software tools may be used to organize, edit, and prepare information for presentation. A student may use a word-processing program, a publishing program, or a hypermedia program (such as HyperStudio, for example) to combine text, graphics, photographs, video, sound, and animation to create a talking slide show, PowerPoint presentation, Web page, database, or other product. With computer tools, students can gather or organize information, create new information, persuade, or entertain.

In planning, the teacher must consider the number of computers available for student use, the time required to complete a project, and the value of the tool to the learning objectives. Many students prefer to use the computer, whether or not it aids in the project at hand. Unless the purpose of the unit is learning to use a technology tool, the teacher must take care that the student does not lose sight of the objectives of the unit. Creative scheduling, staggered assignments, and multiple access points are helpful when planning a unit that requires many students to use tools or programs.

CD-ROMs

Students need help examining and negotiating "edutainment" CD-ROMs. The library media center should have CD-ROMs teachers can take home to examine and preview before sharing with a class. Teachers or the library media specialist should model and demonstrate searches, tools, icons, and special features that can help student researchers get more out of investigations. Teachers should "think out loud" as they practice using CD-ROMs, while students observe with a large-screen monitor. It is helpful to model successful strategies as well as unsuccessful tries.

Teachers and media specialists can gather advice from student observers. "I wanted something on the Revolutionary War, but I didn't want all these things on the Russian Revolution. What could I try to eliminate all those other revolutions?" Or "This search gave me a picture of a dragon, but I really wanted an article about a dragon." Or "There wasn't any information under Babe Ruth. I wonder if I should look under Ruth, Babe." Or "I couldn't find cars, what else can I try?" Their suggestions will show a great deal about how they view the search and research processes.

Media specialists and teachers should discuss pictures and charts. Are they helpful? Do they give additional or essential information? Sometimes CD-ROM encyclopedia pictures are nearly useless and are included primarily because the publisher had the copyright. Students frequently want to print any picture—the bigger, the better, especially if a color printer is available. Discourage wasteful printing without thinking. Explain how to use the "note pad" and how to highlight sections of text for printing. Make it clear that text printed from a CD-ROM is the intellectual property of the author, not the student. With more experienced researchers, guide them to compare multiple sources for currency, completeness, accuracy, and authority.

Internet Sites

The Internet is an alluring playland. Many students have experience using the Internet at home or at the public library. Some students do use e-mail, chat groups, or games, but many more surf the World Wide Web, rapidly clicking and randomly cruising. They may have favorite sites: the home page of a basketball star or lyrics of a popular rock group. They may know about browsers, search engines, key words, hot links, and downloading files, but may not have used them strategically.

Before students use the Internet, the teacher and library media specialist need to share the school or district Internet policy with parents and students. School Internet searches are serious educational business, not time fillers or entertainment. Students should be very clear on the objectives and the responsibilities of using the Internet at school.

Teachers must ensure that students set their purpose for the exploration; they should also provide students with a glossary of special terms and tools. Teachers may model an Internet search offline, using WebWhacker or another capture program. For initial student investigations, teachers may also wish to download selected files to disk using a capture program. Students can explore the features of the whacked page without being online.

Teachers and library media specialists may wish to limit students to "bookmarked" sites, to help them gain familiarity with icons and tools and obtain appropriate content information. Restricting students to a few sites that have been carefully selected by the teacher and library media specialist helps students focus, reduces aimless browsing, and helps the teacher keep track of student progress and problems. As students demonstrate proficiency in using bookmarked sites and exhibit responsibility, the teacher and library media specialist may allow expanded access to the Internet.

CHANGING SCHOOLWIDE STRUCTURE
AND COMMITMENT

Many of the traditional information sources were portable. Find a book, check it out, use it anywhere. All the sources could be housed in a central location and organized on the shelf and in the catalog using agreed-upon conventions like the Dewey Decimal System or Library of Congress. A user with some experience in one library could easily transfer that knowledge to use in another library. The library media specialist provided location information, taught information literacy, and assisted with searches, introducing the special features of more specialized tools. Mini-lessons were targeted to specific users at the point of need. Most reference materials were onsite and always available. There might be some wait to use a particular volume or a microfiche reader, but for the most part, user turnover time was brief. Readers would photocopy the pages in books or magazines or print out articles from the microfiche.

Now, in our technological world, new resources often require elaborate or expensive hardware or online connections, or both. Equipment is frequently dispersed throughout the school: in library media centers, labs, classrooms, offices, and resource rooms. There may be a significant wait to use equipment. The user must negotiate different organizing systems, often without assistance. The library media specialist may not be aware that the chemistry student accessing a resource over the Internet in the science lab is having difficulties. Students and teachers who are sifting through resources, making decisions on what is needed, editing what is found, evaluating, saving for later use, and transforming for presentation require greater blocks of time and access to equipment for longer periods of time.

Some resources, especially Internet resources, are not available on demand, because lines are busy, the server is down, the site is down, the URL is changed, and so on. Print-and-take options may be limited by the location of printers and school restrictions on printing. Saving to disk may be limited by school network software, virus protection software, and school policies. Saving to file may also be limited. The information user is presented with more information, but that information is less organized, less reliable, less transportable, and more time-consuming to use.

The new technologies require that staff and students become information-literate and independent in using both the resources and equipment. Identifying what is useful is no easy task. According to Jamie McKenzie in "Deep Thinking and Deep Reading in an Age of Info-Glut, Info-Garbage, Info-Glitz and Info-Glimmer," "the post-modem school will raise a generation of highly skilled 'free range students,' capable of simultaneously grazing the Net and reading deeply. To achieve this goal, schools must make a dramatically expanded commitment to questioning, research, information literacy and student-centered classrooms." The same article cautioned that "[s]tudents will need a radically different skills array to negotiate the new information landscape" (McKenzie 1997). To meet those increased demands, schools and school districts must determine priorities, examine staffing patterns, alter the schedule, and assess the physical space of the school and the technology capacity of the building.

Technology leads to numerous questions about resources, services, and responsibilities for the library media specialist:

- How will needs be assessed: collection, space, staff, equipment, training?
- Will materials be purchased, leased, used online, borrowed through interlibrary loan?
- Who will determine priorities for space, access to resources, staff time?
- Who will identify new resources, preview existing tools, identify consortia for resource sharing?
- How will the costs be met for upkeep, maintenance, and replacement of hardware, software, networks, lines?
- What building modifications will be necessary to keep up with technology needs?
- How will training needs be met and supported for staff, parents, students?
- Will support and training be provided in-house? By contract? Pay-as-needed?
- How can the limited number of simultaneous access points be prioritized?
- How will the time and cost of staff development and student training be planned?
- How will the quality of resources and review sources be evaluated?
- Who will determine and evaluate student information needs and information literacy?

Given the magnitude of the task, it is obvious that effective implementation of technology requires a school-wide, and even districtwide, commitment. At a minimum, schools need to establish a technology planning team, a scope and sequence for information literacy skills, a comprehensive plan for ongoing staff development, bench-marks, and rubrics for student technology use.

If a school is to fully integrate the use of technology for learning, fundamental changes must be made in school structure and priorities. There must be a schoolwide commitment to:

- Providing planning time for teachers.
- Fostering ongoing collaboration among class-room teachers, subject specialists, library media specialists, and community resource specialists.
- Developing adequate onsite and online resources and technical support.
- Setting priorities for access to and use of staff, resources, and space.
- Hosting staff development for teachers.
- Developing assignments that foster student growth in using technology for learning.
- Developing mechanisms for mentoring: expert to teacher, teacher to teacher, teacher to student, and student to student.
- Providing workshops for parents and interested community leaders.
- Creating some forms of performance-based assessment.
- Continuing assessment, evaluation, and reflection by administrators, staff, and students.
- Keeping current with professional literature and fostering teacher researchers in the school.

CHANGING THE LEARNING

The Nature of Learning with Technology

Because the Internet organizes information in new ways, it does not merely provide more resources; it allows different kinds of learning. Researchers are just beginning to devise experiments to study how the organization of the Internet influences learning. Ian Brown (1998) investigated the effects of "browsing" on learning, providing students with three different common Web page designs. College students with no prior art background were given assigned reading on an art movement: some students received a single page of text organized by the author; others received the information with the addition of "thought questions" or "review questions" to structure the reading; still others were given the text with hyperlinks, enabling students to click at will and find additional information, definitions, or explanations. Text could be accessed in a variety of orders, and students could select when and if additional information or clarification was wanted. After reading, students were tested to see how much they could remember.

The researcher found the single-page hierarchical format best for factual recall; the page with review questions best for answering reconstructive questions; and a small advantage for learning with hypertext, which was outweighed by the improvement caused by the review questions. The author suggested that "jumping" to linked terms may reduce the cohesiveness of the text. However, the author cautioned that additional research is necessary (Brown 1998). Would use of longer passages yield the same results? Were older students successful with the text structured by the author because of their understanding of how to read text, based on past experience with textbooks and other nonfiction reading, and therefore less successful with information that included graphics, sound, or animation in addition to text? Would similar results be obtained with young students; students reading in an area of interest or expertise; students raised on hypertext, the World Wide Web, and computer applications; or students evaluated after a longer period of time?

Technology is also changing the "traditional" interaction between child and book. Eliza T. Dresang and Kate McClelland, in an article in *Booklinks*, suggested, after observing children who have grown up in this electronic world, that

> there is an alteration in the way they think, learn, and give, receive and create information.... For these children, words are becoming pictures and pictures are becoming words. They are able to gain information from bytes and text fragments that are not organized exclusively in a straight line from beginning to end or from left to right.

The authors applied the term "non-linearity" to these books. The authors further suggested that

> books that have special appeal to computer-literate young people share many of the characteristics that are intriguing to those using a computer: graphics in exciting new forms and formats, words and pictures that reach new levels of synergy, nonlinear and non-sequential organization and format, interactive and connection possibilities, open-ended conclusions, and a multiplicity of layers of meaning (Dresang and McClelland 1996, 40).

At the same time many traditional books are changing in structure and organization, the tools for writing are also changing how students read and produce text. One 1990 study, by Christine M. Neuwirth and others, found that

> writers using word processing alone—both student writers and more experienced professional writers—engaged in significantly less

> initial planning, conceptual planning, and total planning than when they used pen and paper, and that this phenomenon was related to the difficulty experienced writers reported in getting a sense of their texts and recalling them when using word processing. Findings of the project suggest that student writers be explicitly taught how to exploit the benefits and avoid the weaknesses of both word processing and pen and paper media (McKenzie 1998b).

The new generation of writers and readers then may need explicit instruction in strategies and skills that past readers and writers gained implicitly through repeated exposure to reading and writing text. Teachers will need to help students develop and articulate a deliberate process and an understanding of how text is structured.

Children need to practice "reading" media and deconstructing media to examine how the elements are used to alter what is perceived. Teachers should also be aware that familiar strategies might not generalize across media. A child who can take notes from a book may not know how to take notes effectively from a video or CD-ROM. A student familiar with watching a video for entertainment may not know how to use the visual images and narration to further research activities. Students who can follow directions in text may be unfamiliar with icons.

When unknown elements are added, students must have time to practice. Activities that compound unknown content with unknown strategy and unfamiliar tools make comprehension difficult. Extra time must be built into the schedule when technology is part of any project or unit. The assignment should also contain alternative activities as well as flexible aspects or choices, in case something does not work or is unavailable at a particular time or place.

Technology has the potential to change the very nature of the learning experience in schools. Scientists from the Institute for the Learning Sciences (ILS) described five different ways of teaching and learning in "The Five Teaching Architectures" (ILS 1994b):

- Simulation-Based Learning by Doing—students learn skills by doing
- Incidental Learning—building programs that impart incidental information while engaging the learner in fun and interesting tasks
- Learning by Reflection—the teacher's job is to muse with the student
- Case-Based Teaching—useful knowledge is built into stories
- Learning by Exploring—students get involved with problems of their own choosing, following up study with self-generated questions.

These scientists provide examples of software and learning programs for each of the learning architectures, using hypertext to connect the reader to examples and more information. The information is included in a book-length text called *Engines for Educators*, which is also presented in hypertext (ILS 1994a).

Information Literacy

Developing students who can function in a technological world should be the focus of schools committed to integrating technology with learning. Jamie McKenzie urged development of students who are navigators in the real world of information: children who can think, explore, and make meaning of the world for themselves (McKenzie 1994a). He proposed activities and problems that will stimulate intellectual growth. Fostering this kind of growth in students necessitates a broader, more comprehensive emphasis on information literacy. Important first steps include projects that emphasize developing strategies, generating questions, evaluating student performance, and reflecting on tools, process, and product. The projects should be structured so that students assume greater responsibility for their own learning.

In an online ERIC Clearinghouse document entitled "Computer Skills for Information Problem-Solving: Learning and Teaching Technology in Context," Michael B. Eisenberg and Doug Johnson clearly delineated how effective information skills can be integrated with technology and content. The authors noted, "Effective integration of information skills has two requirements: 1. The skills must directly relate to the content area curriculum and to the classroom assignments, and 2. The skills themselves need to be tied together in a logical and systematic information process model." The ERIC document detailed the kinds of tasks students will need to perform to demonstrate the new information literacy (Eisenberg and Johnson 1996).

The new national Information Literacy Standards from the American Association of School Librarians (AASL) and Association for Educational Communications and Technology (AECT) require that students become competent locators, developers, evaluators, and users of information in many formats (AASL and AECT 1998b). Students should have both the information-gathering strategies and the critical thinking skills to select, discard, synthesize, and present information in new ways to solve real-life problems. The task becomes more complicated when students must negotiate not only text, but also media images and multiple formats. In "The Information Literate School Community," Jamie McKenzie explored three main elements of information literacy, all of which "contribute to

learners being able to 'make up their own minds'"
(McKenzie 1998a). He labeled these elements:

- **Prospecting:** the ability to locate relevant
  information, sift it, sort it, and select
- **Interpreting:** the ability to translate the data
  and information into knowledge, insight,
  understanding
- **Creating New Ideas:** Developing new insights.

McKenzie continued the discussion of new strategies in online articles appearing in *FNO: From Now On: The Educational Technology Journal*, "Grazing the Net: Raising a Generation of Free Range Students—Part One & Part Two" (McKenzie 1994a and b). McKenzie coined the term "infotective" to describe "a student thinker capable of asking great questions about data (with analysis) in order to convert data into information (data organized so as to reveal patterns and relationships) and eventually into insight (information which may suggest action or strategy of some kind)." He noted that an infotective solves puzzles and riddles using many new technologies and follows problem solving with synthesis (invention) and evaluation. McKenzie discussed how the constructivist classroom lends itself to using the full potential of the Internet, by framing searches using "essential questions," à la Ted Sizer. He stressed that if research is to be meaningful, student questioning must be intense before, during, and after visiting cyberspace (McKenzie 1994a).

McKenzie also concluded that the classic information problem-solving model of Eisenberg and Berkowitz (The Big6™) is more appropriate "when collecting information to match clear targets" than for investigating challenging questions. For the latter, the author noted, the steps must be revised, "encouraging students and classes to form information collaboratives designing and implementing research on issues like acid rain." He then proposed new student competencies needed for cyberspace, including changing course, exploiting serendipity, and screening and compacting garbage.

If schools hope to create information-literate students, increased emphasis must be placed on teaching them skills that extend beyond location and access. Students must be taught:

- How to write essential questions to focus the search for information.
- How to locate useful new sources and determine how materials in a variety of formats are organized and best accessed.
- How to use strategies, search engines, and key word searches effectively to identify useful information and reduce the amount of nonproductive information "noise."
- How to critically evaluate information producers, authors, and sources.
- How to distinguish factual text from opinion, design, and content.
- How to access information online safely and ethically without putting themselves in danger or violating the rights of others; how to reduce hacking, "spamming," "flaming," and deliberate viruses; how to diligently follow the ethical guidelines in responsible use policies; what constitutes fair use.
- How to document sources and use information ethically without plagiarism.
- How to organize, make sense of, and synthesize the information gathered.

- How to transform information and present it in new formats.
- How to reflect on and evaluate their own research process.
- How to develop into independent information searchers.

Teachers and media specialists can provide modeling and scaffolding for students as they are learning information literacy skills. For example, in a unit in which students are expected to use the Internet, the teacher or library media specialist may model a search on the Internet using a large-screen monitor. The students record on an Internet Planning Sheet the key words selected, the topic they are searching, and the search engine being used. Students should use Internet evaluation sheets such as those posted by *MidLink Magazine* (1997/1998), Kathy Schrock's Guide (1998), or other sources listed at the end of this chapter. After the search, students record the number of "hits" found and examine with the teacher the first few hits to determine if they meet the students' needs. Then students consider: Are there too many hits? Too few? The wrong sort? Should key words be refined or a different search engine be selected? Are there problems with the Internet service provider? Does the screen freeze, say "URL not found"? Problems are a part of the search process and should be discussed when encountered.

Internet explorations should include opportunities to practice in small groups or pairs, as well as to develop a plan and discuss before, during, and after searches. Filling out a planning sheet or an evaluation sheet helps focus attention on the source and the strategies, and it reduces quick clicking. The outcome of investigation should be not only useful sites with valuable information, but also useful strategies that can be applied in future searches. Students who use the Internet for research should be able to explain the decisions they made and the strategies they used in conducting their search.

From Traditional Research to Inquiry-Based Learning

In the pre-technology era, beginning research for elementary students often entailed gathering facts, usually from a discrete source (for example, a textbook, almanac, or encyclopedia). The questions had "right answers" and the teacher knew the answers. The students filled in fact sheets; learned to use text-structure guides (index, glossary, table of contents); developed basic notetaking skills; and practiced documenting sources with footnotes and bibliographies.

More advanced students developed a hypothesis, created an outline, and fleshed out a narrative supporting or refuting the hypothesis using print resources gathered from the school or public library. Frequently students worked backward, first identifying conclusions that could be supported given available books and periodicals, and *then* selecting a hypothesis that could be defended or refuted based on available data, developing an outline that linked the conclusion and hypothesis, and pasting in notes from the print sources. The science fair might be the only event in which "research" actually meant inquiry, original observation, or experimentation. Frequently even science projects were not research, but replication of experiments already conducted and documented in books and periodicals.

With the information explosion and the availability of vast quantities of data (both processed and unprocessed), as well as sophisticated tools for gathering data and nearly instant access to scientists (both specialists and charlatans), the world has changed for the student researcher as well as for the average adult in the workplace and community.

Doing research and surviving in a technological world mean negotiating too much information in too many formats from too many sources and too quickly. Both questions and answers are fluid. Several models for the new process of research have emerged.

- The Research Cycle of Jamie McKenzie described in "The Post Modem School in the New Information Landscape" (McKenzie 1996)
- Constructivist learning models, described by Elizabeth Murphy in "A Constructionist Learning Environment" (Murphy 1997)
- Problem-solving models. Example provided in Lanphier Curriculum Center (LCC n.d.)

These models have many common features. For instance, students have greater control over the questions they study and the process by which they learn. Students address complex problems and issues to which there are no easy or absolute answers. Projects tend to be collaborative rather than individual. Students reflect, in writing or in discussion on the issues or questions they are investigating, the tools and information selected and the process by which information is gathered, summarized, evaluated, modified, and reformed. A variety of information sources and tools are used. Students participate in determining the product or outcome, the vehicles for sharing what they have learned, and evaluation of their work process and product. Students speculate on how the project or process could be improved.

The teacher or adult mentor provides an introduction to tools, strategies, and content, and mini-lessons as needed. The teacher and library media specialist provide guidance along the way, helping students focus and refine their strategies for information gathering, tool use, evaluation and synthesis of information, and use of information to answer questions. The teacher and library media specialist provide scaffolding for the research process. As students become more experienced, students work with less imposed support, so that "research" or "inquiry" more closely mimics the information search in everyday living or the world of work.

McKenzie proposed a Questioning Toolkit and urged that students' questioning skills be developed in kindergarten and strengthened throughout the K-12 years so students can bring powerful questioning technologies and techniques with them as they arrive in high school and further expand and refine techniques in high school. In a Web page titled, "Filling the Tool Box: Classroom Strategies to Engender Student Questioning," McKenzie and Hilarie Bryce Davis offered strategies tested by teachers for "shift[ing] the focus of classrooms from teacher-orchestrated mastery and memory of information to student processing of information to create understanding and improve problem-solving" (McKenzie and Davis 1997).

Beginning Projects in Inquiry

In the beginning, whether adapted from those on the Internet or locally developed, the research projects should be of short duration, with clear teacher scaffolding, restricted resources, specified outcomes, and substantial time for reflection and dialogue. A rubric that elaborates what is required and permits the student to review progress and resubmit work is helpful. The teachers provide graphic organizers, templates, time lines, flowcharts, rubrics, checklists, editing guides, and other tools to support the learner. Modeling, thinking aloud, and role playing can also be used by the library media specialist and teachers to assist students.

Students may use response journals to keep records of their progress, questions, and concerns. Thinking about process helps students develop metacognitive skills. The journals provide teachers with authentic work samples and progress reports. They also help the teacher determine needed mini-lessons, such as how to take notes from a video, how to read a graphic, how to use hypertext, how to find out who created that document, and what to do if you get no hits or 10,000 hits. Student strategies are posted on charts around the room so other students can use them if they get stuck.

The library media specialist, in cooperation with the school planning team, should develop an inventory of useful templates from teachers, print sources, and the Internet which teachers can use and adapt. Many useful sample documents can be found in *Power Tools: 100 + Essential Forms and Presentations for Your School Library Information Program* by Joyce Kasman Valenza (Valenza 1998). The looseleaf work is especially user friendly, and it comes with a CD-ROM of most forms that can be printed, adapted, and edited to fit local needs.

The teachers also should provide information for parents so they are clear about the progression of skills and strategies, requirements, student progress, deadlines, and expectations. It is important that parents understand what is expected and how they can support their children's learning.

Assessment and Reflection

Inquiry demands greater attention to assessment and reflection than traditional research because in this mode students assume a much more responsible role in their own learning. Carol Kuhlthau and other authors, writing in *Assessment and the School Library Media Center*, suggested ways to make the research process concrete in students' minds. Kuhlthau's article, "Assessing the Library Research Process," advised helping students to become more self-aware and to reflect on their experiences with the research process using four areas for student reflection: Evidence of Focus, Use of Time, Use of Sources, and Use of the Library Media Specialist (Kuhlthau 1994).

According to Kuhlthau, the focus should be clearly stated in the introduction of the research paper and should be supported throughout the report with facts and ideas gathered from library sources. Students should also reflect on the use of time in a project, thinking backward to when the assignment was given and then reconstructing their work piece-by-piece until the final product is complete. Likewise, a reflective narrative on the use of sources will help students reconstruct their thought processes and become more aware of their pattern of use of library resources and the intricacies of the sources used. Finally, students should reflect on the use of the library media specialist. Students should think about the kind of help required at different stages in the project. According to Kuhlthau, "[i]nteraction with the librarian is part of the research process and students can learn when and how to request information from the librarian" (Kuhlthau 1994, 63).

Kuhlthau recommended additional postresearch techniques to assess the research process, including developing a time line or a flowchart, participating in a one-to-one conference, and writing a summary statement. The most successful projects begin with advance planning by the library media specialist and teachers: setting the objective and desired outcomes, reviewing available resources, establishing who will teach what, developing time blocks for instruction and practice, and providing students with a rubric for assessing their work before beginning the project.

Although rubrics are helpful for many standards-based performance assessment activities, they are especially important for advanced information literacy projects. In an open-ended research project, students must assume greater responsibility for their own learning. A rubric can guide them. Jamie McKenzie's "Information Skills Rating Scale," developed for Oak Harbor, Washington, is useful for assessing student performance on the Research Cycle (McKenzie n.d.). Librarians may also wish to examine the State of Wisconsin's "Model Academic Standards for Information and Technology Literacy" (State of Wisconsin 1998).

CHANGING THE TEACHING

A Schoolwide Focus on Inquiry

Inquiry learning is a whole-school teaching strategy requiring instruction, practice, and layering year after year. To make investigative learning a regular, automatic part of a student's repertoire, practice and strategy instruction must begin in kindergarten and be continued through twelfth grade. Practice must occur in all subject areas, and projects should become increasingly sophisticated while scaffolding and supports are gradually reduced until the student is an independent investigator. Moving from a traditional environment to new learning models requires schoolwide dialogue and commitment. An examination of information skills "scope and sequence" documents and rubrics from other localities and schools is often a helpful first step. *The Information Literacy Standards for Student Learning* published by the American Association of School

Librarians and the Association for Educational Communications and Technology provides a good beginning (AASL and AECT 1998a). Some useful resources for information literacy skills can be found on the Internet in the writings of Jamie McKenzie (McKenzie n.d.), Doug Wright (Wright 1998), and the Northwest Regional Educational Laboratory (NREL 1998).

The "scope and sequence" selected should nest comfortably with other documents (for example, the school comprehensive education plan, mission statement, district or city policies, and state and professional content standards). It is usually easier to modify an existing document than to begin planning from scratch. After identifying a model, teachers, administrators, parents, and in some cases students should be brought into dialogue about appropriate benchmarks. Everyone in the education community needs to be clear on expectations. The planning team should:

- Investigate school-based resources for information technology, including computers, laser disks, CD-ROMs, DVDs, cable access, satellite, print, video, computer software, online services, Internet access points, and experts. Note the location, whether in library, computer lab, classroom, office, or department. Develop a resource guide.
- Investigate community resources that might support student learning: public library, museum, college, business, government, and the like. Develop a data file of resources.
- Develop a needs assessment: materials, infrastructure, staff, training, rubrics for students and staff.

- Examine existing tools in use by teachers: flow-charts, time lines, templates, mini-lessons, check-lists, rubrics.
- Analyze the calendar and schedule, looking at how both can be adjusted to maximize learning, planning, staff development, and resource utilization.
- Identify possibilities for additional resources: grants, equipment, technical expertise.
- Align curriculum content, information scope and sequence, comprehension education plan, assessment, and student outcomes.
- Establish benchmarks and a time line for students. Create baseline assessments and target a grade or grades to begin infusing the information curriculum.
- Determine mechanisms for including students in assessing their own work and in tutoring and mentoring peers.

Requirements for Staff Development

Providing resources through technology alters the instructional roles of the library media specialist and the classroom teachers, because students are able to access a broad range of material over which the teacher has little control. Every student should be taught to analyze (e.g., in terms of source, ownership, currency) and evaluate (e.g., in terms of authority, accuracy, bias) that information. Library media specialists and teachers must also learn and teach new formats (linear and nonlinear) and nontraditional or constantly changing points of access as the media and sources evolve. The paperless aspect of technology and the fact that students have access from home make it difficult for teachers and library media specialists to observe student strategies and intervene when needed. The ease of access to and manipulation of information make it difficult to monitor plagiarism.

Technology, then, has placed increased demands on teachers' own information literacy skills, their ability to facilitate learning, their capacity to teach critical thinking and inquiry, their determination to empower students to be responsible for their own learning, and their own technological skills. Because technology has placed higher demands on teachers, it has also engendered a critical need for staff development. The CEO Forum, STAR (School Technology and Readiness) Report issued in 1997 indicated: "Well-trained teachers are the key to successful classroom integration. Without a teacher's guiding hand, networked computers are expensive investments with questionable returns" (CEO Forum 1997, Appendix A). School systems must commit significant amounts of staff time and dollars to staff development if integration of technology in teaching and learning is to be achieved. Individual teachers must also commit personal time and personal resources for ongoing staff development. Membership in professional organizations, attendance at conferences, and purchase (and reading) of technical literature are continuing obligations of the library media specialist. A home computer with CD-ROM drive and Internet access is also essential. Continuing professional development is a requirement rather than an option for the library media specialist of the twenty-first century.

Brand, in "What Research Says: Training Teachers for Using Technology," reported key elements and essential requirements of teacher training in the instructional uses of technology, including adequate time, opportunities to collaborate with peers, ongoing support, and tasks related to the curriculum (Brand 1998). More about what makes for effective staff development can be found in "What We Learned" (Mink 1997). This report to Congress detailed what works and what does not work in federally funded teacher training programs. Jamie McKenzie described a districtwide staff development project in "Secrets of Success: Professional Development That Works" (McKenzie 1998c). An extensive bibliography of sources can also be found on the *Education Week* Web site from the "Issues Page: Professional Development" (*Education Week* n.d.). Online opportunities for staff development are abundant. The American Association of School Librarians' ICONnect site (n.d.) provides online courses, as did TeachNet (1998). Certainly, there are no easy answers for finding the time and dollars for providing effective training, but continuing staff development is everyone's responsibility.

Often teachers will be learning as they teach their students, so the library media specialist and planning team should identify, publicize, and promote professional resources available in the school and community as well as those available through the Internet and distance learning opportunities. Internet resources include professional journals, research reports, online courses, reading lists, interactive projects, mentors, experts, help lines, listservs, sample lessons, and rubrics.

To help identify technology self-development goals and needs, educators may find helpful a rubric by Doug Johnson, used for evaluating the computer literacy of staff, reprinted from the *School Administrator* (Johnson 1998b). Additional rubrics for staff development may be found by visiting the home page of Doug Johnson, District Media Supervisor for the Mankato Public Schools, Mankato, Minnesota, available at <http://www.isd77.k12.mn.us/staffdir/staf72/Johnson_Doug.html>. The School Technology and Readiness Chart (STAR Chart 1998) provides an additional self-diagnostic tool to help schools evaluate the technological needs and strengths of staff and students.

The current teaching staff will need to make special efforts to become effective users of technology, but within the next decade, those computer-literate students of the last decade who grew up with a computer at home and Internet access in the public library will become the teachers in the classrooms down the hall. A decade beyond that, some will move into administrative positions in the school and district. Many more will become parents or school board members and lobby for their children or constituency.

LEARNING IN THE FUTURE

Continuously Evolving Technology

Before we can even become familiar with existing technologies, the tools, processes, and content have moved on. However, some new features can help reduce the information overload. Software is available to help the user customize the data received from Web sites. For example, the "Cybertimes" section of *The New York Times* asks the reader to fill out a profile of special interests and then sends a customized daily e-mail newspaper to the reader's e-mail address. This practice of allowing the viewer to customize or specify information to be received can ease the information glut.

At the same time, software companies are using software to customize advertising to target markets. Some companies (e.g., "LikeMinds") provide "objective filtering," which the marketer uses to target "an objective characteristic [that] directly relates to a consumer's interests" (LikeMinds Technology 1997). If objective filtering does not result in the desired outcome, "collaborative filtering technology can incorporate objective filtering to narrow results down to specific categories." Whole new fields that are currently evolving will make the job of the library media specialist in teaching information literacy much more challenging.

Other tools may help ease the library media specialist's task. For example, the Dublin Core by Stuart Weibel, which is a 15-element metadata set, is intended to facilitate discovery of electronic resources. Librarians and experts from information and content area specialties are building an interdisciplinary, international set of descriptors that can be applied to Web sites. The authors describe the product as "roughly equivalent to a catalog card for electronic resources" (Weibel 1998).

New Ways of Promoting Learning

Educators are focusing on new ways of using computers to promote learning. In an online article (Carvin 1998), Andy Carvin described several such projects, including:

- Computer as Learning Partner Project (CLP), which provides a full-fledged physical science curriculum for middle school students using computer-assisted instruction
- Kids Network, which links students and classes around the world in interactive science projects
- RAND Microworlds, involving students in simulations and inquiry-based learning techniques
- The National Geographic Kids Network, a pay-for-participation series that partners students around the world in collecting real-world data and using the data in a mentored environment
- MidLink, an online teen publication, one of many opportunities for children to publish stories, poems, art, and reflections.

Carvin cautions, however, that innovative projects may come with problems. Some projects are pay-for-service, or by subscription, like National Geographic Kids Network; others require the purchase of software or more powerful machines. Most require multiple, fast access lines and a method for organizing, sending, and receiving e-mail.

Online Mentors, Experts, and Pen-Pals

One of the most exciting aspects of the Internet is the many experts and mentors willing to chat with students online, providing students with authentic reasons to read and write. KIDLINK (1998) has involved more than 48,000 students in 77 countries since 1990. Help lines such as AASL's KidsConnect (AASL, n.d.) provide K-12 students with question-answering and referral services.

Interactive Learning Projects

MIT Media Laboratory Epistemology & Learning Group Projects (n.d.) offer an array of activities for children that use "constructivist" learning theories. Some of the projects include:

- Toys to Think With—programmable beads that help children discover the concepts of size, shape, numbers
- Programmable Bricks—LEGO bricks that children can use to build autonomous robots and active rooms and conduct personal science experiments
- Beyond Black Boxes—enables students to create their own scientific instruments
- Project Lighthouse—uses computer technology to create different ways of learning
- Virtual Worlds—includes a graphical MUD
- Participatory Simulations.

Changes in Learning from Technology

Anecdotal accounts, teacher observations, and research studies indicate that technology changes what students learn and how they learn. The change is escalating, exciting, and worrisome:

- How will schools provide equitable access?
- How will schools pay for the new technologies?
- How will schools train teachers and students to use technology effectively?
- How will schools help children make sense of a world beyond our imagination?

Teachers and researchers must strengthen the commitment to investigating how technology is changing learning and how the power of technology can be harnessed to enhance learning for all children. Seymour Papert called the computer "the children's machine" in his book, *The Children's Machine: Rethinking School in the Age of the Computer*; there he noted that children currently in public schools and colleges do not remember a world without computers. They are comfortable with computers in a way that anxious adults find mystifying and amazing (Papert 1994). Perhaps, then, the question is not "how will *we* help the *children* make sense of a world beyond our imagination?" but rather, "how will *children* help *us* make sense of a world beyond our imagination?"

REFERENCES

American Association of School Librarians. N.d. ICONnect Homepage. <http://www.ala.org/ICONN/SLMS21st1.html> (accessed December 5, 1998).

——— . N.d. KidsConnect. <http://www.ala.org/ICONN/ kidsconn.html> (accessed December 5, 1998).

American Association of School Librarians and Association for Educational Communications and Technology. 1998a.

Information Literacy Standards for Student Learning. Chicago: American Library Association. (ISBN 0-8389-3471-4).

————. 1998b. *Information Power: Building Partnerships for Learning*. Chicago: American Library Association. (ISBN 0-8389-3470-6).

AT&T. 1998. Resources for Educators: Acceptable Use Policies. <http://www.att.com/edresources/accept.html> (November 4) (accessed December 5, 1998).

Brand, Glenn A. 1998. "What Research Says: Training Teachers for Using Technology." *Journal of Staff Development* 19, no. 1 (Winter): 10–13.

Brown, Ian. 1998. "The Effect of WWW Document Structure on Students' Information Retrieval." *Journal of Interactive Media in Education*. (December 2) <http://www.jime.open.ac.uk/98/12/> (accessed December 5, 1998).

Carvin, Andy. 1998. EdWeb: Exploring Technology and School Reform. <http://metalab.unc.edu/edweb/> (September 19) (accessed December 5, 1998).

Center for Democracy and Technology. 1998. <http://www.cdt.org/> (December 4) (accessed December 5, 1998).

CEO Forum. 1997. *STAR (School Technology and Readiness) Report: From Pillars to Progress*. Washington, D.C.: CEO FORUM. <www.ceoforum.org>.

Distance Education Clearinghouse. N.d. Other Information Sources. <http://www.uwex.edu/disted/websources.html> (accessed December 5, 1998).

Dresang, Eliza T., and Kate McClelland. 1996. "Radical Changes." *Booklinks* 5, no. 1 (July): 40–46.

Education Week. N.d. Issues Page: Professional Development. <http://www.edweek.org/ewhome.htm> (accessed October 3, 1998).

Eisenberg, Michael B., and Doug Johnson. 1996. "Computer Skills for Information Problem-Solving: Learning and Teaching Technology in Context." *ERIC Digest* EDO-IR-96-04. March. <http://www.ed.gov/databases/ERIC_Digests/ed392463.html> (November 30, 1998) (accessed December 6, 1998).

Electronic Frontier Foundation. 1998. <http://www.eff.org/> (December 1) (accessed December 5, 1998).

Electronic Privacy Information Center. 1998. <http://www.unc.edu/~jsenat/medialaw/privacy.html> (September 3) (accessed December 5, 1998).

Engineering Outreach. 1995. College of Engineering, University of Idaho. Distance Education at a Glance: Guide #4 (October). <http://www.uidaho.edu/evo/dist4.html> (December 1, 1998) (accessed December 5, 1998).

Heisel, Odile. 1997. Internet Acceptable Use Policies. K12. <http://falcon.jmu.edu/schoollibrary/netpolicy.htm> (January 30) (accessed December 5, 1998).

Institute for the Learning Sciences. 1994a. *Engines for Education*. "Engines for Educators. A default view of the book on how people learn and what that says for how we should educate them." <http://www.ils.nwu.edu/~e_for_e/nodes/I-M-NODE-4121-pg.html> (August 29) (accessed December 5, 1998).

————. 1994b. *Engines for Education*. "The Five Teaching Architectures." <http://www.ils.nwu.edu/~e_for_e/nodes/NODE-36-pg.html> (August 29) (accessed December 5, 1998).

Johnson, Doug. 1998a. Ethical Issues Surrounding Technology Use in Elementary Schools. <http://www.isd77.k12.mn.us/ethics.htm> (November 11) (accessed December 5, 1998).

————. 1998b. "Rubrics to Gauge Your Staff's Computer Literacy." In *The School Administrator* 55, no. 4 (April). <http://www.aasa.org/SchoolAdmin/apr9802.htm> (accessed December 6, 1998).

KIDLINK. 1998. The Kidlink Network. <http://www.kidlink.org/english/general/overview.html> (Copyright 1998 Kidlink) (November 17) (accessed December 6, 1998).

Kuhlthau, Carol Collier. 1994. "Assessing the Library Research Process." In *Assessment and the School Library Media Center*, ed. Carol C. Kuhlthau. Englewood, Colo.: Libraries Unlimited. (ISBN: 1-56308-211-X).

Lanphier Curriculum Center. N.d. Problem-Based Learning. <http://www.springfield.k12.il.us/schools/pbl/index.html> (accessed December 6, 1998).

LikeMinds Technology. 1997. Objective Filtering. <http://www.likeminds.com/technology/comparison/> (Copyright 1997) (accessed December 5, 1998).

McKenzie, Jamie. 1994a. "Grazing the Net: Raising a Generation of Free Range Students—Part One." *FNO From Now On: The Educational Technology Journal*. <http://fromnowon.org/text/grazing.html> (accessed December 5, 1998).

————. 1994b. "Grazing the Net: Raising a Generation of Free Range Students—Part Two." *FNO From Now On: The Educational Technology Journal.* <http://fromnowon.org/grazing2.html> (accessed August 4, 1998).

————. 1996. "The Post Modem School in the New Information Landscape." *FNO From Now On: The Educational Technology Journal* 6, no. 2 (October). <http://fromnowon.org/oct96/postmodem.html> (accessed December 6, 1998).

————. 1997. "Deep Thinking and Deep Reading in an Age of Info-Glut, Info-Garbage, Info-Glitz and Info-Glimmer." *FNO From Now On: The Educational Technology Journal* 6, no. 6 (March). <http://fromnowon.org/mar97/deep.html> (accessed December 5, 1998).

————. 1998a. "The Information Literate School Community." *FNO From Now On: The Educational Technology Journal* 8, no. 1 (September). <http://fromnowon.org/sept98/infolit.html> (accessed December 6, 1998).

————. 1998b. "The Missing Piece: Strategic Teaching." *FNO From Now On: The Educational Technology Journal* 8, no. 1 (September). <http://fromnowon.org/sept98/infolit4.html> (accessed December 6, 1998).

————. 1998c. "Secrets of Success: Professional Development That Works." *FNO From Now On: The Educational Technology Journal.* Reprinted from *eSchool* (March). <http://fromnowon.org/sept98/infolit3.html> (accessed December 5, 1998).

————. N.d. "The Oak Harbor, Washington: Information Skills Rating Scale." *FNO From Now On: The Educational Technology Journal.* <http://fromnowon.org/libskill.html> (accessed December 6, 1998).

McKenzie, Jamieson A., and Hilarie Bryce Davis. 1997. "Filling the Tool Box: Classroom Strategies to Engender Student Questioning." *FNO From Now On: The Educational Technology Journal* (April 14). <http://fromnowon.org/toolbox.html> (accessed December 6, 1998).

Mediacy. November 26, 1998. Ontario Association for Media Literacy Newsletter. <http://www.screen.com/mnet/eng/med/class/support/mediacy/index.htm> (accessed December 5, 1998).

MidLink. 1997/1998. Rubrics and Tools for Evaluating Multimedia, Documenting Internet Research, and Keeping Students Accountable on the Internet. July 9, 1998.

<http://www.ncsu.edu/midlink/rub.pres.html> (October 11, 1997) (accessed December 5, 1998).

Mink, Pat, chair. 1997. "What We Learned." Washington, D.C.: Subcommittee on Oversight and Investigations of the Committee on Education and the Workforce, Crossroads Hearing Focus: Teacher Training Programs (July 8). <http://www.house.gov/eeo/oversight/cr78sumhrg.htm> (accessed December 6, 1998).

MIT Media Laboratory Epistemology & Learning Group. N.d. Themes. <http://el.www.media.mit.edu/groups/el/elthemes.html> (accessed December 5, 1998).

Murphy, Elizabeth. 1997. A Constructionist Learning Environment. <http://calvin.stemnet.nf.ca/~elmurphy/emurphy/minds.html> (Summer) (accessed December 6, 1998).

Northwest Regional Educational Laboratory. 1998. The Library in the Sky. <http://www.nwrel.org/sky/librarian.html> (May 5) (accessed December 5, 1998).

Owston, Ronald D. 1997. "The World Wide Web: A Technology to Enhance Teaching and Learning?" Draft version of an article that appeared in *Educational Researcher* 26, no. 2 (March): 27–33. <http://www.edu.yorku.ca/~rowston/article.html> (accessed December 5, 1998).

Papert, Seymour. 1994. *The Children's Machine: Rethinking School in the Age of the Computer*. New York: Basic Books. (ISBN 0-4850-10638).

Privacy Rights Clearinghouse. 1998. <http://www.privacyrights.org/> (November 18) (accessed December 5, 1998).

School Technology and Readiness (STAR) Chart Self Diagnostic Tool. 1998. <http://www.ceoforum.org/self-diag.htm> (July 31) (accessed December 5, 1998).

Schrock, Kathy. 1998. Kathy Schrock's Guide for Educators. <http://www.capecod.net/schrockguide/> (August 8) (accessed August 10, 1998).

Setzer, Valdemar W., and Lowell Monke. 1998. Computers in Education: Why, When, How. Sponsored by the State of São Paulo Research Foundation grant 93/0603-1. <http://www.ime.usp.br/~vwsetzer/comp-in-educ.html> (January 11) (accessed December 6, 1998).

State of Wisconsin, Department of Public Instruction. 1998. Wisconsin's Model Academic Standards. <http://www.dpi.state.wi.us/standards/> (April 9) (accessed December 6, 1998).

TeachNet 101—An On-Line, Four-Week Internet Course for Teachers. 1998. Available July 1996 and August 1996. <http://www.teachnet.org/docs/4wkcrse.htm> (August 4, 1998) (no longer active December 6, 1998).

Trotter, Andrew. 1998. "Internet Access Raises Issue of Student Privacy." *Education Week on the Web* (25 February). <http://www.edweek.org/ew/vol-17/24web.h17> (accessed December 6, 1998).

Valenza, Joyce Kasman. 1998. *Power Tools: 100 + Essential Forms and Presentations for Your School Library Information Program*. Chicago: American Library Association. (ISBN 0-8389-0717-2).

Weibel, Stuart. 1998. "The Helsinki Metadata Workshop: A Report on the Workshop and Subsequent Developments." *D-Lib Magazine* (February). ISSN 1082-9873 DC-5. <http://www5.cnri.reston.va.us/dlib/february98/02weibel.html> (accessed September 24, 1998).

Wright, Doug. 1998. "Rubrics for Restructuring." In *Technology Connection* (January). <http://www.isd77.k12.mn.us/resources/dougwri/Rubadv.htm> (February 2) (accessed December 6, 1998).

ADDITIONAL RESOURCES

Books

Anderson, Mary Alice, ed. *Teaching Information Literacy Using Electronic Resources for Grades 6–12*. Worthington, Ohio: Linworth, 1996.

Angle, Melanie J. *Teaching Electronic Information Skills: A Resource Guide for Grades K–5*. McHenry, Ill.: Follett, 1993. (ISBN 0-695-62100-9).

Anstey, Michele, and Geoff Bull. *The Literacy Labyrinth*. New York: Prentice Hall, 1996. (ISBN 0-7248-0704-7).

Atwell, Nancie, ed. *Coming to Know: Writing to Learn in the Intermediate Grades*. Portsmouth, N.H.: Heinemann, 1990.

Barclay, Donald, ed. *Teaching Electronic Information Literacy*. How-To-Do-It Manuals for Librarians # 53. New York: Neal Schuman, 1995. (ISBN 1-55570-186-8).

Chapman, Anne, ed. *Making Sense: Teaching Critical Reading Across the Curriculum*. New York: College Board Publications, 1992. (ISBN 0-87447-470-1).

Eisenberg, Michael B., and Robert E. Berkowitz. *Information Problem Solving: The Big Six Skills Approach to Library and Information Skills*. Norwood, N.J.: Ablex, 1990.

Joyce, Marilyn Z., and Julie I. Tallman. *Making the Writing and Research Connection with the I-Search Process*. New York: Neal-Schuman, 1997. (ISBN 1-55570-252-X).

Junion-Metz, Gail. *K-12 Resources on the Internet: An Instructional Guide*. Internet Workshop Series # 5. Berkeley, Calif.: Library Solutions Press, 1996. (ISBN 1-882208-14-5).

Keim, Nancy, with Cindy Tolliver. *Tutoring & Mentoring: Starting a Peer Helping Program in your Elementary School*. San Jose, Calif.: Resource Publications, 1993. (ISBN 0-89390-259-4).

Loertscher, David V. *Reinvent Your School's Library in the Age of Technology: A Guide for Principals and Superintendents*. San Jose, Calif.: Hi Willow Research, 1998. (ISBN 0-931510-69-4).

Owen, Trevor, and Ron Owston. *The Learning Highway: Smart Students and the Net*. Toronto, Ontario, Canada: Key Porter Books, 1998. (ISBN 1-55013-905-3).

Popp, Marcia S. *Learning Journals in the K-8 Classroom: Exploring Ideas and Information in the Content Areas*. Mahwah, N.J.: Lawrence Erlbaum, 1997. (ISBN 0-8058-2430-8).

Porter, Lynnette R., and William Coggin. *Research Strategies in Technical Communication*. New York: John Wiley & Sons, 1995. (ISBN 0-471-11994-6).

Salmon, Sheila, Elizabeth K. Goldfarb, Melinda Greenblatt, and Anita Phillips Strauss. *Power Up Your Library*. Englewood, Colo.: Libraries Unlimited, 1996. (ISBN 1-5 308-357-4).

Stripling, Barbara K., and Judy M. Pitts. *Brainstorms and Blueprints: Teaching Library Research as a Thinking Process*. Englewood, Colo.: Libraries Unlimited, 1988.

Wagner, Roger, and Michael O'Keefe. *Hyperstudio: Software for a Mediacentric World*. Illus. Jeff Kelley and Donald McIntosh. El Cajon, Calif.: Roger Wagner Publishing, 1988–95. (ISBN 0-927796-49-X).

Whitin, Phyllis, and David J. Whitin. *Inquiry at the Window: Pursuing the Wonders of Learners*. Portsmouth, N.H.: Heinemann, 1997. (ISBN 0-435-07134-9).

Wisconsin Library Information Skills Guide. Madison, Wis.: Wisconsin Library Association, 1992.

Periodicals

Carter, Kim. "Who Does What in Your District . . . And Why."
Technology & Learning (March 1997): 30–36.

Coburn, Janet. "Kids in Charge." *Technology & Learning* 19, no. 1
(August 1998): 24–36.

Farmer, Lesley, S.J. "Training for Techies: A Schoolwise
Commitment." *Technology Connection* 5, no. 1 (March 1998):
14–18.

Farwell, Sybil. "Successful Models for Collaborative Planning."
Knowledge Quest 26, no. 2 (February 1998): 24–30.

Halzberg, Carol S. "What Works: Teaching Your Teachers Well:
Successful Strategies for Staff Development." *Technology &
Learning* (March 1997): 34–40.

Harada, Violet H. "Building a Professional Community for
Student Learning." *Knowledge Quest* 26, no. 3 (March/April
1998): 22–26.

Howe, Eleanor B. "Integrating Information Technology Into and
Across the Curriculum: A Short Course for Secondary
Students." *Knowledge Quest* 26, no. 2 (February 1998):
32–40.

Jacobson, Frances F., and Greg D. Smith. "Teaching Virtue in a
Virtual World: Internet Ethics for Students." *School Library
Journal* 44, no. 3 (March 1998): 100-103.

Jones, A. James, Carrie Gardner, and Judith I. Zaenglein.
"Desperately Seeking Standards: Bridging the Gap from
Concept to Reality." *Knowledge Quest* 26, no. 3 (March/April
1998): 38–42.

Kamp, Sue. "How Does 'Fair Use' Apply to Software Being
Used in Schools?" *Technology Connection* 5, no. 1 (March
1998): 19.

Kotar, Michael, Cris E. Guenter, Devon Metzger, and James L.
Overholt. "Curriculum Integration: A Teacher Education
Model." *Science and Children* 35, no. 5 (February 1998):
40–43.

Leu, Donald J., Jr., and Patrick V. Iannone. "Exploring Literacy
on the Internet." *Reading Teacher* 51, no. 5 (February 1998):
438–43.

Loertscher, David V., and Blanche Woolls. "Current Research:
Information Literacy: Teaching the Research Process vs.
Mastery of Content." *Knowledge Quest* 26, no. 2 (February
1998): 48–49.

McKay, Martin D. "Scheduling the Computer." *Technology Connection* 5, no. 1 (March 1998): 17–18.

Meyer, Michael. "Why Size Doesn't Matter: In the Fast-Changing World of Telecommunications, Cutting-Edge Technology Is What Really Counts." *Newsweek*, August 10, 1998, 44.

Milone, Michael. "Technology Integration Master Class." *Technology & Learning* 19, no. 1 (August 1998): 6–19.

Minkel, Walter. "Lost (& Found) in Cyberspace: How to Make Search Engines Work for You." *School Library Journal* 43, no. 3 (March 1997): 102–5.

Moscovici, Hedy, and Tamara Holmlund Nelson. "Shifting from Activitymania to Inquiry." *Science and Children* 35, no. 4 (January 1998): 14–17.

Siegel, Barbara. "A Model for Teacher-Directed Technology Training." *Technology Connection* 3, no. 9 (January 1997): 16–30.

Stone, Brad. "Coming Soon: www.newsweek.moon?" *Newsweek*, August 10, 1998, 12.

Internet Resources

[*Note:* These Internet sites may be viewed online in hypertext organized alphabetically and by topic by using the URL <http://www.panix.com/internetresources.htm>.]

Birkerts, Sven P. The Gutenberg Elegies: The Fate of Reading in an Electronic Age. <http://www.ou.edu/class/standers/4970web/birkerts.html> (August 12, 1998) (accessed December 6, 1998).

CEO Forum on Education and Technology. <http://www.ceoforum.org>.

Confronting Technology Home Page. <http://www.public.iastate.edu/~lmonke/homepage.html> (November 18, 1998) (accessed December 5, 1998).

Education Issues Series. Performance Assessment. <http://www.weac.org/resource/may96/perform.htm> (June 17, 1998) (accessed December 5, 1998).

Follansbee, Sari. The Role of Online Communications in Schools: A National Study. Center for Applied Special Technology (CAST). <http://www.cast.org/publications/stsstudy/index.html> (August 17, 1998) (accessed December 5, 1998).

Gordon, Janice, and Bram Moreinis. Draft: Promises and Problems: Getting Real about School Technology. Institute for Learning Technologies. <http://www.ilt.columbia.edu/k12/tpi/techkit/essay.html> (November 3, 1996) (accessed December 5, 1998).

Johnson, Doug. Building for Tomorrow. <http://www.isd77.k12.mn.us/resources/dougwri/building.html> N.d. (accessed December 5, 1998).

———. Rubrics for Restructuring. In *Technology Connection* (January 1998). <http://www.isd77.k12.mn.us/resources/dougwri/Rubadv.htm> (February 2, 1998) (accessed December 5, 1998).

———. Some Design Considerations When Building or Remodeling a Media Center. <http://www.isd77.k12.mn.us/resources/dougwri/buildingquestions.html> (March 10, 1998) (accessed August 10, 1998).

LION: Librarians Information Online Network. School Library Facilities: Design, Renovation, and Furnishings. <http://www.libertynet.org/lion/facilities.html> (February 2, 1998) (accessed December 5, 1998).

Matson, Lisa Dallape, and David J. Bonski. "Do Digital Libraries Need Librarians? An Experiential Dialog." *Online* (November 1997). <http://www.onlineinc.com/onlinemag/NovOL97/matson11.html> (accessed December 5, 1998).

McCullen, Caroline. Multimedia Mania! SAS Institute, in collaboration with Teachers Connect, North Carolina Department of Public Instruction. <http://www2.ncsu.edu/unity/lockers/project/ligon/mmania.how.html> N.d. (accessed December 5, 1998).

McKenzie, Jamie. "The Question Is the Answer." *FNO From Now On: The Educational Technology Journal* (October 1997). <http://www.fno.org/oct97/question.html> (accessed September 24, 1998).

———. "The Remedy: 'First the purpose ... then the design!'" *FNO From Now On: The Educational Technology Journal* 8, no. 1 (September 1998). <http://fromnowon.org/sept98/infolit3.html> (accessed December 5, 1998).

Mendels, Pamela. "Education: After Years of Research, Study on In-Home Computers Leaves Questions." Technology, Cybertimes *The New York Times.* <http://www.nytimes.com/library/tech/98/07/cyber/education/22education.html> (July 27, 1998) (accessed December 5, 1998).

————. "Education: Education Secretary Defends Technology in Schools." Technology, Cybertimes *The New York Times.* <http://www.nytimes.com/library/tech/98/07/cyber/articles/30schools.html> (July 30, 1998) (accessed December 5, 1998).

NCEF: National Clearinghouse for Educational Facilities. <http://www.edfacilities.org/index.html> (September 30, 1998) (accessed December 5, 1998).

Problem-Based Learning @ Lanphier Curriculum Center. <http://www.springfield.k12.il.us/schools/pbl/index.html> (May 28, 1997) (accessed December 6, 1998).

Shupe, Gordon. Automate Your Authentic Assessment! How to Score a Rubric on a Computer Using Any Decent Database. <http://stone.web.brevard.k12.fl.us/html/d.b.rubric.html> (February 4, 1996) (accessed December 6, 1998).

————. Automating Authentic Assessment with Rubrics: Technology. The Future of Education. <http://stone.web.brevard.k12.fl.us/html/comprubric.rubric.html> (January 22, 1995) (accessed December 6, 1998).

The Stanton/Heiskell Center for Public Policy in Telecommunications and Information Systems, Project Tell (Telecommunications for Learning). <http://ptell2.gc.cuny.edu/tell.html> (July 18, 1995) (accessed December 6, 1998).

Teacher Magazine on the Web. "Special Assistance: Technology Is Revolutionizing Instruction for Disabled Students." <http://www.teachermag.org/sreports/tc/class/cl-s1.htm> (1997) (accessed December 6, 1998).

Viardero, Debra. "Few Schools Use Technology Well, 2 Studies Report." *Education Week on the Web.* <http://edweek.org/ew/vol-17/07/tech.h17> (July 31, 1998) (no longer active December 6, 1998).

————. "A Tool for Learning." *Teacher Magazine on the Web.* <http://www.teachermag.org/sreports/tc/class/cl-n.htm> (1997) (accessed December 6, 1998).

Wyns-Madison, Peggy. Technology 101: Models/Formats for Professional Development. <http://www.teachnet.org/docs.cfm/dcs/tech101/models.htm> (n.d.) (accessed December 6, 1998).

————. Technology 101. Schools in the Information Age: A Planning Workshop. <http://www.teachnet.org/docs/wyns.htm> (August 4, 1998) (accessed December 6, 1998).

Part III

Context of Collaborative Planning and Teaching

5

Collaboration in Teaching and Learning

Donna L. Peterson

INTRODUCTION

"Collaboration—working with others—is a key theme in building partnerships for learning" (American Association of School Librarians and Association for Educational Communications and Technology 1998). This statement, from *Information Power: Building Partnerships for Learning*, describes a concept that has become a foundation for school library media programs as well as for many other types of organizations. Human service agencies, government, and community groups have embraced the concept of collaboration as a means to address common goals, build support among stakeholders, and maximize shrinking resources. Business and industry place a high value on collaboration as an effective way to promote creativity and achieve better productivity. Many school reform efforts identify collaboration and consensus building as important elements in changing and improving schooling.

Why is collaboration such a hot topic in so many different arenas? A simple conclusion might be that it is a good way for people to work together successfully in organizations. In the context of school library media programs, however, the answer is more complex—and perhaps critical to the survival of the profession. To this end, this chapter defines *collaboration* in the context of school library media programs, explains why collaboration has become an important element in working with teachers, examines the significant barriers to collaboration, and provides some strategies for using collaboration to improve teaching and learning in schools.

WHAT IS COLLABORATION?

The term *collaboration* is commonly used interchangeably with similar terms, such as *partnering, teamwork, cooperation, connection*, or *coordination*. When this occurs, the meaning is still basically the same—people working together. Loertscher (1998, 9) defined *collaboration* as existing when "two partners, the teacher and the library media specialist, team to exploit materials, information, and information technology to enhance a learning activity." A teacher and a library media specialist discussing a project or planning a special event together reflect a basic level of collaboration. When they plan a unit of instruction, they initiate a longer-term interaction that will, it is hoped, result in the integration of curriculum content and information literacy skills. Collaboration, at its simplest level or at its most complex, is desirable and important in the educational setting. No matter what it is called, collaboration should be cultivated and nurtured to the fullest extent possible.

In the *Collaboration Handbook*, developed by the Amherst Wilder Foundation to improve joint human service collaborations, Winer and Ray (1994, 24) defined *collaboration* as "a mutually beneficial and well-defined relationship entered into by two or more organizations to achieve results they are more likely to achieve together than alone." Winer and Ray emphasized the importance of growth in a collaboration. As in all relationships, collaboration grows over time, building from one experience and accomplishment to the next. Winer and Ray compared it to a journey that involves a progression of levels: *cooperation, coordination,* and *collaboration.* In school library media programs, all three levels of collaboration are needed in order to communicate and implement a given program effectively.

The *cooperation* level is the simplest form of interaction. It is informal, with few defined goals and a minimally organized effort to work together. The interaction is positive, yet requires relatively little commitment from the individuals involved, who remain, for the most part, autonomous. In a school library media example, cooperation occurs when the library media specialist sends the library schedule to teachers so that they can see when students can come to the library media center, and a teacher responds by notifying the library media specialist when a class is scheduled for research. The teachers and library media specialist cooperate because they need to share information. Significant joint planning and/or teaching has not occurred at this level.

When the relationship is deepened to the *coordination* level, a more formal arrangement exists. The focus at this level is on a specific team effort approached separately yet equally by the participants. Coordination is more organized than cooperation and requires a higher degree of planning, open communication, and a division of roles. In this scenario, the library media specialist and the teacher both have goals related to a student research unit in the library. For example, the teacher may assign a report on famous scientists. Knowing this, the library media specialist executes a lesson for students about the use of selected reference works. The teacher and library media specialist coordinate their separate efforts in order to achieve their particular instructional objectives. Full integration of information literacy processes and curriculum content is not achieved at this level.

At the *collaboration* level, the participants, even though they may have separate agendas, are fully committed to working together on a common mission with a new structure. Activities at this level are more long-range in scope, are more time-intensive, and require comprehensive planning in which all parties share both the power and the risk. In this scenario, the teacher and library media specialist work together over time, and as a result, establish trust and respect for each other's skills and knowledge.

Cooperation and coordination are important precursors to collaboration, where the library media specialist, in what used to be called the role of instructional consultant, now becomes a full instructional partner with the teacher. This is a new structure that requires different, more complex behaviors. At this level, full commitment is made to integrating information literacy skills into the curriculum. The teacher and the library media specialist create instruction that will improve student learning by helping students become critical thinkers and problem solvers. The teacher and library media specialist jointly select curriculum goals and objectives, plan learning outcomes, identify and locate resources, create an assessment plan, and share leadership responsibilities and accountability. They achieve a level of collaboration that has a greater degree of instructional impact and therefore is more likely to be repeated and sustained.

THE CHANGING ROLE OF THE LIBRARY MEDIA SPECIALIST

The role of the library media specialist as an instructional partner in collaboration with the teacher reflects a relatively recent change in the job description. The expectation that teachers and library media specialists will work together as an instructional team is not the way teachers have traditionally been trained for the classroom. Unfortunately, the stereotype of the school library as a collection of resource materials managed by a well-trained but non-teaching librarian is still a misconception held by some teachers, administrators, and community members. In the school library media profession today, significant changes have occurred. The library media program has shifted its emphasis from collections and services to student learning. Helping students to achieve through information literacy is viewed as the most important goal of the program. The implementation slogan for the new *Information Power* guidelines, "Information Power: Because Student Achievement IS the Bottom Line" provides evidence of this focus (American Association of School Librarians 1998).

The 1988 edition of *Information Power: Guidelines for School Library Media Programs* (American Association of School Librarians and Association for Educational Communications and Technology 1988) described a multi-faceted role for the library media specialist. *Information Power* was widely received in the school library media profession as the visionary document for the 1990s: one that focused on the library media specialist as a teacher and instructional consultant as well as on the more traditional role of information specialist. *Information Power* greatly expanded the view of how school library media programs contribute to the learning process and how library media specialists can be important instructional partners in teaching. It is important to note that *instructional consultant*, the term used to describe the instructional role in the 1988 edition, was replaced by the term *partner* in the 1998 *Information Power* edition. This is a good example of the power of language; *partner* is a better choice of terms to reinforce the concept that teachers and library media specialists should collaborate as equals.

It is also important to note that the term *collaboration* was not used extensively in the text of the 1988 version, nor was it listed in the index. By contrast, the 1998 *Information Power* edition contains the word *collaboration* hundreds of times. Chapter 4 outlines principles that guide library media specialists in achieving library media program goals for student learning. Collaboration is a specific methodology cited in all ten of the learning and teaching principles. Throughout the book, library media specialists are instructed to work collaboratively; to collaborate with teachers, administrators, and others; to use collaborative inquiry; to support collaborative work; to collaborate regularly; to practice collaborative teaching—and the list continues. Collaboration is stressed as one of the three central ideas in the *Information Power* vision of an effective library media program. It is emphatically a unifying theme for the library media program. "Effective collaboration with teachers helps to create a vibrant and engaged community of learners, strengthens the whole school program as well as the library media program, and develops support for the school library media programs throughout the whole school" (AASL and AECT 1998, 51).

CHANGING VIEWS OF LIBRARY MEDIA PROGRAMS

Why is collaboration emphasized so strongly in the literature as a foundation for quality school library media programs? An obvious answer is that collaboration is an effective method for improving learning through information literacy instruction. Another, perhaps more troubling, answer involves the health of school library media programs. The full potential of the library media program cannot be realized in a passive service-oriented environment. The library media specialist who waits for customers to request help may find that the customers have gone elsewhere, especially in the age of the Internet and the café-style bookstore. To create a dynamic, responsive program—therefore, a foundation for lifelong learning—the library media specialist must rigorously collaborate with teachers in the task of educating students. This goal will not be achieved until library media programs are considered essential to schooling.

Think back to *A Nation at Risk*, the widely publicized 1983 report about the deterioration of public education (National Commission on Excellence in Education 1983). School libraries were not mentioned in that report, an important indicator of the prevailing attitudes toward school library media programs at that time. Had school libraries been cited as a factor in the decline of public education, it might have had the positive effect of creating a national debate and plan for school library media program reform. Responses to the report on behalf of libraries were, for the most part, from librarians who published in the professional literature. One exception came from the U.S. Department of Education (1984, 9): "Because of the phenomenal explosion of knowledge, because of the value given increasingly to resources other than books, because of the stern necessity of students to learn how to find and apply information, the library media center should become a magnet for teacher and student alike." This call to action from long ago has yet to be fully implemented in all our schools today.

Nearly fifteen years later, a special feature about the state of education was published by *Time* magazine (Wulf 1997). Though not meant to be another *Nation at Risk* report for educators, its critical assessment of public education was viewed by many more readers and had the same effect . Once again, school library media programs were not mentioned. It is clear that the competition for resources in schools (time, energy, space, and money) is too intense to maintain programs that are considered nonessential to the goal of increased student learning. If the library media program is viewed as supplementary to the instructional program, it follows that support for materials, staffing, facilities, and equipment is subject to erosion, which weakens the program and jeopardizes students' opportunities for learning.

Although most library media professionals recognize that the traditional model of the school library must be replaced by the *Information Power* model, the evolution of the library media center into the essential learning hub for the school will not be easy. Many educators seem barely aware that the new model exists. There are many examples in the library literature about research-based instruction created by talented, collaborating library media specialists and teachers. Common to these articles are examples of authentic learning, fully engaged students, high-interest topics, and well-planned activities resulting in successful outcomes. Unfortunately, articles about this kind of collaboration, though plentiful in school library literature, are nearly invisible in the professional journals that teachers and administrators read.

"In the public's mind, schools are defined by classroom teaching and learning, and teachers and administrators are at the core of it. In that picture, librarians are not perceived as teachers or instructional consultants" (Hartzell

> Why is the performance of the instructional consultation
> role by the library media specialist critical to learning infor-
> mation skills by students? Because, unless there is a signif-
> icant and profound change in the way in which schools
> operate, the classroom will remain the front line of the
> instructional process. Through acting as an instructional
> consultant, the library media specialist gains access to the
> instructional process as it occurs in the classroom, and this
> access is vital" (Turner 1991, 14).

1997, 25). Efforts should be made to link the library media program with research on collaboration, effective teaching, and student achievement. Information about these important connections should be made available to administrators and teachers at the school level and also in the professional literature. Creating a link between classrooms, student achievement, and the school library media program will be the major task of the national *Information Power* implementation effort now under way.

Now more than ever, the pressure is on to improve student learning where most perceive it lives—in the classroom. As educational standards are being developed nationwide for nearly every subject area, new textbook-based materials aligned to these standards are being sought to fill the resource gap in classrooms rather than library media centers. By using collaboration to link the classroom to the library, library media specialists can successfully gain access to teachers and students so that information literacy instruction can be deliberately and purposefully taught. To make significant changes in the way students acquire, analyze, and utilize information, library media specialists must assume the role of instructional partner, an essential person on the instructional team and a strong contributor to the learning process.

COLLABORATION AS A MODEL FOR IMPROVING LEARNING

The nature of learning is based on authentic settings where students are engaged in higher-order thinking and problem-solving skills. In this setting, students are participants in the educational process, connecting new learning to old, exploring the interconnectedness of knowledge, creating new meanings that have relevance, and connecting their school learning to situations and experiences beyond the school. Collaborative planning and teaching will help students acquire the skills necessary to make connections across the curriculum and learn more effectively. Information literacy is an important foundation for this kind of learning.

Student learning in the information age demands new skills. With the global spread of robust networks and growing computing power, coupled with the explosion of the Internet and the World Wide Web, events that seemed futuristic one year ago are not only believable, they have already happened. National education technology standards have recently been developed by the International Society for Technology in Education (ISTE 1998). Their purpose is to provide teachers with a framework of technology skills that all students should have. The inside cover of the document is a battle cry for change in schools. It reads:

> Ready or not...Our educational system must produce Technology Capable Kids. All Kids Must Be Ready for a Different World. Tools are different...The World is Different. Communication is different...Work is different...Kids are different...Information is different...And Learning is Different.

Knowledge about how students learn today and predictions about how students will learn in the future create

> Learners of tomorrow will function in a nonlinear environment fostered by access to electronic resources and tools that enable them to explore relationships and create knowledge within nonlinear frameworks. Learners will engage in real world projects, collaborating with others in their local school, community and around the world using global connections that allow multimedia communications.... The learning program of the future values process equally with content knowledge, and information literacy is recognized as a basic skill along with reading, writing, and calculating (Pappas 1997, 32).

serious challenges to the way schools create and provide education for our youth.

The lack of faith in public education and declining test scores have rallied the nation to set higher, more definitive expectations about what students should know and be able to do. Standards for basic skills have become the foundation for public school reform. Schools use them to review teaching practices; parents use standards to follow their child's growth and development. National information literacy standards have been developed to guide instruction and provide performance indicators of what students should know and be able to do as information-literate learners (AASL and AECT 1998, 8). The standards will further promote and give impetus to collaborative planning and curriculum development involving information literacy. An important next step for AASL will be to introduce the information literacy standards to teachers and administrators and begin to ask some essential questions. Is there agreement that students should be information literate? If so, how will they be taught? Who will be responsible for the instruction? How will we know when students have achieved the standards that have been set?

One district study determined the degree of support for information literacy instruction by involving staff and students in a series of interviews (Willeke 1998). The purpose was to identify the attitudes of staff and students regarding the library media program and, by so doing, help direct the study of the library media program in the district. Most teachers interviewed (89 percent) reported that they expect students to locate and use information beyond the resources provided in the classroom. When asked why this is important, teachers talked about the need for students to become independent learners, to apply a research process, and to become information literate. Although most of the teachers interviewed had not articulated these views prior to the interviews, they were clear that they wanted their students to be information literate. The teachers said that they made assignments that required students to use information literacy skills, and that they expected students to use their skills to locate and use resources that support curriculum in the school library media center.

Many of the teachers, however, were reluctant to support district-wide information literacy standards because they feared it would increase their teaching load. With such strong agreement that information literacy is important, but less definitive support for how it will be taught, the district is working on a plan to articulate a library media vision for all students and faculty that is embedded in existing curriculum. Central to this effort is the collaborative planning and teaching model.

As the nature of learning dramatically changes, the nature of teaching must change also. The information age brings new technical challenges as well as educational practices for teachers, students, administrators, parents, and library media specialists. The pace of technology requires that everyone become responsible for his or her own learning well past the age of K-12 public education. "Students must become more active and responsible participants in the learning process. While teachers will still function as instructional leaders, their dispensing knowledge to students will be replaced by collaborative, cooperative experiences that will sometimes even blur the role of teacher and student" (Parry 1997, 35).

Central to the shift from passive to active cooperative learner is the student's ability to access, evaluate, interpret, appreciate, and communicate information—the skills of information literacy.

> Our changing society and the changing needs of students demand that schools no longer be content with student learning confined to the lower-level of recall of discrete and often unconnected facts. Instead, today's students must be equipped to deal effectively with the information flood that threatens to overwhelm them. In short, today's students must develop the knowledge, skills, and habits that enable them to locate, evaluate and use information to solve problems (Keegan and Westerberg 1991, 9).

The library media specialist and the teacher must assume joint responsibility for the concepts and skills of information literacy instruction. It is the heart of learning.

BARRIERS THAT INFLUENCE COLLABORATION

Although a case can be made that collaboration is an effective means to achieve better learning through integrated information literacy skills, it rarely occurs naturally in schools. In a culture that rewards individual effort, collaboration is not a well-practiced habit. Collaboration requires at least two persons. Library media specialists, though well prepared and well intentioned, cannot collaborate by themselves. If teachers do not wish to plan and teach with library media specialists, it will not happen. What factors influence the desire and ability of teachers to work collaboratively with others? How do these factors shape the strategies library media specialists can use to build influence with teachers?

Norms of Teaching

A six-year investigation of schoolwide action research in urban high schools revealed that the teaching norms of privacy and isolation, as well as basic notions about working together, were problematic for educators. Teachers also were reluctant to open their classrooms to outside study, because they are accustomed to teaching in private behind closed doors. "While teachers generally valued working together with their grade-level or subject-area peers, most schools found it difficult to convince people of the importance of a school-wide focus" (Allen and Calhoun 1998, 707). These results are substantiated by a body of research on the culture and beliefs that are strongly held about teaching (Wittrock 1986). These beliefs (norms) garnered from Wittrock's research, though not uniform in all teachers and in all schools, can be translated into implications for library media specialists who have difficulty getting teachers to plan with them.

- Norm: The teacher is the ultimate authority figure in the classroom. The teacher keeps a distance from students and maintains discipline.

- *Implication: Students are not assigned to the library media program; they belong to the classroom. Library media specialists must find ways to estab-*

lish credibility with the teacher and assume direct responsibility for student learning. Library media specialists must demonstrate their skills, knowledge, and commitment to student achievement in order to build trust and create bonds with teachers.

- Norm: Typically, teachers work in isolation. The traditional egg-crate arrangement of classrooms in most schools, as well as the scheduled blocks of specifically allotted time periods, significantly reduce the opportunities for teachers and library media specialists to pause and interact. Although they can be visible and interact with others during the day, teachers seldom use these interactions to collaborate on shared teaching problems. Teachers may be on friendly terms and still not ask for help because it may suggest failure. A complementary norm discourages teachers from telling their peers how to do something differently.

- *Implication: Autonomous behavior and time constraints make it difficult for library media specialists to gain access to teachers. Expectations that teachers will stop during the day to sit down to create a plan are unrealistic. Many strategies must be employed to create connections and understandings so that when opportunities do arise, readiness is not an issue. Planning as a part of scheduled team meetings is effective, but plans can also be discussed in the hallway or lunchroom as well.*

Time

An important factor in collaborative planning is time. In fact, time is often cited by library media specialists and teachers as a significant barrier to collaboration. Because other instructional tasks must be accomplished during the school day, time for collaborative planning may not be considered a priority. A survey of high school teachers cited by the Center on Organization and Restructuring in Schools (1992) indicated that 46 percent of high school teachers spent less than one hour a month meeting with colleagues on curriculum and instruction planning. Relatively small amounts of time spent on collaborative planning are not likely to change the quality of instruction for students.

A possible way to address the time issue is to infuse collaborative planning into regular unit planning. It is critical that teachers know that integrating information literacy concepts, such as problem-solving skills, is a way to enhance the quality and effectiveness of instruction. "The unit plan is also a critical tool. It is perhaps the best instrument for emphasizing problem solving and critical thinking. In general, experts recommend that critical thinking be taught in the context of complex problem-solving units, not as discrete skills taught in isolation" (Glatthorn 1993, 4).

Though collaboration is a joint effort, it is critical that the library media specialist assume leadership and major responsibility for its success. However, if the library media center has a fixed schedule of classes all day long, collaboration will be difficult to accomplish. Time and fixed scheduling become significant obstacles to success. "Perhaps the best scenario for the implementation of the consultation and teaching roles defined in *Information Power* includes flexible scheduling, with a full-time certified library media specialist who meets with teams of teachers to plan for instruction" (Tallman and Van Deusen 1994, 37). Flexible scheduling of the library media center will ensure that the library media specialist has the opportunity to meet with teachers who have limited time and opportunities to plan. If collaborative planning is to be effective, principals and other school leaders should address how time can be provided for that purpose and how time can be used more productively.

Change

The challenges that face library media specialists who wish to improve student learning through collaboration and integration are significant because they involve change. The essence of change is that deeply-ingrained behaviors must be altered. Change automatically means resistance, especially in the field, where the basic behaviors of teaching have not changed much in 100 years.

The key factor in changing to collaborative planning is what it means to the teachers and library media specialists who must implement it. "Planning is a solitary activity for teachers. Planning in concert with the school library media specialist may be unwelcome because it is unfamiliar. Until teachers come to expect such a collaborative relationship, school library media specialists may be charting new territory in forging planning partnerships" (Wolcott 1994, 163). A comprehensive compilation of research on school librarianship and the implementation of change suggests that the shift to collaborative planning will be difficult because it involves creating changes that will inherently be opposed. However, the research can also be used as a reliable source of information and as important guidelines for the institutionalization of library media programs (Haycock 1995).

Most of the energy in an organization is invested in maintaining the existing order of things; change is always resisted, internally and externally. Seventy-five years of research confirm in theory what library media specialists

have sadly experienced in practice for a long time (Orlosky
and Smith 1972).

1. Changes in methods of instruction are more
   difficult than changes in curriculum or administration.
   *Is it easier to use a new text than to teach a
   different way?*

2. If a change requires teachers to abandon an
   existing instructional practice, it is in danger of
   defeat.
   *Teachers don't want to give up what is comfort-
   able and known.*

3. If retraining is required, success is threatened
   unless strong incentives are provided.
   *Training is hard work and failure is always a
   possibility—motivation is important to any
   change in behavior.*

4. Efforts to change curriculum by integrating or
   correlating the content are resisted and are especially at risk.
   *Big changes require big effort, and it's just easier
   not to do it unless it's required.*

5. The cost of the change is a significant factor in
   determining the permanence of the change. If
   the change puts a strain on school personnel,
   or if it requires a substantial investment in
   learning new facts and procedures, it is not
   likely to persist.
   *Hard work in this circumstance means that
   the sooner it can be discarded, the easier life
   will be.*

These are formidable obstacles to the degree of change needed for naturally autonomous teachers to become instructional team members. What facilitates the adoption and implementation of change in a teaching environment? What strategies can library media specialists use to overcome the natural resistance to change that is reflected in schools?

First, change that requires little new behavior has a better chance of being accepted. The successful library media specialist initially can contribute a greater share of the work to make things go smoothly until the teacher experiences firsthand how collaboration can be beneficial. Second, collaboration must not be viewed as difficult to attain. "Teachers must not only want to implement a change, they must feel that they can achieve it. They need to see change not only as appropriate for students and as promising better learning but also as something practical that they and their school can manage" (Evans 1996, 85).

Finally, if collaboration is not viewed as essential to their success, teachers will be much less likely to want to create any changes in their behavior. They should know clearly what is to be gained from making the change. This is the WIIFM (What's In It For Me?) principle in action (Hartzell 1997). The teacher must understand the value of integrating information literacy skills into classroom content. The important questions for teachers are: "Will my students learn more effectively?" "Are these skills important to students' academic success?" "Does my teaching improve as a result of working with the library media specialist?" Library media specialists must be able to articulate the answers to these questions for the teacher and use this information to get the teacher to the planning table and into the library media center. Library media specialists must be strong advocates for their programs and exert appropriate leadership skills to build support. Provisions should be made for open, two-way communication to take place between the library media specialist and the teacher. The library media specialist must know and understand the concerns of teachers and must use a gradual, flexible approach (Owens and Steinhoff 1976).

COLLABORATION REQUIRES KNOWLEDGE AND SKILLS

Knowing How Teachers Plan

Understanding obstacles to change is an important first step in overcoming them. Knowing how teachers plan is an important way to get in sync with the culture of the school and to pave the way for positive interactions that lead to collaboration. In order for library media specialists and teachers to work together to deliver integrated units of instruction, it also is essential that library media specialists understand how teachers plan. "Instructional consultation is a function that has been widely endorsed, but not widely practiced. School library media specialists may be only marginally involved in the instructional process because they lack an understanding of how teachers plan" (Wolcott 1994, 161). Teachers use different types and styles of planning. They plan so that they can be prepared, but primarily to create a framework that guides instruction. The most important kind of teacher planning is creating units of instruction; less effort is spent on daily written lesson plans unless they are required. Predictably, teachers start planning by using published curriculum materials. What is somewhat surprising is that much of the planning process for teachers is mental and nonlinear. Linear models of instructional design typically involve the basic steps of (1) identifying goals and objectives, (2) selecting and organizing learning activities, and (3) evaluating. The nonlinear planning method starts first with teachers thinking about the subject matter; objectives and evaluation are of lesser importance (Glatthorn 1993).

This information reveals why it may be cumbersome for library media specialists to plan with teachers using linear-type models as prescribed in the library literature. These methods could be counter to the way teachers, and also library media specialists, normally plan. It is not advisable to throw out the linear models in favor of some intuitive, spontaneous mental alternatives; however, the wisdom here is found in the increased knowledge and understanding of the planning environment. Library media specialists can use the linear model as a guide to help fill in the gaps for teachers and improve the quality of instruction. Understanding how teachers plan is an important consideration for library media specialists who, in the role of instructional partner, must accommodate varied teaching approaches and personalities. This is a key element in successful collaborative practice.

Interpersonal Relations Are Important

Collaborative planning is built on the degree to which teachers and library media specialists possess the personal attributes needed to work together as adults and colleagues. Most teachers have not been trained to integrate and infuse information literacy into their instructional planning. They need the expertise of the library media specialist, who is skilled at planning and who must also be warm and welcoming. Connections between colleagues should be nurtured and developed in the same way as personal friendships. Sometimes the sole reason why teachers work with the library media specialist—and vice versa—is because at some time a small favor was offered, a thoughtful gift of information exchanged, or a new resource shared. These are small events but important ones. Like

Ten Collaborative Planning Strategies

1. Establish friendships. Engage in "teacher talk" to establish trust, create ideas, and identify common ground.
2. Initiate rather than wait. The teacher workroom or team meeting is a good place.
3. Take advantage of informal opportunities, but schedule formal ones too.
4. Use reflection and dialogue to help articulate the planning methods and thinking that is unique to each teacher. Listen and ask questions.
5. Identify the way the teacher likes to plan. Is it orderly? Intuitive? Last-minute? Long-range? Be adaptable and fill in the gaps in the plan.
6. Use curriculum content (texts and guides) as a starting point. Then get the resources to match. This is where library media specialists can really excel, because they have the materials that teachers want and need.
7. Do not force linear behavior that may not be welcomed. Flexibility is essential.
8. Keep the paperwork simple. For collaborative planning, use forms that you are willing to complete. The planning process is a means to an end, not an end in itself.
9. Be patient. Plans evolve over time through interconnected ways. Teachers who are satisfied will come back. Sometimes it isn't all in one place at one time.
10. Always try to say yes first. Forgive last-minute thinking—we all do it.

building blocks, collegial relationships are built slowly and with care. Library media specialists who are successful at creating collaborations are also successful at creating positive interpersonal relations and knowing how to build influence with their colleagues.

Creating a Collaborative Vision

The collaborative model has been established as an effective way to create meaningful connections between the library media program and the classroom. It is essential for the successful integration of information skills and curriculum. Barron and Bergen (1992) connected the *Information Power* library media program with elements that are important to the restructured school: improved achievement, the importance of information literacy, the goal of lifelong learning, and the importance of collaboration. It is common to read about school reform efforts that have identified teacher collaboration as a means to achieve positive instructional change. Teachers need time to talk to each other, compare notes, encourage, discuss, revise, and try out new ideas. This naturally collaborative activity builds supportive bonds and empowers teachers collectively to reach a higher level of teaching. Research indicates that teachers who work together have seen significant improvements in student achievement, behavior, and attitudes. Where collaboration is practiced in schools, students benefit from program coherence and consistency. Improved student behavior and achievement may well be a response to a more collaborative learning environment (Morton 1993).

Central to the success of any major change in curriculum or teaching methodology is the degree of shared belief that there is a need for the change and that there is a good opportunity to achieve results. Administrators are essential leaders who are in the best position to promote and support changes, including collaborative efforts, in their schools. They can help the faculty to see the importance of the library media program to student achievement. They can ensure open access to the library media center, provide adequate support staff, and create schedules that promote collaborative planning in the whole-school culture. A body of evidence indicates that a climate of "cooperation, collaborative planning and collegial relationships among staff is one of the important factors that differentiates academically effective from less effective schools" (Bell and Totten 1991, 293). Administrators should use this research to their advantage.

Providing the climate and support for collaborative unit planning will pay dividends by providing an organizing structure for learning, improving the quality of the units, improving the depth of professional expertise, supporting classroom practices (e.g., interdisciplinary curriculum, teaming, research-based instruction, cooperative learning), integrating information across disciplines and within process skills, utilizing a wide range of print and nonprint resources to meet varied student needs and interests, encouraging shared decision making, helping create healthy school communities, and improving the collegial relationships among faculty members.

One notable school reform model that focuses on improving teaching and learning through effective school library media programs is the National Library Power Initiative, a $40-million effort supported by the DeWitt Wallace-Reader's Digest Fund. Library Power is built around the concept that collaboration, involving all members in the learning community, will help students achieve better learning.

> Because the Library Power model is built around collaboration, teaching has also been substantively affected in many schools. Teachers are working with each other and with the library media specialist to develop and teach units that integrate content and information literacy skills.

Many of these units are interdisciplinary. Some teachers have given up strict control over the learning process in order to facilitate students learning on their own. Some principals have recognized the effectiveness of collaborative teaching and have honed their own ability to lead through facilitation rather than authority (AASL and AECT 1998, 141).

Library Power succeeded best where the concept of collaboration was used to create a community-wide vision, plan grant activities, involve others in decision making, and implement the program with all stakeholders.

Lessons Learned

In 1996, the American Association of School Librarians (AASL) sponsored a "Meeting in the Middle," during which teams of middle school teachers and library media specialists were gathered to foster collaboration. An analysis of the responses from the eleven teams revealed some lessons to be learned about collaboration. The list mirrors research and provides a checklist of beliefs about what actually works in practice (Grover 1996).

Lesson 1: School culture must support collaboration.

Lesson 2: Flexible scheduling is a vital component of the collaborative planning and work.

Lesson 3: The library media specialist can and should be a leader of the efforts to collaborate.

Lesson 4: Expect apathy and/or dissent among faculty.

Lesson 5: Members of the collaborating group must share an understanding and respect for each other.

Lesson 6: It takes a whole team at every meeting to have real cooperation.

Lesson 7: Things will not go smoothly all of the time.

Lesson 8: Every level within the school (administrators, teachers, library media specialists) must participate in decision-making.

Lesson 9: School administrators and other decision-makers must support the concept of collaboration.

Lesson 10: The group is flexible in the way it organizes and accomplishes its work.

Lesson 11: Staff development is essential.

Lesson 12: Collaborating group members communicate often, openly discuss issues and convey necessary information to one another and to people outside their group.

Lesson 13: Goals and objectives of the collaborative group must be attainable and understood by all group members.

Lesson 14: Essential resources (time, facilities, learning resources, budget) must be provided to assure success.

SUMMARY

The school library media program succeeds to the degree it affects teaching and learning. Collaboration is the vehicle that connects the classroom to the library media center. To ensure the survival of the library media program, important, meaningful connections in the form of collaborations must be made with administrators, teachers, and other members of the learning community. Though the library media program has changed to focus more on student learning than on resources, these changes are not apparent to the entire educational community. Library media specialists have been reluctant to assume the role of instructional partner and teachers have also been slow to adopt reform efforts that focus on collaboration and facilitation. Adoption of the collaborative model is difficult and will remain so because the obstacles are well entrenched in the structure of the school and the culture of teaching. One key to success lies in the interpersonal skills of the library media specialist. The support of the school principal is critical in order to have the schedule, resources, credibility, and opportunity to plan collaboratively.

A major concern involves the absence of knowledge in the literature and in teaching institutions about the contributions of the library media program and the benefits of integration of content and information literacy to student achievement. Administrators must create a climate for change that supports the library media program and its goals for students. Creating a collective information literacy vision for students is an important schoolwide task for the entire faculty; however, it is the library media specialist who is charged with the major responsibility for information literacy instruction in schools. Collaboration—working with others—is an important ingredient of any organization. It is the foundation of school library media programs.

REFERENCES AND ADDITIONAL RESOURCES

Allen, Lew, and Emily F. Calhoun. 1998. "Schoolwide Action Research: Findings from Six Years of Study." *Phi Delta Kappan* 79, no. 9 (May): 706–10.

American Association of School Librarians. 1998. *Information Power: Because Student Achievement IS the Bottom Line, A National Plan for Coordinating the Implementation of* Information Power: Building Partnerships for Learning. Chicago: American Library Association.

American Association of School Librarians and Association for Educational Communications and Technology. 1988. *Information Power: Guidelines for School Library Media Programs*. Chicago: American Library Association.

———. 1998. *Information Power: Building Partnerships for Learning*. Chicago: American Library Association.

Barron, Daniel, and Timothy Bergen. 1992. "Information Power: The Restructured School Library for the Nineties." *Phi Delta Kappan* 73, no. 7 (March): 521–25.

Bell, Michael, and Herman L. Totten. 1991. "School Climate Factors Related to Degrees of Cooperation Between Public Elementary School Teachers and School Library Media Specialists." *Library Quarterly* 61, no. 3: 293–310.

Center on Organization and Restructuring of Schools. 1992. "Collaborative Planning Time for Teachers." *Brief* no. 2 (Winter).

Evans, Robert. 1996. *The Human Side of School Change*. San Francisco: Jossey-Bass.

Glatthorn, Allan A. 1993. "Teacher Planning: A Foundation for Effective Instruction." *NASSP Bulletin* 77, no. 551 (March): 1–7.

Grover, Robert. 1996. *Collaboration* (Lessons Learned Series). Chicago: American Association of School Librarians.

Hartzell, Gary. 1997. "The Invisible School Librarian." *School Library Journal* 43, no. 11 (November): 24–29.

Haycock, Ken. 1995. "Research in Teacher-Librarianship and the Institutionalization of Change." *School Library Media Quarterly* 23, no. 4 (Summer): 227–33.

International Society for Technology in Education. 1998. *National Education Technology Standards for Students*. Eugene, Ore.: Author.

Keegan, Bruce, and Tim Westerberg. 1991. "Restructuring and the School Library: Partners in an Information Age." *NASSP Bulletin* 75, no. 535 (May): 9–14.

Loertscher, David V. 1998. *Reinvent Your School's Library in the Age of Technology*. San Jose, Calif.: Hi Willow Research & Publishing.

Morton, Inger. 1993. "Teacher Collaboration in Urban Secondary Schools." *ERIC/CUE Digest No. 93*. New York: ERIC Clearinghouse on Urban Education (September).

National Commission on Excellence in Education. 1983. *A Nation at Risk: The Imperative for Educational Reform*. Washington, D.C.: United States Department of Education.

Orlosky, Donald E., and B. Othanel Smith. 1972. "Educational Change: Its Origins and Characteristics." *Phi Delta Kappan* 53, no. 7: 413–14.

Owens, R. G., and C. R. Steinhoff. 1976. *Administering Change in Schools*. Englewood Cliffs, N.J.: Prentice-Hall.

Pappas, Marjorie L. 1997. "Library Media Specialists and Teachers in the School of Tomorrow." *School Library Media Activities Monthly* 13, no. 8 (April): 32–34.

Parry, James D. 1997. "Reshaping Schools for the Information Age." *What's Noteworthy on ... Education Issues in the Heartland*. Mid-Continent Regional Educational Laboratory (Fall): 30–40.

Tallman, Julie I., and Jean Donham Van Deusen. 1994. "Collaborative Unit Planning—Schedule, Time, and Participants." *School Library Media Quarterly* 23, no. 1: 33–37.

Turner, Philip M. 1991. "Information Skills and Instructional Consulting: A Synergy?" *School Library Media Quarterly* 20, no. 1: 13–18.

United States Department of Education. 1984. *Alliance for Excellence, Librarians Respond to A Nation at Risk*. Washington, D.C.: Government Printing Office.

Willeke, Marjorie J. 1998. "Library Media Programs, Results of Student and Teacher Interviews, 1997-1998." Lincoln, Neb.: Educational Service Unit No. 18 Evaluation Team (June).

Winer, Michael, and Karen Ray. 1994. *Collaboration Handbook: Creating, Sustaining and Enjoying the Journey*. St. Paul, Minn.: Amherst H. Wilder Foundation.

Wittrock, Merlin C., ed. 1986. *The Handbook of Research on Teaching*. 3d ed. New York: Macmillan.

Wolcott, Linda L. 1994. "Understanding How Teachers Plan, Strategies for Successful Instructional Partnerships." *School Library Media Quarterly* 22, no. 3 (Spring): 161–65.

———. 1996. "Planning with Teachers: Practical Approaches to Collaboration." *Emergency Librarian* 23, no. 3 (January–February): 9–14.

Wulf, Steve. 1997. "How to Teach Our Children Well (It Can Be Done)." *Time*, 27 October, 62–96.

6

Standards-Based Teaching in the Library Media Center

Sheila Salmon

INTRODUCTION

A dynamic school library media program, led by a library media specialist working collaboratively with teachers, is a catalyst that reaches beyond the library media center into the classrooms. As schools develop initiatives designed to improve and assess student learning, thoughtful library media specialists not only participate in planning the initiatives but also serve as mentors and colleagues in teaching and learning. Teaching is a major function of school library media specialists and may be the most visible aspect of our work. This visibility can positively influence teachers who see us teaching with strategies that engage students in active learning. When teachers observe our teaching methods and collaborate with us in planning and delivering instruction, we have powerful opportunities to introduce effective models of authentic learning experiences for students.

School library media professionals are examining their role in teaching as they and other educators throughout the country focus on raising student achievement. The American Association of School Librarians' publication of *Information Power: Building Partnerships for Learning* (AASL and AECT 1998a), with its embedded piece, *Information Literacy Standards for Student Learning* (AASL and AECT 1998b), defines nine information literacy standards with indicators, levels of proficiency, and examples of integration into library media specialists' work with students and teachers.

Standards by themselves cannot effect student learning. Schools must create the conditions that can make learning happen. Lauren B. Resnick, director of the Learning Research and Development Center at the University of Pittsburgh, has enumerated certain basic conditions called "Principles of Learning" that, when implemented, create powerful learning environments. Principles of Learning (Institute of Learning 1998) grew out of the New Standards project (New Standards 1997), which was developed by Marc Tucker and Resnick to identify performance standards and create assessment techniques to evaluate student work. The principles are designed to specify the conditions that support the different learning styles and academic needs of all students and give them the time and conditions for optimal learning.

These principles can provide library media specialists with a conceptual framework for examining our practice and developing strategies for engaging students in active, in-depth learning. This chapter defines the principles most relevant to the library media center and discusses their implications in our work with teachers and students.

EFFORT-BASED LEARNING

Resnick's first principle—that learning is effort-based rather than dependent on native ability—may be a radical departure from traditional beliefs in many schools. Organizing for effort maintains that hard work determines success. If students work as hard as they need to and have the time to refine and revise their work, they will reach the standards and achieve success. Schools should grade students by comparing them to a set of standards rather than to each other. This principle is in direct opposition to the bell-curve theory that suggests that only a small percentage of students will excel. Grading children by comparing them to each other rather than against standards creates the bell-shaped curve. The curve encourages the belief that many students must have a low performance level. It also leads to rewarding high achievers by organizing schools around their needs and by offering challenging curricula only to those students who score well on achievement tests.

The learning principles, in contrast, are based on the idea that effort can create achievement. Aptitude is only one aspect of learning. The capacity to learn can be affected by giving students the proper learning environment and appropriate instruction. Educators need to reorganize schools both to provide the extra time some students may need to meet the standards and to develop a school culture that believes that effort-based education can transform the tracking system that accepts poor performance from students at the lower end of the curve.

Practices that support effort-based education include creating "accomplishment" standards that students can attain through their own efforts. These might include reading twenty-five books or completing a community service project or revising work until it meets the standards set for the work. Celebrating the work of all students who attain standards is another important part of a school culture that expects all children to learn.

Implications for the Library Media Center

- *Involve all students in projects and assignments that require higher-order thinking skills.*

  Library media specialists know from experience that many students who are considered "slow" or unable to learn perform well when they work in the library media center with a committed, skillful practitioner. The practitioner who believes that students are able and gives them the extra support they may need is rewarded by the self-fulfilling prophecy that they do well. However, in many schools the students who are most active in the library media center are those who are already academically successful. They are given the challenging assignments and are likely to benefit most from the resources and teaching attention from classroom teachers and the library media center. Other students are given less challenging assignments, or no assignments at all, that require library media resources.

  The library media specialist can collaborate with teachers to design projects for all students to build reading, writing, and information literacy skills that result in standards-based work over a period of time. Library media specialists can spread the concept of effort-based learning throughout the school by articulating it to colleagues, offering to team teach, and giving students time in the library to work on their assignments.

• *Provide opportunities for all students to reach performance standards.*

One performance standard formulated by the New Standards Project that is particularly suited to the library media center is that of reading twenty-five books a year. It applies to all students and can be attained by the effort of the learner, as there are no requirements for specific books and students can select according to interest and readability. The library media specialist can help students reach the standard by suggesting appropriate titles and helping them create a database of their reading records. Library media specialists can also spearhead reading incentive activities that benefit and provide enjoyment to the whole school community.

Other aspects of the New Standards for reading include student engagement in author and genre studies. Library media specialists are particularly able to lead the instructional design of projects in these two areas and should be attentive to the collection needs that will support the resulting increase in reading.

• *Structure mini-lessons in the classroom or in the library media center.*

When planning collaborative projects with classroom teachers, library media specialists may identify specific reading, writing, or information literacy skills that will enable students to reach the targeted performance or content standards. A mini-lesson on notetaking from interviews, printed material, or visual material might be appropriate for the whole class or only for a small group of students. The teacher or the library media specialist might teach the lesson. Library media specialists will also provide additional learning opportunities to bring students who are less proficient up to standard.

- *Establish working groups that fit the learning needs of the students.*

    Working with a small group can be an effective way for students to help each other learn, as well as to benefit from the richness of thinking that develops from brainstorming and teaming. Library media specialists can support teachers when they organize cooperative learning groups, pair students who work together, or set up peer teaching situations. The library media specialist can facilitate learning by leading group discussions; asking probing questions; and helping students organize their work, find resources, and prepare presentations.

CLEAR EXPECTATIONS

We need to define what we expect all students to learn, and we must make our expectations clear to students and the school community. Not only do students need to know what is expected, but they also must have the supports they need to reach the standards. Students need time to reflect on and perfect their work, and teachers need to create benchmarks of progress so that advancement can be measured in small increments. This makes the expectations less daunting and gives students recognition for achievements leading to full attainment of the standard. In addition, "every student must be expected to meet the same standards" (Rothman 1996, 4-1).

Implications for the Library Media Center

- *Design assignments with rubrics so students know what is expected and can measure their progress.*
  Collaborating with teachers on the design of a project should include planning the assessment. Rubrics are an effective method. A *rubric* is a set of descriptive statements with a measurement scale for each component. *Information Literacy Standards for Student Learning* (AASL and AECT 1998b) sets three levels of proficiency—Basic, Proficient, and Exemplary—and has indicators in each category. A teacher/library media specialist assignment may have a rubric that relates to content, style, sources, organization, searching strategies, and presentation. Students may help develop the rubric and may also be involved in assessing themselves and their fellow students according to the rubric. The rubric should clearly cite the evidence needed to establish how well the work meets the standard.

- *Create opportunities for students to have additional instruction and time to perfect their work.*
  When students are expected to attain high standards, they need the supports to reach mastery. Often, additional time or instruction is not available, and students fail or turn in substandard work. The library media center program can be organized to provide that

needed extra support. A flexible, open-access library on the elementary level can provide time for individuals and small groups, and the library media specialist can instruct or bring volunteers into the facility to give students more support.

Opening and staffing the secondary school library before or after school, during lunch hours, or (in some rare situations) on days when schools are normally closed is another way to add instructional time to the school day. Library media specialists who have collaborated with the classroom teacher to design the assignment have the information they need to clarify tasks and assist students with their work.

ACADEMIC RIGOR IN THE THINKING CURRICULUM

Two vital aspects of pedagogy are combined in these principles: rigor in subject and development of thinking skills. Both are interdependent in an effective curriculum. Subject content should be organized around essential questions and/or concepts rather than expecting students to learn a series of related facts. Students must have opportunities to learn content and demonstrate to others what they have learned. They need to make hypotheses, engage in research and study to test the hypotheses, and engage in problem solving that uses their knowledge to draw conclusions.

The thinking curriculum is organized so that it deepens progressively, putting new concepts into the context of previous learning and adding new understandings to build knowledge. A key implication of academic rigor is that of revising work until there is a quality finished product that reflects correctness in detail and ideas.

Implications for the Library Media Center

- *Develop assignments that demand academic rigor.*

    Developing challenging assignments for students using the library media center is perhaps the single most difficult area for the library media specialist and teacher. Too often, research assignments require students to fill in an outline of information gathered from an encyclopedia or one or two sources. Students gather information, but do not use that information to develop hypotheses, draw conclusions, make judgments, or generate questions that would lead to further study. Working with teachers to design assignments that require students to ask the questions that necessitate gathering data and lead to using the data to construct meaningful work is a challenging task.

    Assignments can, in fact, be driven by questions that range from the simple to the complex. "What is the best pet for our classroom?" can lead children to charting the pets' environmental needs and comparing those needs to what the classroom can support. A complex question, such as "What are the potential social, political, and economic benefits and problems related to the recent success in cloning a mammal?" entails sophisticated data gathering, evaluation of sources, and making of informed judgments.

    Assignments that require academic rigor also demand that library media specialists teach the thinking skills necessary for the inquiry process. Teaching of inquiry skills should be built into the assignments, so that students develop techniques to perform each step of the process thoughtfully, from determining prior knowledge to creating their own understandings and presenting their new learning.

- *Use graphic organizers.*

  Venn diagrams, KWL (what you Know, what you Want to learn, and what you have Learned), QAR (Question, Answer, Relationship), and webbing are excellent tools for the practitioner to teach to students so they can construct a model for their inquiry projects. The organizers can give a structure that relates directly to the questions asked and is an effective alternative to the standard encyclopedia format many students use because they have no other models.

- *Encourage reflection and revision.*

  The thinking curriculum necessitates time for reflection. Students need to make critical judgments about their work. They need to get feedback and suggestions for improvement from the library media specialist, their teachers, and their peers. Library media specialists can facilitate reflection by forming study groups of students who work on related topics, asking critical questions, having students share their research strategies with each other, or suggesting people or organizations outside the school who may bring other insights to the work.

Library media specialists can be critical friends to students on an individual basis as they work to complete and perfect an assignment. This special time with a knowledgeable and supportive adult can be very important, particularly to the struggling student.

Students often finish their work just before or perhaps just after the due date. There is no time to revise and students are given a final grade on a product that needs improvement. The principle of academic rigor demands that students revise their work until it reflects a high standard of accomplishment. The library media specialist can assist by working with students on revisions, giving them suggestions, encouragement, and time in the library media center.

- *Expect students to be knowledge producers.*

The idea that children are empty vessels into which teachers pour knowledge is obviously false. Children come to school with a body of knowledge, and what they learn in school is mixed with what they already know. The teacher's job is to find ways to help children use the knowledge we want them to learn so that they really own it, demonstrate that they know it, and can use that knowledge to build more complex understandings and concepts.

When students produce their own knowledge, the role of the teacher changes from that of knowledge giver to coach. The teacher suggests improvements and gives students the techniques and strategies for improvement. The purpose of the teacher is to enable students to become more proficient at building on prior knowledge to develop their own new understandings.

- *Develop a resource-rich facility.*

    If the library media center is to support students in their learning, the collection must reflect the diversity of needs, the changing curricula, and the technological capacity to search and produce the results of the search in up-to-date formats. It also means that the teaching function of the library media center expands to include the broad range of technological tools housed in the library media center.

- *Model coaching behavior for teachers and students.*

    The role of coach in the library media center is a familiar one to library media specialists who, in their work with individuals and small groups, encourage independent research and suggest strategies for improvement. Working with teachers may also give library media specialists the opportunity to model coaching with peers. Facilitating discussions, settling differences of opinion diplomatically, offering suggestions, and team teaching are techniques known to many library media specialists, who can model these behaviors for teachers who may have little experience with collaborative planning and teaching.

- *Collaborate with teachers to provide opportunities for students to share their research findings with others.*

    Here again, library media specialists have an important teaching function that may begin in the library media center but reaches far beyond its walls. Helping students learn the principles of presentation—including selecting the material, deciding on the form of the presentation, coaching their performance, and finding venues for them to share their work—is an exciting part of the library media specialist's work.

ACCOUNTABLE TALK

Lots of talking goes on in a classroom, but the key word in this principle is "accountable." *Accountable* implies that classroom discourse is purposeful, sharpens students' thinking, and leads to building knowledge and reasoning ability. Accountable talk is polite, responsive to others' comments, based on factual content backed up by evidence, and appropriate to the subject matter studied. This includes using mathematical proofs and scientific reasoning, citing reference sources, and applying other methods specific to the disciplines studied.

Implications for the Library Media Center

- *Model accountable talk for students.*

  Conversations about their work should include asking students to explain their reasoning, back up their conclusions with evidence, and justify the sources they used for information. Collaborate with teachers to create opportunities for students to critique each other's work using rubrics and justifying criticism (both positive and negative) with evidence from the work.

- *Participate in accountable talk with teachers.*

  Designing and assessing effective projects is one aspect of accountable talk. Another is the examination of completed student work to analyze students' academic needs. This analysis forms the basis on which teachers and library media specialists can build a curriculum that deepens understanding and lessons that move students forward in their learning. Standards-based teaching has moved beyond the "Well-I-taught-it" mode to teaching based on the identification of specific learning needs and accountability for student success. Participating with teachers in professional discourse brings the library media specialist into the heart of teaching and learning and makes the library media center an essential part of the school.

SOCIALIZING INTELLIGENCE

As with the principle of effort-based education, the principle of socializing intelligence is based on the belief that all but the most severely learning-disabled children can learn at high levels with enough time and the appropriate support. If children, parents, and teachers act on the premise that intelligence is learned and that effort will create students who can ask questions and analyze problems, this will be a self-fulfilling prophecy. Belief in learnable intelligence demands a school culture in which students are held accountable for their work and are expected to succeed.

Implications for the Library Media Center

- *Expect success.*
  With the expectation that children will succeed comes the responsibility to provide the scaffolding that will make success possible. Many of these supports are described in other

sections of this chapter. They include teaching mini-lessons at the point of need, establishing working groups that fit the learners' needs, using graphic organizers, helping students frame research questions, and making all the elements that are needed to fulfill the assignment clear at the beginning of a project or assignment.

In addition to using a variety of instructional techniques, the library media specialist's attitude of "you are smart and you can do it if you are persistent" is important in helping students do their best.

LEARNING AS APPRENTICESHIP

Learners learn best when working beside an expert who models skilled practice and encourages and guides the learners as they create authentic products or performances for real audiences. Students need the support of experts in their subject area, whether they are teachers in the school, scientists contacted via the Internet, or community members who share their interests and knowledge. The best learning environment gives students the opportunities to make products that meet quality standards and a venue in which to share their work with others, both inside and outside the school building.

Implications for the Library Media Center

- *Explain your own thinking process as you help students craft questions, create a search strategy, or decide on a presentation model.*

  Thinking out loud is a way to model an approach to a problem for students: "If I were doing this I might...." Letting them hear your own thought processes, your own errors, as you brainstorm and then reject or accept certain courses of action helps students see that they do not have to have the right answer to every problem. They learn that the thinking process may be convoluted and that it is all right to make a mistake. Encourage students to think out loud with you, asking their own questions and finding their own solutions. As they practice doing this, they will need less support and become more independent.

- *Set clear expectations for professional accountability.*

    We library media specialists and teachers need to be clear about our own teaching practice. The worksheet in figure 6.1 is designed for use by practitioners to help focus attention on the way we implement learning standards, provide a look at our own teaching methodology, and serve as a basis for devising a rubric as we reflect upon our own work with students.

CONCLUSION

Library media specialists, more than ever, must join with teachers to build partnerships that improve teaching and learning. The struggle to build the professional image of the library media specialist as a colleague who is skilled both in teaching and librarianship is important to our vision of ourselves. Being seen as a colleague who has not only specialized information literacy skills, but also teaching skills that enhance and expand the opportunities for children to learn, will make us truly essential members of school communities.

Figure 6.1. Evaluation form

Evaluating Standards-Based Planning and Teaching Assignment

List the learning standard or standards addressed:

    Content:

    Performance:

    Information Literacy:

Describe how the assignment addressed student learning styles and individual needs.

What were the criteria for success? Were students involved in determining the criteria?

List the lessons taught or scaffolding provided (e.g., tracking sheets, checklists, hyperlinks) to help students fulfill the assignment.

How did you monitor student progress? Journals? Conferences? Interim evaluations?

Did you meet with peers to plan the assignment? Share teaching responsibilities?

Did you evaluate the assignment based on student work and success in meeting the criteria?

REFERENCES AND ADDITIONAL RESOURCES

American Association of School Librarians and Association for Educational Communications and Technology. 1998a. *Information Power: Building Partnerships for Learning.* Chicago: American Library Association.

———. 1998b. *Information Literacy Standards for Student Learning.* Chicago: American Library Association.

Brandt, Ron. 1994. "On Creating an Environment Where All Students Learn: A Conversation with Al Mamary." *Educational Leadership* 51, no. 6: 24–28.

Fitzpatrick, Kathleen A. 1997. *Indicators of Schools of Quality.* Schaumburg, Ill.: National Study of School Evaluation.

Institute of Learning. 1998. "Learning Principles." Pittsburgh, Pa.: Learning Research and Development Center, University of Pittsburgh.

Mitchell, Ruth, Marilyn Willis, and Chicago Teachers Union Quest Center. 1995. *Learning in Overdrive: Designing Curriculum, Instruction, and Assessment from Standards. A Manual for Teachers.* Golden, Colo.: North American Press.

New Standards. 1997. *Performance Standards.* Washington, D.C.: National Center on Education and the Economy and the University of Pittsburgh.

Resnick, Lauren B. 1995. "From Aptitude to Effort: A New Foundation for Our Schools." *Daedalus* 124, no. 4: 55–62.

Rothman, Robert. 1996. "Organizing So All Children Can Learn: Applying the Principles of Learning." In *Organizing for Results.* New York: National Center on Education and the Economy.

———. 1997. "How to Make the Link Between Standards, Assessment, and Real Student Achievement." In *New American Schools.* Arlington, Va.: NAS.

Secules, Teresa, C. Cottom, M. Bray, and L. Miller. 1997. "Creating Schools for Thought." *Educational Leadership* 54, no. 6: 56–60.

Shriner, James G., J. E. Ysseldyke, M. L. Thurlow, and D. Honetschlager. 1994. "'All' Means 'All'—Including Students with Disabilities." *Educational Leadership* 51, no. 6: 38–42.

Sternberg, Robert J. 1997. "What Does It Mean to Be Smart?" *Educational Leadership* 54, no. 6: 20–24.

7
Creating Meaningful Assignments for Student Learning

Denise Rehmke

The students are at work on computers. Some are writing their science lab reports, describing in detail each of the product tests they designed and carried out; others are graphing and charting the results of those product tests. Which brand of paper towel is more absorbent? Which cereal stays crisp the longest in milk?

The unit began with students locating and reading reviews in consumer magazines of various goods and products. Students were then charged with designing and executing a series of tests on several brands of a household product of their choosing. They were to follow stringent lab protocol, document and analyze the data, and report their findings.

Authenticity. Relevancy. Appropriateness. Variety. As we develop instructional units for students, we strive to challenge them with thoughtful, effective learning activities. The assignments we give students and the tasks we ask of them have a great deal to do with their development into thoughtful, lifelong learners. Assignments should be designed to allow students to cultivate their current interests and skills and discover new ones. Assignments should teach not only content, but also processes. Assignments should demand increasingly more sophisticated thinking skills of students. Assignments should be created with an eye to the real world. In short, assignments should be meaningful.

Library media specialists working collaboratively with classroom teachers are in a position to develop meaningful assignments. Information problem solving—the research and production skills, strategies, and techniques of our trade—is at the heart of survival and success in our information-rich society. When carefully integrated into a well-crafted curricular unit, information problem solving can enrich and add significant value to the learning activity.

Several factors must be considered when planning meaningful assignments for students. The classroom teacher and the library media specialist each bring necessary background and expertise to the planning session when these factors are discussed: purpose, content objectives, and information literacy objectives (see figure 7.1).

PURPOSE

What is the purpose of this learning activity? What will the students gain from the experience? First, realize that the purposes the teacher and library media specialist have in mind may differ somewhat from how the students ultimately perceive the purpose. The teacher likely has a particular content and often specific skills or techniques students are to learn or understand or demonstrate. The library media specialist likely has research or production resources, tools, skills, techniques, or strategies for students to learn and apply.

The student, however, may interpret the purpose differently. If students are to "buy into" and thereby commit to an activity, they need to understand and accept the relevance of the task. Students, particularly older ones, often complain about the pertinence—or lack thereof—of tasks assigned to them. "I'll never use this!" they moan. Clearly, if an activity replicates a plausible, realistic experience or situation, students can more easily see the significance of it. Students in a government class can be quite motivated when their task is to select and research an issue of interest, investigate the current legal status regarding that issue, then write a letter to the appropriate official (congressperson, city council member, school superintendent, CEO, store manager) expressing their research-based views. Drinking age. Driving age. Curfews. Minimum wage. Local option sales tax. Curbside recycling. Students are engaged and challenged when they can see that their efforts might make a difference. But this type of activity is not always possible, nor feasible.

If an activity is set up as a problem-solving task, though, it will have a more real-world essence to it. Most students recognize that outside the school setting, they have to (or will have to) solve open-ended problems: identify the problem, issue, or situation; gather information; make choices; and live with the decisions. If the task is presented as a problem to be solved, students are more likely to be motivated and engaged by it.

CONTENT OBJECTIVES

What content do the students need to learn during the course of this activity? In an ideal problem-solving environment, the students would select and develop their own topics of interest. They would choose topics for which they had a great deal of curiosity, perhaps even passion. They

Figure 7.1. Planning guide

Iowa City West High School

Planning Guide
Library Research and Production

Course _____   Teacher _____

Period(s) _____   Number of Students _____

Monday	Tuesday	Wednesday	Thursday	Friday

Facility   _____ library 1st floor   _____ east area   _____ west area

_____ library 2d floor   _____ Mac lab   _____ PC lab

_____ open area

Unit Overview/Description/Purpose _____

_____

_____

Content Objectives _____

_____

_____

Information Literacy Objectives_____

_____

_____

Resources _____

_____

_____

Figure 7.1. Planning guide (continued)

Responsibility Checklist

Task	Teacher	Librarian	Student

Things to consider next year . . . _____

_____

_____

_____

_____

would be motivated to learn, engrossed in their discovery. The reality is, however, that the content of a particular unit—the topics or subjects addressed in a specific activity—is often curriculum-imposed. The classroom teacher has to assign topics that will compel students to address the specified content during their research and study or presentation.

It is generally the classroom teacher who makes the decision about content, whether the topics are teacher-assigned and highly defined; whether the content is entirely open to student selection; or whether the content falls somewhere in between, with teacher-set parameters, but some student choice as well.

A world history teacher wants students to research the ancient Greeks. She wants to offer the students some choice, yet she recognizes that she needs to set the content parameters so that the information critical to the unit is addressed. Therefore, she develops a list of broad topics relating to the ancient Greeks—such as art and architecture, literature, theater and drama, sports and games—and allows groups of students to choose from the list. Using this controlled list, she can direct students toward the more, or less, challenging topics, depending on their abilities.

The library media specialist can provide assistance in developing these topic lists, based on knowledge of available resources, and the tools and skills necessary to access these resources. Is a given topic "researchable" by the intended students? Are there enough relevant resources, in the proper format, at an appropriate intellectual level?

INFORMATION LITERACY OBJECTIVES

What information literacy skills can be addressed in this activity? What research skills—concepts, strategies, techniques, tools, resources—are required for students to undertake the project effectively? What production skills do students need to create products that demonstrate and communicate what they have learned?

Many factors help determine which information literacy elements are relevant to a particular unit. First, the content of the unit dictates to some extent what aspects of the information literacy curriculum are to be addressed. Students undertaking literary research—investigating authors, writing styles, motivations, backgrounds, and influences, then delving into criticism and analysis of the authors' writings—need to know the scope and depth of particular resources and tools and how to use them (many are quite specialized). Students researching contemporary controversial issues need to be able to distinguish fact from opinion and objectivity from bias in sources, whether these sources are in print or on the Internet. Students conducting product reviews and comparisons need to know which resources—periodicals, Web sites, and so on—evaluate or review products, and how to access those resources efficiently using print or electronic periodical indexes or search engines.

Next, the prior learning of the students is a consideration. What information literacy skills do the students already know? New learning requires time for formal guided instruction and practice. However, if the students have already been introduced to a skill or a resource, a quick refresher or reminder is enough. With older, more experienced students, a research guide or pathfinder might be enough to get them started independently (see figures 7.2 and 7.3). Students in an upper-level foreign-language class could independently research prominent Latinos with a simple pathfinder identifying key resources and including a few searching tips. It becomes increasingly critical to keep a record of which skills students have learned and

Figure 7.2. Biography pathfinder

Getting Started with Research About People

Print Resources

R 031 Various General Encyclopedias are always good starting points . . .

R 920.02 CUR Current Biography has been issued one volume per year since 1940. Use the cumulative index volume.

R 920.03 Encyclopedia of World Biography provides brief articles on prominent individuals throughout history from around the world. We have 2 editions—the 1998, as well as the 1973 set.

R 920.073 DIC Dictionary of American Biography is a comprehensive resource which includes prominent Americans who are dead. **DAB** consists of the main set plus a series of 10 supplemental volumes. Use the index.

R 920.72 Notable American Women This four-volume set includes brief bios of prominent women from the earliest to the 1970s.

Specialized Biographical Reference resources are available in many different areas: musicians, artists, scientists, reformers, writers, etc. These are scattered throughout the reference collection by Dewey Decimal number.

General Collection Biographical resources Full-length biographies are located in the "B" section (after the fiction books). Collected biographies have the Dewey **920** designation. And some bio info is found scattered throughout the nonfiction collection in different Dewey areas. How do you find these resources efficiently? Use the **West High Library Catalog** on InfoNet.

which they have not yet experienced, not only at their current school level, but at other levels in the school as well. A matrix based on the district's information literacy curriculum or model in which the appropriate grade levels and integrated subject areas can be recorded is a useful tool.

Another factor to consider in determining which information literacy skills to address is the students' level of cognitive development. Consider at which levels the students have performed previously. Consider pushing them

Figure 7.2. Biography pathfinder (continued)

Getting Started with Research About People

Electronic Resources

Encyclopedia Americana 98 is available on PC workstations in the library and lab. Same info as the print edition. Includes WWW links with most articles.

MAS is available through the InfoNet icon on PC workstations in the library and lab. It indexes more than 400 general index magazines (including *Time*, *Newsweek*, *People*, *Sports Illustrated*, etc.) from 1984 to the present. It has full-text articles for about 1/3 of the magazines. We subscribe to many of the magazines and they are available for checkout at the circ desk.

World Wide Web access is on all Mac and PC workstations in the library and labs. Select a search engine such as AltaVista or Excite and do a search. Or try this Web site as a starting point:

http://www.hisp.com/

HISPANIC Online is the Web site of **HISPANIC Magazine**, a monthly magazine for and about Hispanics. It covers news, events, and issues of interest to the Latino community. Lots of links!! It even has its own Excite search engine.

Remember: Please print selectively! Only print what you really need. Screen it on the screen. Copy and paste relevant info into a Word "notepad," then print from Word.

---

to employ increasingly more sophisticated thinking skills in their research activities.

Likewise, there are factors to examine in determining which production skills are necessary for a given activity. Of primary consideration is the end product the students are to create. What skills do the students need to produce effectively? Are the necessary resources available? Is there enough time not only to teach students how to create the product, but also for them to do it? When end products were primarily written papers or speeches, the production

Figure 7.3. Poetry pathfinder

Getting Started with Research About Poets and Poetry

Print Resources

For **biographical info** on poets...

R 928 Ame *American Writers* is a very authoritative source with biographical info as well as analysis of each writer's work. There are a total of 10 volumes (4 original plus supplements). Check the comprehensive index in the back of the Supplement 3, Part 2 to see which poets are included.

R 928 Con *Contemporary Authors* consists of many volumes about writers—including poets. Use the index volume—a thin blue paperback!

R 928 Kun *Wilson Authors Series* covers writers from the earliest times to now. Titles include
> *European Authors 1000–1900*
> *British Authors Before 1800*
> *British Authors of the 19th Century*
> *American Authors 1600–1900*
> *Twentieth Century Authors* plus *First Supplement*
> *World Authors: 1950–1970; 1970–1975; 1975–1980;*
> *1980–1985; and 1985–1990.*

We don't have a cumulative index—check the contents of the appropriate volume ...

R 928 Vin *Poets*, is part of the **Great Writers of the English Language** series. Includes some bio plus some analysis.

R 920.02 Cur *Current Biography* contains some prominent literary figures. It has been issued one volume per year since 1940. Use the cumulative index volume.

R 920.03 *Encyclopedia of World Biography* provides brief articles on prominent individuals—including literary folks—throughout history from around the world. We have 2 editions—the 1998, as well as the 1973 set.

R 920.073 Dic *Dictionary of American Biography* is a comprehensive resource which includes prominent Americans who are dead. **DAB** consists of the main set plus a series of 10 supplemental volumes. Use the index.

For **poetry analysis, interpretation, criticism**...

809 Mag *Magill's Survey of World Literature* has 8 volumes (6 + supplements) and provides biographical information, general analysis of the writer's work, and more detailed analysis of a few specific works.

Figure 7.3. Poetry pathfinder (continued)

809 Mag *Magill's Survey of American Literature* also has 8 volumes (6 + supplements) and provides the same type of biographical and analytical information on American writers.

810.9 Har *The Oxford Companion to American Literature* and *Benét's Reader's Encyclopedia of American Literature* are each single-volume sources with info on writers and works. Also includes literary terms. See also the other *Oxford Companion* and *Benét's* volumes.

808.8 Mag *Masterplots Poetry Series* is a single-volume work with essays/reviews of 141 famous works of poetry. Check the index.

811.09 Mal *Crowell's Handbook of Contemporary American Poetry* subtitled: *A Critical Handbook of American Poets since 1940.*

General Collection resources Full-length biographies on selected poets are located in the **"B"** section (after the fiction books). Some collected biographies have the Dewey **920** designation. And some bio info can be found in literary books in the Dewey **800s.**

Finally, there are some **terrific** books of analysis/criticism on many of the poets and their works—critical editions from Twayne and Greenhaven, for example. These are located in the Dewey **800s.**

How do you find these resources efficiently? Use the **West High Library Catalog** on InfoNet!!!

For information about **literary terms** ...

803 Sha *Dictionary of Literary Terms*
808.1 Den *Poetry Handbook*
803 Thr *Handbook of Literature*

Need help with poetry terminology? Consult these guides!

For **locating poetry** ...

808.81 Col *Granger's Index to Poetry* is the print resource for locating specific poems by author, title, first line, or on a particular subject. We have the 6th, 7th, 8th, and 9th print editions. This resource is also available electronically. *(See next page.)*

(continued on next page)

Figure 7.3. Poetry pathfinder (continued)

Print Resources (continued)

Poetry books are located in the Dewey **800s**.

    808   Poetry anthologies

    811   American poetry

    821   British poetry

Poetry Anthology = contains works by **different** poets

Poetry Collection = contains works by a **single** poet

Electronic Resources

DISCovering Authors is available through the InfoNet icon on PC workstations in the library and lab. It covers 300 of the most studied writers through full-text articles with biographical information as well as critical essays on their works.

MAS is also available through InfoNet and indexes more than 400 general index magazines from 1984 to the present. It has full-text articles for about 1/3 of the magazines. We subscribe to many of the magazines, which are available for checkout at the circ desk. For more contemporary poets, MAS is useful ...

Columbia Granger World of Poetry is another InfoNet tool. This is the electronic version of the Granger's print reference tool. *(See above.)* Keyword search by poet, title, first line, and subject. Includes a few full-text poems, some quotes, and cites to anthologies and collections.

skills and necessary resources were less of an issue. With the variety of presentation and communication methods now available, the various skills, resources, and time become more critical. American history students used to write papers in which they described the social and cultural significance of the themes and messages in music of the 1960s. Today, they create music videos to depict the themes and messages of those songs. Although the content of this activity remains the same, as do the basic research tools and skills, the production skills and the resources the students

---

Figure 7.3. Poetry pathfinder (continued)

World Wide Web access is on all Mac and PC workstations in the library and labs. Select a search engine such as AltaVista or Excite and do a search.

Or try this **Yahoo** directory as a starting point for browsing:

http://www.yahoo.com/Arts/Humanities/Literature/Poetry/

Other useful Web sites:

*University of Michigan Humanities Text Initiative: **American Verse Project**.* A searchable archive of American poetry, primarily 19th century. Available at:

http://www.hti.umich.edu/bin/amvidx.pl?page=main

A Chronological Index of Poets ... in Representative Poetry Online. From the University of Toronto. Indexed by poet, title, first line, keyword, and criticism. Available at:

http://library.utoronto.ca/www/utel/rp/indexdates.html

Finally, the ***Poet's Corner*** contains links to a number of interesting poetry Web sites. Check it out! Available at:

http://pen.k12.va.us/Anthology/Pav/LangArts/poetcorner.html

Remember: Please print selectively! Only print what you really need. Screen it on the screen. Copy and paste relevant info into a Word "notepad," then print from Word.

---

need to create their products are dramatically different. Students need access to camcorders and video editing equipment. They need instruction in how to use this technology. They need time to work in the video editing labs.

Foreign-language students once wrote and illustrated simple books depicting fables. The books were distributed to young children in a day care program. Today, students create multimedia fables using computer programs (e.g., HyperStudio) along with scanners, CDs, and electronic drawing programs.

Students used to research controversial issues, write position papers, and then summarize and present their viewpoints using visuals such as posters or transparency slides to help explain and enhance the presentation for viewers. Today they create PowerPoint slide shows to accompany and enhance their presentations.

Technology has clearly brought about significant change in production as well as research. But its place in the production end of the information literacy spectrum should be monitored carefully. Variety is important, and it is good that students have the opportunity to learn many new production techniques and skills; nevertheless, some of the old techniques are still viable and valuable. Clear, formal writing should not be abandoned. PowerPoint is, indeed, heavily used in the "real world" to accompany presentations, but it is also true that many make transparency slides from PowerPoint simply to avoid having to move computers and video projectors around.

Consider what types of end products students have been creating in other classes. If the library media specialist knows that many students are already working on papers or videos or multimedia shows in another class, suggest to the teacher that a different type of end product be assigned, or that students be given the option of selecting from various types of end products. Just as with research skills, the types of production skills students have learned and used should be logged, keeping track of the grade level, subject area, and even specific units in which various skills were taught and used.

A caution regarding end products: When the teacher and library media specialist are planning an activity, they should think about the emphasis and relative importance of the various components of the activity—the content, the research, the production—in terms of the total time allotment. If students have an elaborate, time-consuming end product facing them, they might put too little emphasis on the content or the research, in favor of creating a product that is showy but lacking in substance. Give the most time to the most important aspect of the activity.

SUMMARY

An effective, meaningful learning activity will engage and challenge students. Creating a relevant assignment that leads students to higher levels of thinking and performing requires thoughtful collaboration between the classroom teacher and the library media specialist, who together examine and determine the most appropriate content, research skills, and production skills.

SUGGESTED ADDITIONAL RESOURCES

Bleakley, Ann, and Jackie L. Carrigan. 1994. *Resource-Based Learning Activities: Information Literacy for High School Students*. Chicago: American Library Association.

Burdick, Tracey. 1998. "Pleasure in Information Seeking: Reducing Information Aliteracy." *Emergency Librarian* 25, no. 3 (January-February): 13–17.

Jansen, Barbara A. 1996. "Defining the Task: The First Step Toward Success." *School Library Media Activities Monthly* 12, no. 8 (April): 27–29.

Loertscher, David. 1996. "All That Glitters May Not Be Gold." *Emergency Librarian* 24, no. 2 (November-December): 21–25.

Stripling, Barbara K., and Judy M. Pitts. 1988. *Brainstorms and Blueprints: Teaching Library Research as a Thinking Process*. Englewood, Colo.: Libraries Unlimited.

Winn, Patricia G. 1991. *Integration of the Secondary School Library Media Center into the Curriculum: Techniques and Strategies*. Englewood, Colo.: Libraries Unlimited.

8

Making Sense of a Changing World: Digitized Primary Source Documents in Schools

Mark W. Gordon

ARCHIVES ON THE WEB

The Library of Congress began to digitize some of its archival collections of primary source documents nearly a decade ago. There are now more than 40 collections online at <http://memory.loc.gov/ammem>, the American Memory site of the National Digital Library. This effort has been joined by dozens of others. Large universities, government agencies, and public libraries have made available their previously off-limits collections via the Web. Usually many collections reside at each site. To get a taste of the range of possibilities, here is a brief list, randomly selected, of some of these collections:

> **American Slave Narratives**, University of Virginia, <http://xroads.virginia.edu/~HYPER/wpa/wpahome.html>

Inaugural Addresses of US Presidents, Columbia University, <gopher://gopher.cc.columbia.edu:71/11/miscellaneous/cubooks/inaug>

Franklin Roosevelt Documents, Marist College, <http://www.academic.marist.edu/fdr/fdrintro.htm>

Historical Text Archive, Mississippi State University, <http://www.msstate.edu/archives/history/>

Digital Collections, New York Public Library, <http://digital.nypl.org/>

The Urban Landscape, Duke University, <http://scriptorium.lib.duke.edu/diap/>

The California Heritage Collection, University of California at Berkeley, <http://sunsite.Berkeley.EDU/CalHeritage/>

The Tobacco Control Archives, University of California at San Francisco, <http://www.library.ucsf.edu/tobacco/bw.html>

The availability of these collections via the World Wide Web offers both opportunities and challenges for library media specialists. The collections are rich additions to the range of resources school libraries can offer. However, because of the nature of the original items, each of these collections comes with distinctive and often quite limited searching capabilities, and thus the collections pose access challenges for users. Teachers and students may find some of these collections very difficult to use without support. For example, at the American Memory site, checking in at the search options page provides information about some collections that are not even searchable. Some collections are searchable only from (or more deeply from) that collection's home page. Library media specialists who are knowledgeable about the intricacies of these collections can make the difference between the success or failure of any query.

Collections of primary source documents can be thought of as reference collections and thus can be used to support term papers and general research reports by students. But they can be used more powerfully as the focal point around which inquiry curriculum can be designed. Student inquiry lessons using primary source documents offer opportunities for deep reflective and critical thinking, examination of issues such as point of view and bias, and the development of acute visual literacy capacities. Library media specialists' support of these efforts can be decisively important to their success.

It is important to examine the context in which this development is occurring. School library media centers are currently experiencing the effects of two powerful currents in American education. The first is the availability of enormous new information resources, many through the Internet. The second is the effort to make classroom learning more effective and engaging for all students. These currents offer opportunities for school library media specialists to help their schools rethink instructional strategies and work with classroom teachers to improve student achievement, particularly for those who have not traditionally experienced success in school.

COLLABORATION: ARCHIVES IN THE CLASSROOM

During the past two summers at the Library of Congress's American Memory Fellows Institutes in Washington, D.C., teams of teachers and library media specialists designed curricular units built around primary sources. Some of these units are posted at the LC Learning Page site: <http://memory.loc.gov/ammem/ndlpedu/lesson97/lesson97.html>. Library media specialists had a key role in creating and later implementing many of these units.

Kathleen Ferenz, a middle school teacher who is now Director of the Bay Area National Digital Library Project,[1] and her American Memory Fellow partner, Leni Donlan, a San Francisco teacher, created a unit entitled "America Dreams." A description of the unit is on the Web at <http://www.internet-catalyst.org / projects / amproject / toc.html>.

The unit asks students to inquire about the American Dream. What is the Dream? Is it the same for all Americans? Is it a myth? How has the Dream changed over time? Some see their dreams wither and die while others see their dreams fulfilled. Why? What is your dream?

This online unit is designed in the format of a WebQuest.[2] Its goal is to challenge students to investigate the American Dream as they investigate the lives of those who lived before. It is designed around the rich set of primary source documents from the American Memory collections. These include, among others:

- "Life of a City: Early Films of New York, 1896-1906," <http://lcweb2.loc.gov/ammem/papr/nychome.html>
- "Inside an American Factory: Films of the Westinghouse Works, 1904," <http://lcweb2.loc.gov/ammem/papr/west/westhome.html>
- "Before and After the Great Earthquake and Fire: Early Films of San Francisco, 1897-1916," <http://lcweb2.loc.gov/ammem/papr/sfhome.html>

Because students must learn specific research and information literacy skills in order to make meaning from the Library of Congress collections, planning must include ways for students to acquire those skills. Built into the "America Dreams" unit are many suggestions for lessons that allow students to get a sense of what primary sources are and how to begin searching for documents. The collaborating library media specialist plays a key role at this point in helping define and support these introductory lessons. It may be desirable in many classroom contexts to download and place a subset of documents in a folder for students to access, or even to print them out for initial use by students. Although a few teachers may love doing this, bookmarking or downloading documents does not have to be a teacher's responsibility.

To understand these documents, students will need background and contextual information. These secondary sources may be located on the Web or in resources located in the library. Care and attention are needed to help students get a balanced picture. Library media specialists, in collaboration with the teacher, can develop a number of ways of making sure students have access to a balanced perspective, including bookmarking, downloading, flagging catalog records, or pulling books and articles and placing them either in the library or in the classroom.

When students then share their own dream for the future, they also can reflect on what they've learned. Is the American Dream a reality? What can the dreams of others teach you? Why would different people in different times have different dreams? How will your personal dream become part of America's future? So...what is the American Dream? As students formulate their ideas, they defend them by pointing to the primary source documents as evidence of their understanding of others' dreams.

Having students develop understanding about the significance of primary source documents and the way historians work with them is an important goal of "America Dreams." One way Ferenz decided to introduce this was to design an inquiry lesson on "What stories do documents tell?" Ferenz collected many primary documents, such as the Constitution and other digitized primary source documents. She downloaded them from various Internet libraries and printed them on parchment paper. Next, she borrowed magnifying glasses from the science teacher. At each table of four students she placed a box containing lots of different documents, a magnifying glass, and a pair of white gloves, similar to those worn at the Library of Congress whenever anyone handles original documents.

Students assumed the roles of Historian, Rare Document Curator, Equipment Manager, and Archivist. Their goal was to look at each document carefully and ask questions: What do I see? What does it look like? What do various elements mean? Then the students were to figure out why each document was created, find its link in history, date the piece for a time line, and finally, in teams, write out the "story" of at least one document. Students had to present their stories and defend their theories.

Ferenz is a wizard at locating and presenting information from the Web, and most teachers will not have those skills. Nevertheless, good teaching really rests on creating engaging lessons, not on technological prowess. The special skills of combining engaging teaching with technological literacy that Ferenz has modeled in "America Dreams" are ones that should be in the library media specialist's bag of tricks and made available to their collaborating partners at school.

SEIZING THE OPPORTUNITIES

What implications do interdisciplinary and thematic projects like this have on library media centers and schools? Ferenz's experience of teaching this project in middle school in 1998 indicated that students need to acquire information literacy skills that allow them to perform their investigations. Teachers and library media specialists working together need to provide enough time for student reflection on their investigative process. What have they found? Where have they found it? What are the biases of each source of information? Students typically are pleased when they find anything that seems relevant. Only when teachers and students value the process checks will they get the idea that keeping a log and developing answers to questions about authenticity and point of view are important.

Lessons that allow students to develop techniques for uncovering the merit of information sites are often a necessary adjunct to units like this. For example, a quoted official from the Civil War period might be either pro- or anti-slavery. Knowing that piece of information might change the meaning of the quote. Students will take the time to find out only if the structure of the class requires and rewards that activity.

This habit of mind is at the heart of the analytical thinking we prize in students. Library media specialists who understand how information is formed, presented, and used can help ensure that the student inquiry curriculum allows for deep student thinking. For success, students will need teacher and library media specialist planning and support in order to carry out their inquiry in a meaningful and timely way. In virtually every case, library media specialists are key. They understand how to locate and access collections of primary source documents. They know what information literacy skills will be needed and how those skills can be placed within the context of the unit. They routinely support student inquiry.

NEW ROLES AND POSSIBILITIES

The appearance of digitized collections of primary source documents is one example of the sweeping changes the World Wide Web is bringing to schools and especially to library media centers. These changes suggest three new possibilities for library media specialists.

1. Library media specialists now have the capacity to provide two primary entry points to their services for the school community. One is the physical front door; the other, the home page of their library media center's Web site. The discrete items located in the library media center are no longer enough. Neither is it desirable simply to allow access to the World Wide Web to substitute for the selection and management of high-quality information. The ability to master HTML and Web authoring tools sufficiently to be able to pull sites or documents from the Web onto locally produced pages for classroom or library media center use is becoming more and more important. It is an extension of the skills needed for thoughtfully pulling a set of print or multimedia resources for classroom use. It would be wonderful if we could design the library media center's online search screen to query both the library media center's online catalog *and* a set of carefully selected World Wide Web sites, in such a way that the results of *both* searches appeared as a single integrated hit list. Each of these ideas, however, is merely a new facet of the library media specialist's traditional work: providing excellent information resources to support curriculum and promote reading.

2. The information literacy skills needed to make intelligent use of the new technologies for delivering information are needed throughout the school, in every class. They cannot be simply the work that occurs in the library media center. Library media specialists can help their schools craft an information agenda in which appropriate

elements are embedded in every classroom. Because library media specialists understand the way information works, they are the ones who can keep teachers current in skillful, thoughtful use of information. For example, library media specialists have always highlighted new books, bringing them to the attention of particular teachers or displaying them prominently. There are analogous ways to promote new primary source document collections and other network-based resources.

3. Library media specialists are already masters of the methods of personalization, integration of ideas across subject disciplines, and support of inquiry. As schools seek to redesign the work they do to incorporate these ideas in classroom practice throughout the school, library media specialists must be prepared to offer and share what they know about this. There is no substitute for the insight library media specialists can bring to the school's restructuring, curriculum, or technology committees. The purpose of all of these is to promote the improvement of student achievement. This exactly parallels the library media center's goals, so the library media specialist should be a key participant.

Units such as "America Dreams" raise the ante for library media specialists. This curriculum is student-centered: kids drive the inquiry, and the outcome is unpredictable. To be successful and sustainable, classrooms characterized by this kind of work require close collaboration between teachers and library media specialists. The library media specialist's role as a manager of information in both print and electronic form is crucial. The library media specialist's experience in supporting student inquiry, with all its attendant skills and techniques, must become a resource for the whole school as it makes the transition to more student-centered pedagogies.

Without library media specialists playing this larger role, it is unlikely that long-term improvement in school performance can be sustained. Teachers may have the desire and inclination to experiment with new technology and teaching methods, but that will not be enough to sustain new curricula and teaching methods. Too much is happening and time is too limited. The rapidly changing information picture requires the library media specialist to be the mediator and organizer of information resources, as well as the partner with teachers in providing an information literacy agenda throughout the school.

NOTES

1. The Bay Area National Digital Library Project (BANDL) is part of the school reform efforts of the Bay Area School Reform Collaborative. Its purpose is to promote successful use of information technology in classrooms and to enhance the role of the library media specialist in a school's reform efforts. More information can be found at <http://www.wested.org/basrc/bandl>.
2. Information about the WebQuest design can be found at <http://edweb.sdsu.edu/webquest.html>.

REFERENCE

Donlan, Leni, and Kathleen Ferenz. 1998. "America Dreams... Through the Decades." <http://www.internet-catalyst.org/projects/amproject/toc.html> (accessed May 25, 1998).

9
Assessment: A Tool for Developing Lifelong Learners

Jean Donham and Barbara Barnard Stein

When we assess student performance, we are gathering information about what students are learning, to help us know better what and how to teach. Because we base our assessment on their performance of tasks or assignments, a discussion of assessment is also a discussion of assignments.

Several questions face us in considering assessment in the library media center:

- Why is assessment of interest to library media specialists?
- What are the purposes of assessment and who is the audience?
- What assessment techniques are particularly useful to school library media specialists?
- What is the relationship between assessment strategies and assignments in developing information literacy?

SCHOOL LIBRARY MEDIA SPECIALISTS' INTEREST IN ASSESSMENT

Several key concepts have moved assessment into the spotlight in recent years. Most relevant to the school library media program are authenticity, process, curriculum integration, complex thinking, and independent learning.

Authenticity

An intention to prepare students not merely for school (first grade as preparation for second grade, and so on) but rather for life has generated concern for authenticity in students' schoolwork. In real life, tests—whether they lead to employment, promotion, or privileges—are not multiple choice; instead, they are performance-based. Schools are seeking similar performance-based assessment.

A goal for library media programs is that students develop the skills, knowledge, and attitudes necessary to be learners not just in school but throughout their lives. What do learners do? Learners pose questions, access and evaluate information, apply information to decision making and problem solving, and assess whether the information has met their need. These life skills are the heart of the information literacy curriculum; that focus on life skills lends authenticity to the information literacy curriculum as well. Newmann and Wehlage (1993) suggested several attributes of authentic tasks:

- higher-order thinking: application, analysis, synthesis, and evaluation more than knowledge and comprehension
- depth of knowledge: learning integrated across disciplines rather than in fragmented collections of isolated facts (e.g., designing a wildlife park

habitat to accommodate various species of plants and animals rather than collecting isolated facts about animal or plant species to complete a chart as the final product)

- connectedness to the world beyond the class-room: application to real-world problems, whether local or global (e.g., searching for solutions to solid waste disposal)
- substantive conversation: interaction between teachers and students and among students as they make distinctions, form generalizations, and raise questions (e.g., developing a class proposal for a local bike trail, beginning with defining the need, determining the various sources of political support, identifying the obstacles (financial, political, environmental), and continuing to a final proposal).

When students' tasks fit these criteria, the students are working in ways representative of real-life work, not just "schoolwork." This is authenticity. These tasks create a need for information-driven problem solving and provide an ideal circumstance for developing information literacy. Assessment strategies must collect data about how students work to solve these problems; they must address the process as well as the content learning of these experiences.

Process

Knowledge is increasing so rapidly that we cannot expect to prepare students by providing them all the facts they will need for their lifetime. Instead, we must develop in them the skills and attitudes of information literacy. To succeed in the Information Society, they must be learners.

Such a realization has brought a greater respect for the importance of teaching processes, such as decision making, problem solving, and information processing.

For school library media specialists, information processes are central to our curriculum. For example, a ninth-grade language arts class is focusing attention on purposeful information gathering. The students' assignment is to work in teams of four as consultant groups for a corporation seeking to locate its corporate office in some United States city.[1] Their task is to recommend an appropriate city. The library media specialist teaches students strategies for defining their information need, and uses an information process model to help them see how to solve the problem and generate a proposal. By offering students a mental model of the information search process, the library media specialist has provided a framework for their work and made them aware of their own process. Of course, as the students use that framework, the library media specialist will also be suggesting strategies and sources that will help them be successful. What is important is that the process has been made explicit.

Integration of Curriculum

A third development changing the face of assessment is curriculum integration—defining the connections among the disciplines. Curriculum integration requires relating the content and processes of one discipline to those of another and applying skills or knowledge across areas of study. Library media specialists know that information literacy does not develop in isolation; students must apply the skills and knowledge that make up the information literacy curriculum in order to learn them.

In an interdisciplinary sixth-grade unit, students research countries, but their task is not the typical country research because the requirements come from teachers in several disciplines: the social studies teacher requires information on history; the science teacher asks for information about natural resources, especially bodies of water and the economic and social impact that water has in the country; the math teacher requires spreadsheets tracking precipitation and temperature for the country and comparison of those data with Iowa data; the language and fine arts teachers require information about culture and arts in the country; and the library media specialist emphasizes notetaking and organizing information using graphic organizers.[2] This approach creates a meaningful context for student learning.

Complex Thinking and Complex Tasks

Students need many opportunities for applying, analyzing, synthesizing, and evaluating information. Although lower-order thinking skills—recalling and comprehending—still have their place, emphasis on these higher-level processes reflects the increased complexity students will face in an information society. For the school library media specialist, a particularly important higher-order process to teach is evaluating information. Consider the high school chemistry class investigating painkillers.[3] Students receive this scenario:

> You've just smacked your finger with a hammer and are desperately in need of a painkiller. You rush to the medicine cabinet and find the section your very organized mother has labeled "pain killers." But which one will you use: Bayer, Anacin, Aleve, Bufferin, Ecotrin, Excedrin, Advil? You need information—fast!

Each student receives a card with the name of an analgesic; students pair up to search for information on the

Internet. The library media specialist teaches mini-lessons on key word searching on the Web and evaluating the information found there. The teacher provides a set of questions about the chemical makeup, effects, and cost of the drug to guide students in collecting relevant information so that they can make a decision about their personal pain. Teaching students search and evaluation skills at the point of need gives these skills meaning and value. Determining how well students perform these processes requires a new look at assessment techniques.

Independent Learning

Information Literacy Standards for Student Learning (AASL and AECT 1998) states that one dimension of an information-literate person is striving for excellence in information seeking and knowledge generation. To meet this standard, students must develop expertise in self-assessing how well they use information to solve problems or make decisions. By experiencing a variety of assessment techniques during their information work, students gain awareness of the importance of assessing the quality of their work, and can develop a repertoire of strategies and criteria to help them monitor their own work. For students to achieve this standard, opportunities for assessment—by teachers, peers, and themselves—must be frequent.

Given these trends in education, understanding assessment and developing skill in using a variety of assessment strategies become increasingly important for all educators, including school library media specialists.

THE PURPOSES AND AUDIENCES FOR ASSESSMENT

Assessment can serve any of four purposes. (National Council of Teachers of Mathematics 1995). Those purposes are clarified in figure 9.1.

Figure 9.1. Purposes of assessment

Purpose	Formative / Summative	Audience	Sample Assessment Strategy
Improve student growth	Formative	Inform student of progress	Rubric
Improve instruction	Formative	Inform teacher of what instruction is needed or how effective teaching has been so far	Conferencing
Recognize accomplishment	Summative	Inform student (and parent) of how well the student has done	Checklist
Improve a program	Summative	Inform teacher of how well a curriculum is working	Matrix

MATCH BETWEEN ASSESSMENT TECHNIQUE AND PURPOSE

A library media specialist needs a varied repertoire of assessment techniques (Donham 1998). Because some assessments are formative and others are summative, certain assessment strategies work better for one purpose than another. For example, because rubrics show a progression of development, they seem best suited to formative assessment, whereas portfolios sum up a student's progress and can be particularly useful as summative assessment. That is not to say that each assessment strategy is only suited to one purpose or the other; instead, we must consider our purpose and choose a strategy with that purpose in mind.

Improve Student Growth

One purpose of assessment is to improve student growth. Here assessment is a component of teaching, whether the method is the simple yes/no check for understanding so integral to good lesson design or a fully developed rubric. In the library media program, these formative assessments to improve student performance focus largely on information processes. Here, the results of assessment inform the student about his or her progress, answering the question, "How am I doing in relation to the goals we have set and agreed on?" This is an ongoing process. Certain assessment techniques can be particularly useful as tools to give students data about their performance and guidance on how to improve. Techniques most useful for improving student growth are rubrics, conferencing, and checklists.

Rubrics

Rubrics can provide structured assessment. They are particularly helpful when students need a precise and concrete description of successful performance. A rubric describes a range of successful and unacceptable performances. Often, we tell students their performance is excellent or we give them an *A*. This is not descriptive language; this is evaluative language. It only tells the student our judgment, rather than describing success. To develop a rubric, first we must identify the attributes of a successful performance of the task. These attributes must be teachable; that is, teachers must be able to help students increase their ability to perform (Popham 1997). For ninth-graders beginning a report assignment, for example, these three aspects of the planning phase of a research process might be important:

A research question: The topic is focused into a clearly stated, answerable research question.

A search plan: The student creates either a written or a mental plan for identifying potential sources of information.

Criteria-based selection of potential sources: The student applies criteria relevant to the topic in selecting sources of information.

Once we identify these attributes of success, the next step in developing a rubric is to watch or visualize performances at varying degrees of excellence. Close observation helps us recognize less-than-perfect performance so that we can describe it as well as excellence. The final step is to describe performances of varying qualities. The questions posed are: "What does excellent search strategizing look like?" "What does the student do to select potential information sources?" "What processes—thinking and doing— occur?" As these questions are answered, the descriptions of effective and less effective performance within each attribute emerge. Words such as *appropriate, excellent, better*, do not describe—they label. A rubric for the planning phase might then address these three dimensions, as seen in figure 9.2.

There are three crucial conditions for using rubrics:

1. Students must have the rubrics *before* they do the work, to increase success.
2. One-time use of a given rubric misses the point; students need the chance to improve their performances. Using a rubric repeatedly for the duration of a unit or project, as well as reusing a

Figure 9.2. A sample rubric

Task Definition: Developing the Research Question

_____ My topic can be explained by stating a question that begins with "how" or "why."

_____ My topic can be explained by stating a question that begins with "what."

_____ My topic can be explained by a few words or phrases.

_____ My topic can be explained in one word or phrase.

Information-Seeking Strategies: Designing the Search Plan

_____ I made a mental or written list of possible information sources and key words. I put them in order from general to specific.

_____ I made a mental or written list of possible information sources and key words.

_____ I went to several sources I knew about.

_____ I went straight to the library catalog.

Location and Access: Using Criteria to Select Potential Sources

_____ I searched the library catalog and MAS (Magazine Article Summaries) and limited my search to yield no more than 15 hits each by using combinations of key words, publication date, and local availability.

_____ I searched the library catalog and MAS (Magazine Article Summaries) and combined key words with *and*, *or*, or *not* and skimmed the entries to mark which ones to print.

_____ I searched the library catalog and MAS (Magazine Article Summaries) using a key word and printed out the first 10–15 hits on each list.

_____ I searched the library catalog and MAS (Magazine Article Summaries) using a key word and printed out all the hits.

rubric in a new project, both support student growth.

3. Use of rubrics as an assessment strategy is appropriate when the task is complex enough that degrees of sophistication, independence, or excellence can be seen; rubrics are not necessary for yes/no, right/wrong tasks. Such tasks as writing a correct bibliographic citation or using a glossary to locate a term are tasks that one can either do or not. In contrast, a task like key word searching has degrees of performance, in terms of efficiency, accuracy, relevance to the question, and so on.

To use a rubric, then, students receive it at the beginning of their work. It must always be available to them, and as the library media specialist works with each student to "check" on progress, he or she refers to the rubric to say, for example, "Let's read what the rubric says; which of those statements describes what you have been doing?" This becomes a way of engaging students in conversation about their information search process using specific and concrete terms to guide them to improved performance.

Once students have had enough practice with rubrics so that the format and use are familiar, it is possible and effective to include students in the development of rubrics for their projects. After an assignment has been determined and modeled, students can generate degrees of performance. It is important that these be in student language and that continued use and discussion promote refinement. An example of one developed by a third-/fourth-grade class is cited in figure 9.3. Note that the language is student-generated, and it is clear that the students have specific criteria they are assessing.[4]

Figure 9.3. Student-generated rubric

Hyperstudio Rubric

	4	3	2	1
Content	• lots of details • organized • interesting • a lot of information • fun to read • edited	• a few details • organized • a little information • some editing	• no details • little organization • not too interesting • little editing	• no details • not in order • not interesting • not much information • no editing
Presentation	• easy to read • clear picture • good spacing • colorful • organized • obvious button • very neat	• easy to read • good pictures • OK fonts • pretty neat	• not very organized • no pictures • not too easy to read	• blurry picture or none at all • hard to read • bad background and font • messy

Designed by Mrs. Hill's third-/fourth-grade class at Weber Elementary School, Iowa City, Iowa.

Conferencing

Conferencing can help both students and teachers assess progress (Harada and Yoshina 1998). As students work, the teacher or library media specialist can move from student to student to inquire about progress. In informal conferencing, the questions may be, "What is your topic?" "What research questions have you written?" "What sources of information have you found?" "How are you organizing your notes?" "How are you keeping track of your resources for your bibliography?" Questions like these call for the student to explain some aspect of the research process.

Checklists

Checklists can be one more useful tool for assessment that is intended to improve student growth. A checklist given to students at the beginning of the research activity is simply a guide that helps students attend to all aspects of the assignment. It can include elements for the process as well as the product. Each of these items can be checked off the list, providing organization for the student as well as a basis for dialogue between the student and the media specialist. The checklist in figure 9.4 is for upper elementary students. It provides a visual reminder of the expectations of the assignment, and either student or media specialist can tell in a quick glance what has been accomplished and what is yet to be done.

If they have this checklist from the beginning, students can use it as a guide and know from the outset what they must include. The checklist is used again as the final evaluation for the project. An additional benefit of using a checklist is that it gives frequent and specific feedback, clear expectations, and a model of successful performance.

Figure 9.4. Sample checklist

Evaluation of Process

Name _____

Check each resource you use
during your research process.

Resources: Check those you have used.

Classroom	Media Center	Other
_____ textbooks	_____ books	_____ magazines
_____ books	_____ dictionaries	_____ TV
_____ teacher	_____ encyclopedia (print)	_____ personal interview
_____ computer programs	_____ encyclopedia (electronic)	_____ family
	_____ atlas	
	_____ almanac	
	_____ CD-ROM	

Organizational Tools: Check and date what you have completed.

✓	Tool	Date
___	Brainstorming	_____
___	Automated catalog	_____
___	Notetaking	_____
___	Conference with teacher or media specialist	_____
___	Rough draft	_____

Rubrics, checklists, and conferencing are strategies that provide opportunities for dialogue about learning.

Improve Instruction

A second purpose of assessment is to improve instruction. Here the information informs the teacher by answering the question, "How can I use this evidence about students' progress to modify my teaching and thereby improve learning?" Based on information gained via assessment, one can decide what teaching activities should occur for students to progress.

Journaling

Journal writing can be a very simple process in which students just take a few minutes at the end of each session in the library media center to respond to a question or two posed by the library media specialist. The teacher or library media specialist asks questions such as, "What problems did you have today? How did you solve them? Which ones are still unsolved?" These responses are then collected at the end of each class work session in the library media center. On another occasion, the questions might be, "What did you accomplish today? What do you need to accomplish next?" These responses can be simple and quickly recorded on 3 x 5 cards; this need not be an elaborate process. Such journaling will urge students to focus, at least briefly, on the research process as well as the content of their research. In addition, the brief entries can give the teacher and the library media specialist a sense of how students are doing. For example, they may learn that a mini-lesson on some specific skill or strategy should be taught next.

Besides journaling, conferencing with students or using rubrics can also provide information to guide instruction. As the library media specialist sees patterns among groups of students, the need for group instruction on a specific topic may become evident.

Recognize Accomplishment

A third purpose of assessment is to recognize accomplishment. Unlike the first two assessment purposes, recognizing students' accomplishments is summative in nature, coming at the end of an instructional episode. Periodically, teachers will synthesize student progress into a narrative commentary, a checklist, or a grade, to answer the question, "How is this student doing compared to our overall expectations?" Traditionally, grades have been the primary way in which we have recognized student accomplishment. Grades, however, provide students with only a label and a judgment about their work. Other assessment strategies provide students with a more detailed and substantive indication of their success.

Portfolios

Student work can be accumulated over time to show a progression of developing skills and knowledge (Callison 1997). Portfolio development is largely a classroom responsibility, because the teacher ultimately synthesizes the student's achievement into a final report or a grade. Nevertheless, library media specialists will want to maintain awareness of the portfolio and see that assessments of work included within the portfolio represent the information literacy processes as well as the content of the classroom curriculum.

Improve a Program

A final purpose of assessment is to modify or improve the program. At this point the focal length of assessment changes somewhat as we step back and review a unit or an entire program to determine how well it is meeting expectations. Here again, data collected via various assessment strategies are useful in identifying not only how well we are doing, but in what ways we are doing well and in what ways we may need to improve.

Formal Conferencing

At the end of a research activity, formal conferencing may be an appropriate assessment technique for gathering data to help improve the program. A schedule of questions for a formal conference might look like this:

- How did you find your information?
- Can you think of any problems you encountered as you did your research? What was hard about doing research? Where did you get stuck?
- What was most interesting to you about doing this research project?

By analyzing the results of these conferences, the library media specialist can look for patterns that indicate a deficiency in the program or an area of strength.

If time constraints make conferencing impractical, a brief questionnaire to students can serve a similar purpose. The questionnaire in figure 9.5 works for a range of students. Each can fill in his or her own self-assessment, and the media specialist can agree or disagree with that assessment. Both have the opportunity to evaluate performance and both may add comments. The questionnaire can be added to a portfolio, sent home, used for parent conferences, or used as a part of a class set to identify needs of the instructional program.

Matrix

Charting the instructional activities in the library media program can also prove useful in overall program improve-

Figure 9.5. Sample student questionnaire

Student/Media Specialist Evaluation Conference

Student Self-Evaluation	Media Specialist Evaluation

1. I used the automated catalog and refined my search.

Agree Disagree	Agree Disagree
Comments:	Comments:

2. I was able to find useful books about my topic.

Agree Disagree	Agree Disagree
Comments:	Comments:

3. I feel confident about my skills for finding information using the table of contents and index within sources.

Agree Disagree	Agree Disagree
Comments:	Comments:

4. I was able to use nonprint sources like CD-ROM encyclopedias and computer programs.

Agree Disagree	Agree Disagree
Comments:	Comments:

5. Our media collection had enough for this project.

Agree Disagree	Agree Disagree
Comments:	Comments:

ment. By charting what is being taught to each group in the school, the library media specialist can know how comprehensively the program is being delivered, and can then begin to identify weaknesses. Figure 9.6 shows an excerpt from a matrix that records a high school library media program integration of information literacy skills. The entire matrix will include all aspects of the information literacy curriculum, with lines for identifying each unit where that skill is integrated and whether it is introduced, emphasized, or reviewed. Maintaining such a matrix, organized by aspects of the information literacy curriculum, provides a system for monitoring the program. The data collected in that matrix can be used to collaborate with teachers to improve the program by identifying areas of over- or underemphasis.

RELATIONSHIP BETWEEN ASSESSMENT AND INFORMATION LITERACY

Making meaning is the challenge for today's student. Given the vastness of information and information sources, students must integrate an array of ideas. When we provide students with assignments that meet criteria for authentic learning and demand integrative reasoning, we are providing experiences similar to real-life issues they are likely to confront. Such complex tasks provide opportunities for substantive conversation and for in-depth investigation. They also demand complex information processing skills. Developing those skills has never been more important than today, when the question is not, "Can I find enough information?" but rather, "How do I filter, sift, sort, evaluate, and manage the mass of information I have found?"

If we believe the adage that "What gets measured gets taught," then assessment must include elements related to

Figure 9.6. Excerpt from high school skills integration matrix

Topic	Integration into Unit	Level	Introduce/ Emphasize/ Review
Collection Stage			
Identifying possible sources	Humanities: 60s research	11	E
	English 9: Symposium project	9	E
	Government: Social movement research	10	E
	Economics: Marxist research project	11	R
Filtering of sources and information	Humanities: 60s research	11	R
(i.e., distinguishing fact and fiction,	English 9: Symposium project	9	E
skimming, scanning, applying criteria	Biology: Diseases research	9/10	R
such as relevancy, accuracy, and	American Studies: Political leaders of the	9	E
currency)	20th century—Biographical research		
	project		
Etc.			

the information process tasks as well as the curriculum aspects of students' work. Assessing information processes ensures that relevant skills are taught and raises students' awareness of those processes so that they can begin to self-monitor as they grow toward independence as information seekers. Assessment of information processes helps students know not only *whether* they were successful but also *why* they were or were not successful. To develop into independent learners capable of applying information effectively to solve problems and to make decisions, they must be able to assess their own skill in accessing, using, evaluating, and creating information.

CONCLUSION

We began with four questions:

1. *Why is assessment of interest to library media specialists?* Library media specialists have a key role to play in both assignment and assessment design, for several reasons:

 the library media center is by its very nature interdisciplinary

 the information literacy curriculum focuses on processes

 problem solving and decision making are logical outcomes of effective use of information

2. *What are the purposes of assessment and who is the audience?* Assessment provides us with information to improve the performance of students, teachers, and our overall program.

3. *What assessment techniques are particularly useful to school library media specialists?* Each of us needs to have a varied repertoire of assessment

strategies and decide which one(s) to use to accomplish our purposes most effectively.

4. *What is the relationship between assessment strategies and assignments in developing information literacy?* Students will become independent, lifelong learners when they develop skill in using information effectively and assessing their own successes and shortcomings in applying information to problem solving and decision making. By giving students assignments that call for application of information to meaningful problems, and by focusing their attention on their information processing with the use of assessment strategies, these life skills are nurtured.

In collaboration with teachers, library media specialists can help design appropriate authentic assignments to challenge students in life-like ways, and they can help design and carry out assessments that help students gain insight into the processes associated with effective use of information.

NOTES

1. Example provided by Joan Gushiken, Library Media Specialist, Holmen High School, Wisconsin.
2. Example provided by Cindy Kunde, Library Media Specialist, North Cedar Community Schools, Iowa.
3. Example provided by Susan Kientz, Library Media Specialist, Fairfield High School, Iowa.
4. Example provided by Yukiko Hill, Teacher, Weber Elementary School, Iowa.

REFERENCES AND ADDITIONAL RESOURCES

American Association of School Librarians and Association for Educational Communications and Technology. 1998. *Information Literacy Standards for Student Learning*. Chicago: American Library Association.

Callison, Daniel. 1997. "Portfolio." *School Library Media Activities Monthly* (October): 42–44.

Donham, Jean. 1998. *Assessment of Information Processes and Products*. McHenry, Ill.: Follett Software.

Harada, Violet, and Joan Yoshina. 1998. "The Missing Link: One Elementary School's Journey with Assessment." *School Library Media Activities Monthly* (March): 25–29.

National Council of Teachers of Mathematics. 1995. *Assessment Standards for School Mathematics*. Reston, Va.: Author.

Newmann, Fred M., and Gary G. Wehlage. 1993. "Five Standards of Authentic Instruction." *Educational Leadership* (April): 8–12.

Popham, W. James. 1997. "What's Wrong—and What's Right—with Rubrics." *Educational Leadership* (October): 72–75.

Part IV
Context of Library Media Programs

10

Developing a Collaborative Access Environment: Meeting the Resource Needs of the Learning Community

Sandra M. Hughes and Jacqueline C. Mancall

THE ENVIRONMENT OF INFORMATION SERVICES

The cover story on the February/March 1998 *Bulletin of the American Society for Information Science* pictured the new information professional as "pioneering, flexible, agile and empowered" (Griffiths 1998, 8). José-Marie Griffiths, author of the cover story, described this individual as a "guide in the face of an uncertain future, a collaborator ... someone who understands the core capabilities of one's organization, work group and colleagues" (Griffiths 1998, 8). Griffiths's keen insights are helpful in understanding the revolutionary times we are moving through—times that call for new definitions of basic beliefs and practices.

Griffiths called our attention to a schema in which the information professional as guide provides intellectual, physical, and procedural access to resources in a world where no one is sure precisely what will be available and where (Griffiths 1998, 8). The role of guide is a curious but appropriate one, as it does not always include being the expert. The contemporary school library media professional can no longer be the sole proprietor of a self-contained, one-stop shopping establishment. Even extending the metaphor to operating an information supermarket is inappropriate. We must learn how to manage electronic kiosks on the information superhighway: kiosks that are staffed by a variety of experts, carry a minimal and ever-changing stock, and provide instant access to other stores of items and resource people (wherever they are located). We must learn what it means to "understand the core capabilities of one's organization, work group, and colleagues" (Griffiths 1998, 8).

A number of factors influence how we build and manage what we have traditionally referred to as *the collection*. Paramount among them is the proliferating body and nature of information that is available. As important as the explosion of information is the paradigm shift in learning theory that is changing the teaching/learning climate of the school, with its implications for the types of resources needed to enable the learning process. New national standards support an already complicated picture. *Information Power: Building Partnerships for Learning* calls for a collaborative environment in which the school library media professional is identified as an information specialist who plays a key role on teaching and learning teams (AASL and AECT 1998). This has major ramifications for practice and the roles of collector and manager of the school library media center as a resource place.

As the context in which school library media specialists work continues to change, assumptions about the role of the collector must also change. To provide resources that meet the requirements of the learning community, school library media specialists must reimagine the collection and create access environments that reflect the characteristics of the learner, the teaching/learning context of the school, changes in the knowledge base, and partnerships with the broader learning community. To do this, collectors must become change agents, resource guides, leaders, and learners.

THE PARADIGM SHIFT AND ITS EFFECT ON THE TEACHING/LEARNING ENVIRONMENT

During the last decade, our view of teaching and learning has undergone a change. At all levels of education, kindergarten to college, there is a growing awareness of what it means to enable learning. Treating students as passive receptors of knowledge has not been universally successful. Making teachers better speakers and lecturers has not produced better learners. The paradigm has shifted from an emphasis on good teaching to an emphasis on enabling learning. This has major implications for school library media programs and library collections, as well as for the collector.

Traditional theories of learning, which have influenced teaching and learning for more than a century, view education and learning as external processes. Students learn a prescribed body of knowledge through memorization and drill, with knowledge viewed as true and unchanging. The focus is on the teacher as the source of knowledge and students as recipients. The aim is to provide students with a common core of concepts, skills, and knowledge (Walker and Lambert 1995; Brooks and Brooks 1993; Barr and Tagg 1995).

In traditional classrooms, the focus is on developing the conventional academic intelligences (Gardner 1983).

Table 10.1. The Traditional View of Learning

Traditional Theory of Learning	Traditional Learning Context
• Learning is viewed as an external process	• Students are viewed as empty vessels to be filled by the teacher
• Knowledge is viewed as true and unchanging	• Focus is on providing students with a common core of concepts, knowledge, and skills
• Knowledge comes in "chunks" and "bits" and is delivered by teachers	• Direct instruction is the primary teaching strategy; textbooks provide bulk of content
• Outcomes of learning are uniform	• Teachers determine the outcomes and learning is measured by standardized tests

As Table 10.1 shows, direct instruction is the primary teaching strategy. Teachers establish learning goals, determine the criteria for success, deliver the content in "bits" and "chunks," and evaluate student progress using standardized tests. Curricular activities rely heavily on textbooks (Walker and Lambert 1995; Brooks and Brooks 1993; Barr and Tagg 1995).

As we progressed through the twentieth century, a new theory of learning emerged. This theory, known as constructivism, views education as "an internal process in which learners use prior knowledge and experience to share meaning and construct knowledge" (Walker and Lambert 1995, 20). Central to constructivism is the belief that knowledge is not a static body of information, but rather a process. The role of the teacher is to bring preexisting knowledge to the surface, provide learners with experiences that challenge their current understandings,

Table 10.2. The Constructivist View of Learning

Constructivist Theory of Learning	Constructivist Learning Context
• Learning is viewed as a process	• Students are treated as thinkers with emerging theories about the world
• Knowledge is viewed as constantly changing; knowledge and beliefs are formed within the learner	* Students are involved in authentic learning tasks; use of multiple intelligences is stressed
• Learning is a social activity that is enhanced by shared inquiry	• Students are engaged in cooperative learning
• Knowledge is constructed by the learner through interactions with ideas, objects, and people	• Inquiry and Socratic dialogue are primary teaching strategies; primary resources and manipulatives are used
• Outcomes are varied and often unpredictable	• Students and teachers together determine outcomes; assessment involves students in self-reflection and demonstrations

and make learners aware of the processes they use to create new structures (Walker and Lambert 1995; Brooks and Brooks 1993; Barr and Tagg 1995). The aim of constructivism is "education for understanding" (Gardner 1983).

As Table 10.2 shows, constructivist classrooms look different. Constructivism advances the idea that learning is a social endeavor requiring engagement with others. Students work in groups to solve problems together. Inquiry and Socratic dialogue are the primary teaching strategies. Curricular activities rely heavily on primary sources and manipulatives. Students and teachers establish learning goals together and assessment involves self-reflection and demonstrations. In this environment, prejudgments about resources become difficult, because the interests, talents, and abilities of the learner will affect judgments about the potential utility of resources.

IMPLICATIONS FOR THE COLLECTOR

Traditional Collection Development

In schools that operate under the traditional learning paradigm, the library media center may be perceived as the old corner store—the place where the proprietor (the school library media specialist) knows exactly what should be stocked. The focus of the collector is on buying *the best*, what external experts have identified as the most appropriate for particular age and user groups. Suggestions from teachers and students are considered useful, but collaboration is not a high priority in making resource decisions. The library media specialist functions as the school's expert, knows which selection tools to consult, and controls the budgeted funds for materials. As media formats become more diverse, the best traditional settings expand the corner store metaphor to become resource supermarkets. Quality remains the overriding issue, though, with increasing collection size the predominant quality indicator. Although the variety of formats collected expands to include electronic ones, in most instances the library media specialist predetermines them. Collections built in this mode focus on resources *just in case* they may be needed.

The traditional collection development model is thus a *just-in-case* model. The collection, as an entity to be perfected, is at the heart of the process. Typically, the parts of the process include a policy statement that explains how the mission of the school is achieved through collection and collection services. Criteria for collection of materials are part of the policy, as are broad references to acquisi-

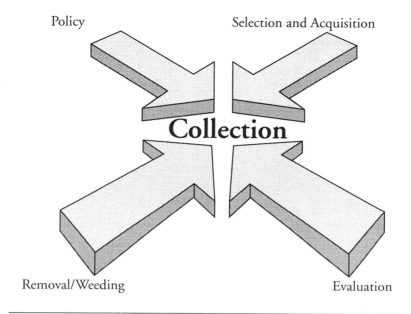

Policy
Selection and Acquisition

Collection

Removal/Weeding
Evaluation

Figure 10.1. Collection-centered model

tion procedures. The health of the collection is maintained through removal of outdated and useless materials, and ongoing evaluation is assumed to be part of the overall process. Knowledge of user behaviors is not totally ignored in making decisions, but the collection as an entity is the major concern.

The collection-centered model (Mancall 1994) places the collector in the position of supporting traditional expectations for the student as learner (see figure 10.1). Many teachers who embrace the traditional learning paradigm are comfortable with traditional formats of materials and with teaching a research process that focuses on the format of the tool. Even when the collector introduces new information formats, such as electronic encyclopedias or the Internet, the teacher's concern is still with the item itself, rather than with helping students understand the need to vary their search strategies according to the format, organization, and search capability of the resources as those resources relate to the particular issue students are researching.

Constructivist Collection Development

Under the constructivist paradigm, the library media center must be reimagined. The focus of the collector is on learning rather than on dissemination of information (AASL and AECT 1998, 1). The physical collection and access to resources are determined through collaboration with all members of the learning community. The library media specialist is aware of what is going on in the classroom and brings to the learning community resources that match the learners' characteristics and the teachers' expectations for what is to be achieved. Students' interests play a heightened role in this environment. The interests and capabilities of the students, matched to the requirements of the classroom, are used to suggest resources available internally and from the external community or virtual world.

The following two diagrams show the intellectual stages we have followed in moving our view of collection development to a constructivist approach. The first stage in rethinking the collection and access issues placed the user in the center of the picture and relabeled the pieces of the puzzle (see figure 10.2). In this model the characteristics of the users became one piece of the collector's mental model. Their types, ages, and backgrounds became a critical concern. The knowledge base became another piece of the collector's intellectual framework. The idea was to match the characteristics of the users to the knowledge base available. The collector's concern was making the appropriate match between the broad capabilities of

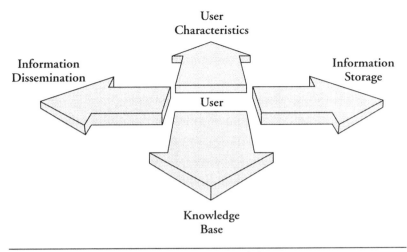

Figure 10.2. The user-centered model

the user and the resources that exist in the knowledge base.

The horizontal arrows in our user-centered model reflect the ongoing decisions the collection manager makes in determining which material formats to store and make available internally and how information of all types can be disseminated to users. Dissemination includes all processes, from the well-accepted in-house circulation of materials from a central collection, to providing access to remote databases, or directing users to appropriate Web sites (Mancall 1994, 10).

The next model we developed is pictured in figure 10.3. The change in the model's central label was integral to our changing conceptual framework. Our focus shifted from the *user* to the *learner*, and our concept of learner continued to expand to include all members of the learning community.

Neither of these models is meant to imply that the collector is unaware of current publication, production, and

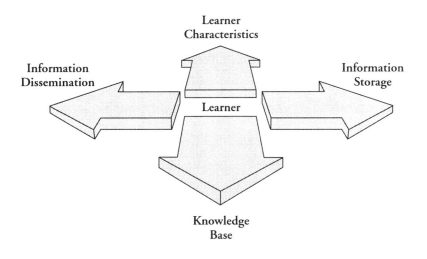

Figure 10.3. The learner-centered model

expanded access possibilities. In fact, it is just the opposite. The collector in the user-centered and learner-centered models must be connected at all levels: to what is being published and produced (print, nonprint, and electronically); to what is physically available in the broader community in which the school sits; to what is obtainable via the Internet; and to potential expansions in the networked environment that will bring information directly to the classroom or the home, as well as to the school library media center.

THE COLLABORATIVE ACCESS ENVIRONMENT EMERGES

The final model that emerged clarifies the forces that are present in a dynamic setting. This model, which we titled the Collaborative Access Environment, functions like a successful open-systems model. It is influenced by constantly shifting patterns in its internal and external

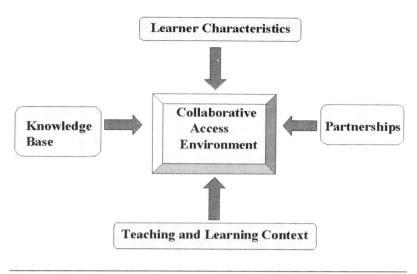

Figure 10.4. Collaborative access environment model

relationships. There is no beginning point and no set of linear steps for the collector who operates within this configuration. Instead, the collaborative access environment is controlled by systematic reactions to changing multiple forces. In our diagram the forces are labeled Learner Characteristics, Teaching and Learning Context, Knowledge Base, and Partnerships (see figure 10.4). Each of these forces requires data to support decision making and policy to clarify relationships and expectations. The successful collector in this model is a *guide* who understands the needs, interests, and capabilities of the organization and its work groups.

Learner Characteristics

The learners in our model include all the members of the school community: the students, the teachers, the administrators, the parents, and the caregivers. Available socioeconomic data describe the broad characteristics of these individuals and provide one frame of reference that will affect resource and access decisions. Data on student abilities come from information collected by the school describing reading and developmental levels, and from interactions with students, teachers, parents, and caregivers.

Teaching and Learning Context

Data needed to understand the teaching and learning context come from close observation in classrooms, planning meetings with the teaching staff, professional development opportunities, and analysis of units that require resource support. Existing mechanisms for curriculum analysis may be useful first steps in looking at the broad picture and making a first stab at matching materials to the teaching and learning context. (See Eisenberg and Berkowitz 1988.)

Knowledge Base

The knowledge base is in a state of continuous change. This is particularly evident in areas like science, technology, and medicine, but can also be seen in areas like the social sciences, psychology, and fine arts. The growth of the knowledge base has been accelerated by changes in technology. The Internet has made instant access to people, ideas, documents, images, and sounds possible. Members of the learning community can now interact with each other across cultural, social, and distance barriers. This means that they can share information freely and work together to create new understandings.

Partnerships

Teams and partnerships have become key ingredients in successful operations. The resources available to the learning community in the school can be enhanced by formal relationships with other organizations. The public library is a natural partner for access to collections of materials. Community-based organizations, such as local education funds, may support efforts to connect universities, businesses, museums, and other community agencies and their resources to the school.

Within the school, classroom teachers must be central participants in the resource world. Collaboration with classroom teachers is essential to the creation of an access environment that reflects learner characteristics and the teaching and learning context. In addition, classroom libraries, which often include books and access to electronic resources via a local area network, are becoming a reality. If creating classroom libraries benefits students, then the school library media profession must accept them. Classroom libraries are natural allies of the centrally located media center and can be viewed as an extension of it. Library media specialists have a responsibility to help teachers use funds wisely that come to them for classroom materials. By helping teachers understand the principles of selection, school library media specialists can help create classroom collections that reflect the changing developmental, cultural, and learning needs of the students.

Unanswered questions exist about how funds can be used to support resources in the school. Teachers and library media specialists must see themselves as on the same winning team when it comes to selection and maintenance of resources for learning. A new collaborative budgeting model could encourage the sharing of resources and would provide support for the resource allocation process. This process, which would involve all members of the learning community, must include access via the newer technologies.

THE PROCESS OF DEVELOPING A
COLLABORATIVE ACCESS ENVIRONMENT:
AN EXAMPLE

A look at how one school library media specialist developed a collaborative access environment might be useful at this point.[1] The media specialist's first task was to understand how constructivism had changed the teaching and learning context of the school. To do this:

- she familiarized herself with the district's academic content standards and benchmarks
- she attended professional development workshops on standards-based instruction and assessment
- she participated in conversations with teachers to identify what they expected students to know and be able to do
- she engaged the staff at her school in curriculum mapping.

The media specialist's second task was to become familiar with learner characteristics and understand how these characteristics affected the types of resources she needed to make available for students to be successful. She did this by learning more about literacy development; working with teachers on a regular basis to collaboratively plan, teach, and assess standards-based units of instruction; and talking with students informally when they visited the library.

At the same time, the media specialist had to be aware of the changing knowledge base and how to access information from this knowledge base. To do this, she remained on top of new developments in both the electronic and print environments by reading professional journals, attending professional conferences and workshops, and networking with her colleagues.

Lastly, the media specialist began to look for resources that would match teacher expectations and learner characteristics. Her definition of resources expanded to include not only print resources, but also CD-ROMs, Web sites, people, and places in the community. As she identified potential resources, she discussed them with teachers and students to alert them to the availability of these resources and to assess their value to the learning community. She also expanded the quality and amount of information available to teachers and students by developing partnerships with several organizations in the community (specifically, the public library, area museums, a local education fund that provides grants to schools, and several local universities).

Collector Behaviors in the Learning Community

In the preceding discussion, we identified the role of the collector as "guide." According to Griffiths, "guiding an expedition means we are embarking on new territory. And new territory most often requires us to do things in new ways, to change" (Griffiths 1998, 10). Building a collaborative access environment requires changes in the attitudes and behaviors of school library media specialists. As collectors, school library media specialists become, of necessity, change agents, resource guides, leaders, and learners (see Table 10.3).

Change Agent

Building a collaborative access environment demands that school library media specialists, teachers, and other members of the learning community enter into a collaborative relationship and share the authority for collection

Table 10.3. Collector Behaviors in the Learning Community

Required Behaviors

Change Agent

- Brings members of the learning community into the collection/access decision-making process
- Supports members of the learning community in the use of resources
- Models the use of resources to solve instructional problems

Resource Guide

- Collaborates with teaching and learning teams to match desired learner outcomes to resources
- Provides continual assessment of emerging resources and delivery mechanisms
- Facilitates physical and intellectual access to resources in all formats
- Develops mechanisms to alert and connect constituents to resources
- Evaluates, on a continuous basis, the utility of available resources

Leader

- Provides opportunities to develop a collaborative culture in the school
- Revises and updates resource and access policies and practices to reflect the changing information environment
- Creates and manages internal and external cooperative arrangements to meet the needs of the learning community
- Develops a budget that maximizes access to resources

Learner

- Remains current about emerging formats and information delivery mechanisms
- Understands the implications of learning theory on collection and access decisions

and access decisions. Establishing this collaborative relationship requires school library media specialists to act as change agents. According to Routman, moving to true collaboration is difficult: "We have spent so many years working in isolation in our own classrooms that it is a new-found experience to have engaging, professional... conversations with our colleagues" (Routman 1991, 20). To encourage collaboration, library media specialists need to engage in power sharing (Hughes 1998). This means they need to acknowledge and welcome the expertise other members of the learning community bring to the table concerning electronic resources, delivery mechanisms, and even print resources.

At the same time, school library media specialists must share their expertise in using resources with the other members of the learning community. Providing access to information is not enough. As collectors, school library media specialists need to model for teachers how to use new resources to solve instructional problems. They need to "fill in gaps in expertise" and support teachers as the teachers begin to incorporate the use of electronic resources and technologies into their teaching (Fullan and Stiegelbauer 1991; Hughes 1998).

Resource Guide

Providing physical and intellectual access is at the heart of *Information Power: Building Partnerships for Learning* (AASL and AECT 1998). Matching resources to the information needs of clients is what traditionally has attracted the good school library media specialist to the field. This matching concern is also at the heart of our role as evaluators of current publications and productions. The effective guide knows what is being produced and can suggest to the client (i.e., learner) what is most suitable. The dramatic change in the enactment of this role is our inability to closely monitor the exploding resource arena.

Knowledge of appropriate resources is our job, but collecting them just in case is no longer a satisfactory solution. The *just-in-time* idea is the cornerstone for the changing twenty-first century paradigm. This aspect is enhanced in the collaborative environment because the collector works so closely with teaching teams and is intimately aware of students' ability levels, how they will use resources, their learning goals, and requirements. In this respect, the collector alerts all members of the learning community to new developments. She also does this through other targeted activities, such as newsletters, selective dissemination of information services, and links from the school's home page to resources in the broader community.

Leader

Information Power: Building Partnerships for Learning identifies the school library media specialist as a leader (AASL and AECT 1998). Leadership in thinking about the future is implied. As the resource environment changes, schools need leaders who can anticipate and match emerging technologies to needs of the learning community. School library media specialists will be responsible for developing a collaborative approach to collection development, encouraging collaboration skills in other members of the learning community, and revising and updating resource and access policies and practices to reflect the changing information environment.

For a collector, leadership also means planning and managing a program budget that maximizes access to resources. In today's world, access to information defines the difference between wealth and poverty; it is the library media specialist's responsibility as collector to provide access that allows all children to successfully participate in the learning community. In addition, many school library media specialists no longer work in environments that guarantee funding for library resources. As an increasing number of schools have moved to site-based decision making, library media specialists are finding it necessary to develop and present annual program budgets to the school council or site-based team.

Leadership also requires working with others beyond the walls of the school. It is not unusual for groups of librarians from different types of libraries to meet, share concerns, and engage in cooperative negotiations for better pricing with vendors. The arena in which this is becoming the most popular is in the area of serials collecting. The evolving prospect of how serials can be made available provides a perfect opportunity for cooperation. Detailing how this can be done is beyond the scope of this chapter, but advice exists in the literature (Kachel 1996).

Learner

As Griffiths pointed out, we cannot always lead. Sometimes we may need to "follow while someone else steps up for a while and cuts down the forest in front of us, clearing a new path" (Griffiths 1998, 8). Our success as collectors depends on our ability to continue to be learners.

As educators continue to struggle to define the purposes, processes, and structures of education, school library media specialists need to stay abreast of research in the education field (Walker and Lambert 1995). We cannot be successful collectors unless we understand learning theory and its impact on collection and access decisions. We need to know how research is affecting the teaching/learning contexts, what teaching strategies are being used in the classroom, how students are being assessed, and what they are expected to know and be able to do.

The information world also continues to change at a rapid pace. The vendors that collectors deal with are moving quickly to create new products and new markets. The serials example used earlier is just one part of a changing picture. Online searching environments are available commercially that allow user-oriented searching across multiple databases. The best-known reference format, the encyclopedia, is available in multiple formats, including those with photos, videos, animation, documentaries, maps, tables, and sound clips ("Multimedia" 1998, 49). Keeping up with new resources, advances in online searching, and changes in technology and delivery mechanisms has become a necessity for collectors who see themselves as guides to resources.

BECOMING A CHANGE AGENT, RESOURCE GUIDE, LEADER, AND LEARNER: AN EXAMPLE

ICONnect, a technology initiative of the American Association of School Librarians (AASL), offers a second example of how to move from a traditional collection and collector perspective to one that enables collaboration by providing instant access to stores of items and resource people wherever they are located, via the Internet. Its five components include:

1. online courses to educate the school's learning community about use of the Internet
2. curriculum connections to suggest resources as well as tools for Web site evaluation
3. a KidsConnect question-and-answer service (operated in partnership with Syracuse

University) that suggests specific resources and
paths to resources for questions submitted

4. a monetary prize for exemplary collaborative
units, with reference to the resources used

5. a specific component for families that links them
to appropriate sites for locating resources that
meet their needs.

The five components of ICONnect provide one of the
delivery tools we envision for school change, that is, mechanisms that can enhance the collector's role as change
agent, resource guide, leader, and learner. Links to
resources (materials and people) are suggested throughout the five components. Enabling student learning is the
core concept that drives the ICONnect initiative.

Since 1996, AASL has awarded fourteen grants/prizes
to teams of library media specialists for exemplary collaborative units that use Internet technology.[2] One of the
prizes went to a New Jersey middle school team of school
library media specialist and special education teacher who
were change agents in their school.[3] The library media specialist wanted a small, controlled way to introduce use of
the Internet to students and teachers. The special education teacher wanted her fifth-grade students to think about
their future careers and the role of education in meeting
their career interests.

A small item in the school library's newsletter alerted
the learning community to the possibility of applying for an
AASL ICONnect prize. The special education teacher was
intrigued and contacted the librarian. Together, the
teacher and school library media specialist designed a unit
that used print, online, and human resources. It began with
students accessing an online career interest indictor via the

Internet. Each student selected a specific career and brainstormed the questions that he or she wanted answered about it. They followed this by writing letters to professional organizations, requesting information, and they communicated with an expert found through an "Ask an Expert" site. They shared what they learned with key-pals via e-mail and with classmates through oral presentations. Among the desired learning outcomes achieved was knowledge of the amount and type of education required to pursue their career interests.

The library media specialist as collector and collection manager demonstrated the key behaviors we listed in Table 10.3. She brought a teacher into the collection/access decision-making process and supported both the teacher and the class with resources. She collaborated as a member of the learning team by matching desired learner outcomes to the resources needed. She provided continual assessment of emerging resources and delivery mechanisms and evaluated the availability of appropriate resources on a continuous basis. Both teacher and school library media specialist understood how students could create meaningful learning and engaged equally in the design of the student experiences.

The national task force that guides ICONnect believes that stories like this one can be a premier delivery mechanism for advocating for *Information Power: Building Partnerships for Learning* (1998). The behaviors exhibited are evidence of a new collection/access environment that is collaborative in nature.

PRESCRIPTION FOR POSITIVE CHANGE

Is there a potential prescription for matching collection and access decisions to the requirements of the learning community? Can the preceding discussion provide school

Table 10.4. Changing Assumptions

Collector as Expert	Collector as Guide
• Size and ownership equal quality • "Expert" judgment guides selection • Representative formats control purchases • Access to syntheses by experts is a priority • Access to information in a variety of formats is useful but not critical	• Access to virtual world expands quality of information delivery • Learner characteristics and expectations control selection; expertise in selection is developed in learner • Information required dictates collecting decisions • Access to a breadth of ideas is expected, including those in primary resources • Access to information in every format is critical

library media specialists with a philosophy of collection development they can accept and use to make collection and access decisions that not only support the school's curriculum, but also meet the diverse learning needs of students? What are the changing assumptions collectors must accept, and what strategies can they use to develop collections that meet the requirements of the learning community? Based on the arguments offered in this chapter, we believe the paradigm of the collector as expert proprietor is no longer effective. The contemporary resource environment and current learning theories require the collector to act as a knowledgeable guide.

Both of the examples we shared earlier reflect how the school library media specialist works from Griffiths's guide assumption, rather than the traditional view of the collector as resource expert. In Table 10.4, we have shown how other sacred cows are also challenged. We used to believe that the size of a collection was an indicator of its quality. We know now that collection size is not the premier mark of quality. The collection must be judged based on how it is used, and the collection manager must understand how to collect data demonstrating usage patterns (see Drott 1993).[4] In addition, access to the virtual world and primary sources are important quality benchmarks.

The actual and enacted curriculum of the school should dictate what is collected and how long various resources are held. Although reviewers can sort and describe parts of the proliferating information world, they cannot be the primary judges of what should be purchased and maintained. The information needed to deliver the enacted curriculum of the school must dictate what is collected, and broad access to the virtual world of information must be provided to increase the breadth of ideas for students.

MATCHING THE ACCESS ENVIRONMENT TO THE REQUIREMENTS OF THE LEARNING COMMUNITY: STRATEGIES

Rx 1: Understand the Information Needs of the Learning Community

- Collaborate with faculty to identify what students need to know and be able to do (content and process)
- Analyze units of study to determine how students will be expected to show what they have learned (papers, demonstrations, performances, presentations, etc.)
- Collect information about students (demographics, habits, interests, etc.)

Rx 2: Know the Resource and Access Environment

- Follow current publication and production (print, nonprint, electronic)
- Evaluate existing and emerging resources (authority, relevancy, currency, appropriateness)
- Keep current on changes in technology and delivery mechanisms, including advances in online searching
- Stay abreast of intellectual freedom, copyright, and intellectual property issues as they relate to the changing access environment
- Consider storage and decision possibilities
- Develop partnerships with other agencies (public library, university, museums, etc.)

Rx 3: Use What You Know to Select Resources and Access Points Based on the Requirements of the Learning Community

- See figure 10.5 (based on Aversa and Mancall 1989, 75).

CHALLENGES CENTRAL TO THE SUCCESS OF THE COLLABORATIVE ACCESS ENVIRONMENT

Our collaborative access environment model recognizes the importance of partnerships (see figure 10.4). Only by understanding the core capabilities of our organizations, work groups, and colleagues can we relate what is available in the knowledge base to the characteristics of learners and the teaching and learning context of the school. Building a collaborative access environment challenges school library media specialists to change long-held beliefs and attitudes—to act as change agents, resource guides, leaders, and learners.

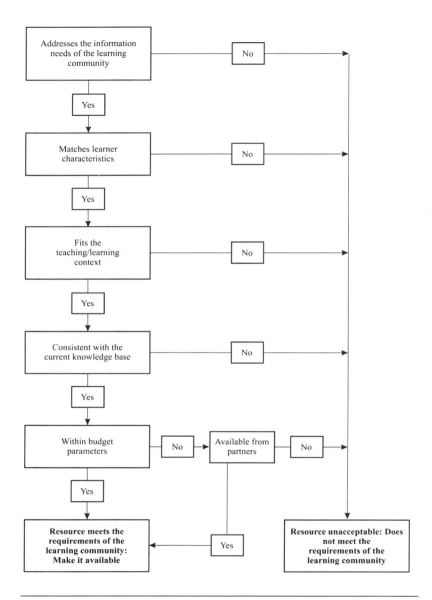

Figure 10.5. Resource and access point selection

The Challenges

1. Physical control of collection development must become a shared process. This shift will be difficult, because this area previously was the sole responsibility of the school library media specialist. However, rather than view this as *giving up power*, school library media specialists need to look at it as *sharing power* that enhances student learning.

2. Constructivist models of learning demand that learners develop strategies to construct their own meaning. The library media specialist must now teach all learners to select, analyze, and evaluate resources, a role that was once the sole province of the school library media specialist.

3. The changing information environment demands that ethical issues such as intellectual freedom, copyright protection, and respect for intellectual property rights receive increased attention. Policy development in these areas must be initiated by the school library media specialist and then become a shared responsibility of all members of the learning community.

4. Knowledge of and access to an expanding resource world is essential. Requests for resources must be handled expeditiously, with provision for instant access to stores of items and resource people wherever they are located. Access to this world demands the creation of partnerships with all relevant community-based organizations, including other schools, public libraries, and institutions of higher education.

NOTES

1. The librarian described is Renee Stroback, A. D. Harrington Elementary School, Philadelphia, PA.
2. Descriptions of the winning units are available on the ICONnect Web site at <http://www.ala.org/ICON/icprize.html>.
3. The winning applicants were Shayne Russell and Ann Kelly, Mt. Laurel Hartford School, Mt. Laurel, N.J.
4. See also *Dr. Drott's Random Sampler* at <http://drott.cis.drexel.edu/sample.DrottHome.html>.

REFERENCES AND ADDITIONAL RESOURCES

American Association of School Librarians and Association for Educational Communications and Technology. 1998. *Information Power: Building Partnerships for Learning.* Chicago: American Library Association.

Aversa, Elizabeth S., and Jacqueline J. Mancall. 1989. *Management of Online Search Services.* Santa Barbara, Calif.: ABC-CLIO.

Barr, Robert B., and John Tagg. 1995. "From Teaching to Learning—A New Paradigm for Undergraduate Education." *Change* (November/December): 13–25.

Brooks, Jacqueline G., and Martin G. Brooks. 1993. *In Search of Understanding: The Case for Constructivist Classrooms.* Alexandria, Va.: ASCD.

Drott, M. Carl. 1993. *Dr. Drott's Random Sampler.* Englewood, Colo.: Libraries Unlimited.

Eisenberg, Michael B., and Robert E. Berkowitz. 1988. *Curriculum Initiative: An Agenda and Strategy for Library Media Programs.* Norwood, N.J.: Ablex.

Fullan, Michael, and S. Stiegelbauer. 1991. *The New Meaning of Educational Change.* 2d ed. New York: Teachers College Press.

Gardner, Howard. 1983. *Frames of Mind.* New York: Basic Books.

Griffiths, José-Marie. 1998. "The New Information Professional." *Bulletin of the American Society for Information Science* 24 (February/March): 8–12.

Hughes, Sandra M. 1998. "The Impact of Whole Language on Four Elementary School Libraries." Ph.D. diss., University of North Carolina.

Kachel, Debra E. 1996. "Improving Access to Periodicals: A Cooperative Collection Management Project." *School Library Journal* 24, no. 2 (Winter): 93–103.

Loertscher, David V. 1996. *Collection Mapping in the LMC: Building Library Media Center Collections in the Age of Technology*. Castle Rock, Colo.: Hi Willow Research & Publishing.

Mancall, Jacqueline C. 1994. "Refocusing the Collection Development Process: Collecting, Cooperating, Consulting." *Taproot* 3, no. 1 (Spring): 8–13.

"Multimedia 2000 Unveils Webster's International DVD Encyclopedia." 1998. *Information Today* 15, no. 9 (October): 49.

Routman, Regie. 1991. *Invitations: Changing as Teachers and Learners K-12*. Portsmouth, N.H.: Heinemann.

Walker, Deborah, and Linda Lambert. 1995. "Learning and Leading Theory: A Century in the Making." In *The Constructivist Leader*, ed. Linda Lambert et al. New York: Teachers College Press.

11
Designing Library Media Programs for Student Learning

Barbara K. Stripling

INTRODUCTION

With apologies to Robert Fulghum, I would have to say that almost everything I really need to know about designing a library media program, I have learned from first-graders.

Although it was early in the school year, the library media specialist and first-grade teacher decided that their young charges needed to learn to find information in the library to answer questions that kept coming up in the classroom. They worked out a plan: when students needed to know something, they would go in groups of four to the library, work with the library media specialist to find important facts that answered their questions, and come back to the classroom to teach their classmates. The library media specialist and teacher hoped the students would like the idea so well they would not be intimidated by their independent trek down the hall to the library.

The first day of this new system, the library door flew open and Jerry, a normally obdurate student, proclaimed for all to hear: "Here are your Searchers!!!"

From Jerry and his classmates, who became accomplished searchers and teachers, I learned the importance of putting students in charge of their own learning. The teacher and library media specialist had high expectations, and the students lived up to them. In fact, they even exceeded the learning expectations when they became the teachers themselves. They were empowered by the responsibility to transmit accurate and complete information to their classmates, and it was important to them that their classmates understood.

I also learned the importance of the connection between the classroom and the library. Students came to the library media center every time they had a burning question; it was interesting how much the frequency of those questions increased as students vied for the opportunity to be the Searchers and Teachers.

Mrs. Davidson, the library media specialist, met with small groups of first-graders on a regular basis to talk about an author and his or her books. For the past few weeks, they had been reading Patricia Polacco books and talking about her life and the importance of family to her. The library media specialist asked probing questions after they read each story and the little ones learned to think carefully about their answers.

One day, they had just started reading another Polacco book when Michael interrupted to say, "Just a minute. I've seen that quilt before." He scrambled to the shelf and pulled off a Polacco book they had read a couple of weeks before. He opened the book to a page with the identical quilt. Mrs. Davidson was impressed at his memory and started to continue reading the story, but Michael was still thinking, "I wonder why the quilt in one book is more faded than in the other." He wrinkled his brow in concentration. Finally he straightened in his chair with a triumphant smile, "I know why. She's trying to show us that it's important to tell the stories of our families. If we don't, they'll fade like the quilt."

Michael taught me that students must be given the opportunity to think and make connections. Mrs. Davidson made time for Michael to think; she provoked his thinking by the questions she asked after each story. Along with thinking, students need opportunities to find personal connections to the learning. Michael did not react to the story as an intellectual exercise; he was absorbed in the book and the author's life and therefore was looking for deeper meaning.

I also learned that reading is the foundation for learning. Library media programs cannot forget reading in this technological age. Students need to hear stories and to read good literature, but mostly students need to develop the love of reading on their own. Library media programs must be designed to grow readers.

LaShanda was an active first-grader who loved recess. Normally she ran and jumped and played the whole time, but this day she was crouched over the sidewalk and barely moving. The teacher bent down to be sure that LaShanda was all right. On the sidewalk, ants in a trail were bearing heavy burdens. Each ant was carrying a small white pellet, which looked somewhat like a grain of sand. "Mrs. Wilcox, what are those white things?" "I don't know, LaShanda." "Can I go to the library to find out? Can I go right now?"

Mrs. Everett, the library media specialist, helped LaShanda find a book that not only had pictures of the "white things," but also explained why the ants carried their eggs out to air in the sun. LaShanda was ecstatic. She eagerly returned to her classroom, brimming with her new information to share.[1]

LaShanda's experience reminded me of the importance of making the joy of discovery central to any library media program. The culture of the school as a whole should encourage students to be curious and to follow up with learning that satisfies their own need to know. The library media program should be designed flexibly so that students can be independent learners who can connect their learning to real-world experiences.

What the first-graders have defined for me are really the "rules" for a culture of learning. A learning environment must support curiosity, independence, connectedness, high expectations, thinking, reading, and collaboration. If we want to create such a culture in our schools and library media centers, we need to pay attention to these natural laws of learning when we make decisions about our programs, policies, and activities.

GUIDELINES FOR EFFECTIVE PROGRAMS

Library media specialists have national "rules" to live by in developing effective programs: the guidelines for school library media programs detailed in *Information Power: Building Partnerships for Learning* (AASL and AECT 1998). These guidelines reflect a change in the philosophy of library media programs—in fact, almost a paradigm shift, from a focus on teaching to a focus on learning. When school libraries were in their initial development stages, the emphasis was on the library itself: setting up a facility and acquiring a centralized collection. Services often revolved around those resources. Gradually, library media programs started focusing on instruction; library media specialists directed their energies toward teaching library skills and the use of resources. In the last few years, however, library media programs have been moving to a primary emphasis on learning. Library media professionals have realized the essential role of information literacy skills in learning all academic content, as well as in lifelong learning.

The shift from instruction to learning requires changes in the culture and practices of the entire school. Certain practices provide evidence that the focus on learning in the library media program has been achieved:

- Full integration of the library media program into the curriculum

- Collaborative planning and teaching

- Use of multiple resources to support learning in all content areas

- A change from didactic instruction to facilitation of learning

- Emphasis on authentic learning and assessment experiences.

The difficulty created by the new national library media program guidelines, as with any standards or guidelines, is understanding them to the point that they can be put into action. Usually the language has to be clarified. Always a task analysis has to be done on each standard, to lay out the steps of development necessary to achieve the standard. We do this instinctively for students, but we rarely allow ourselves the same luxury of orderly development over time. If we hope to bring our programs to a higher level of effectiveness, we must develop a long-term plan for improvement.

One way to define an orderly development process is through a rubric. A rubric essentially describes criteria in terms of what they would look like if they were being accomplished at a beginning, proficient, or exemplary level. The rubric included at the end of this chapter (see figure 11.1 offers a view of library media program development that is focused on achieving the national guidelines in *Information Power* (AASL and AECT 1998).[2] The rubric was created based on a structure initially developed in Colorado[3]; numerous school library professionals across the country have contributed to its revision.

Embedded within the rubric are elements that will lead to learning-centered library media programs, including those that were so important to Jerry, Michael, and LaShanda. These elements can be added or enhanced over time as the expertise, resources, and collaborative efforts of the school increase. The rubric actually delineates a plan for development. For example, one of the guidelines is that the school library media program integrates information literacy standards into content learning ("Learning and

Teaching: 2"). A library just beginning that process of integration features lessons on the use of library materials related to content being taught in the classroom, but the students are taught only the traditional locational skills. As the library program develops to the Proficient level, teachers assume joint responsibility with the library media specialist for information literacy skills, and the definition of those skills broadens beyond location to include analysis, evaluation, and the use of information. Most units in the school include some information literacy skills. In an exemplary library program, the teachers and library media specialist assume joint responsibility for information literacy skills and every appropriate unit includes those skills. The definition of *information literacy* is expanded to include learning-how-to-learn skills (inquiry, synthesis, and expression). Information literacy is recognized as essential to content learning throughout the school.

USING THE RUBRIC TO GUIDE PROGRAM DEVELOPMENT

The rubric can provide an impetus for developing a culture of learning within the library and the school. It should be used as a development tool, not an evaluation instrument. The rubric should never be superimposed over an existing program for the sole purpose of determining how that program measures up. Nor should the rubric be used as a cookie-cutter approach to library programs.

Each school library in the country is unique, with different areas of emphasis depending on the needs and strengths of the students, teachers, administrators, and library media specialists in that school. Finding the right match between national guidelines and local culture is the essence of library media program design.

If the rubric is to have a positive effect on program development, certain provisos must be kept in mind:

1. *Focus on the program.*

   The rubric focuses on the school library media program, not on the library media specialist. Much of the success of a library media center depends on teachers, administrators, and students working with the library media specialist in all aspects of the program. In fact, if the library media specialist has assumed sole responsibility for the program, the program has failed in its essential mission: to fully integrate into the curriculum to support student learning throughout the school.

2. *Select certain criteria.*

   The rubric cannot drive change on all criteria at once. Any change process must be focused on only a few areas. Schools must determine priorities based on the importance of specific Target Indicators to the learning needs within that school.

3. *Involve other educators.*

   Library media program assessment and development must be driven by a committee of teachers, administrators, and the library media specialist, not by the library media specialist alone. Just as teachers and administrators are essential for achievement of library media center goals, so must this collaborative effort drive the planning process. The conversation generated by the rubric is rich and can serve as a learning experience for the educators themselves. The collaboration leads to high-quality ideas and a shared sense of ownership.

4. *Target only what is possible.*
   Some aspects of the rubric are out of the hands of the school. For example, if the district provides no funding for paraprofessionals, schools probably do not have the wherewithal to override that decision. If such an externally controlled criterion seems especially important, efforts can be made to change the external conditions, but the path will probably be more difficult than creating change within the school.

5. *Use descriptors as guidelines.*
   The descriptors under Basic, Proficient, and Exemplary should be used as guidelines, not invariable characteristics. A program can be rated Proficient on a particular indicator if most of the activity falls within that level. Missing characteristics under Proficient can then form part of the library improvement goal. After all, the purpose of using the rubric is not to classify a library according to its level of development, but to gauge progress and set future goals.

6. *Develop school priorities.*
   Rarely, if ever, will a school library media program exhibit exemplary characteristics for every guideline. Different programs will have different areas of focus and priority. What is essential, however, is that the school community understand what the focus and priorities are and that all members of the community unite in working toward those priorities.

PROGRAM DEVELOPMENT PROCESS

Before the program development process begins, the library media specialist should pause for reflection, to clarify his or her own responses to some fundamental questions:

- What do I think are the strengths of the library media program?
- What are some areas I am concerned about?
- What is my relationship with most of the teachers at the school? What do I want it to be?
- How well do the students and I get along? What do they need the most from the library program?
- Why do I want to begin a process of library media program development?
- What do I want the library media program to look like in five years? Ten years?

Once the library media specialist has clarified the focus and purpose of program development, a process should be delineated. Just as the research process is rarely linear, so the program development process may take dips and turns along the way. Any linear process that is developed, therefore, must be interpreted as a structure from which to vary, as need dictates. The following steps provide a procedure that leads to thoughtful development and shared ownership of the library media program. These steps are written as personal tips to library media specialists, because the process is, above all, determined by the dynamic personal relationships forged by the library media specialist in each school.

Step One: Meet with Administrator(s)

Meet with your building administrator(s) to share the rubric and exchange your visions of the library media program. With luck and perhaps some work, your relationship will be honest enough that you can both identify areas of strength and concern and discuss the reasons for those. You need to make clear that your purpose is to impact student achievement by improving the library media program.

This conversation helps cement your administrator's support for the process. Together, you and the principal may decide that some of the descriptors on the rubric are not appropriate for the situation in your school. If so, change or eliminate the descriptors before using the rubric.

Step Two: Form Library Advisory Committee

With the principal's advice, form a library advisory committee comprised of the principal, teachers, students (if appropriate), and community members or parents (if appropriate). You and each member of the advisory committee individually assess the library media program based on the rubric. You can use the template in figure 11.2 (at the end of this chapter) to indicate the current status of the program on each target indicator, with examples that offer evidence of your rating.

Step Three: Develop Shared Vision

Call the committee together to talk about each indicator and the individual members' perceptions. Make sure that the conversation during this meeting (or meetings) is rich, honest, and probing. You are trying to make several things happen during these meetings: to help teachers understand the vision of an exemplary library media program; to generate a sense of shared ownership; to identify consensus areas of strength; to take note of areas for improvement; to come to a group understanding about the interrelationship of the library media program and the work of the school to improve student achievement.

Step Four: Select Areas for Improvement

Once the committee understands the vision and the current status of the program, the committee selects one to three areas where you want to direct your energies toward improvement. Choose these areas based on your previous conversations, your school's overall improvement plan, the needs of your students and teachers, and the resources that are available. For example, if the school has decided to implement inquiry-based learning, then the committee may choose to focus library efforts on information literacy skill development, collaborative planning and teaching, and development of a collection to support inquiry learning. If the school, however, has extremely limited funding for library resources, then developing the collection may not be a feasible goal for that year. Be sure that part of the consideration in setting the goals is your own personal preference (or passion, if you will) and your professional expertise, because you will be the spark behind the whole process of change.

Step Five: Develop Action Plan

Once the advisory committee has come to consensus on the targets for the year, the committee's next step is to determine its recommendations about what actions will be taken and what resources will be needed to achieve the targeted goals. Although committee members cannot mandate actions by the entire faculty, they can think through the action plan carefully enough that they will be able to gain whole-faculty buy-in.

It is quite possible for the whole process to fall apart at this point, either because the action plan is too ambitious to be accomplished or because the plan is not complete enough to be carried out. For example, if the committee has chosen to focus on developing collaborative units, setting an action plan that calls for collaboration between the library media specialist and every teacher on every unit is neither feasible nor desirable. Likewise, if the action plan calls for a more reasonable level of collaboration, but includes no professional development opportunities or time for collaboration, then the plan will be equally difficult to implement.

Step Six: Share with Entire Faculty

Once the committee has come to consensus on the action plan, you and the committee present your proposed goals and action plan to the entire faculty for discussion. Because teachers will have responsibilities for accomplishing the goals, they will want to discuss the plan in depth. Everyone should have a clear idea of the potential impact on the teaching and learning of the school. The entire faculty should be brought to consensus on the (perhaps revised) plan.

Step Seven: Implement Action Plan

Implementation begins, and you are driving the process. Rely on your principal to ensure that the process has the support (both resources and effort) to succeed. Depend on the advisory committee to meet throughout the year to assess progress and the need for changes in the plan.

A lot has been written about the change process and the speed at which change should occur. The school should set the goals high with the realization that implementation occurs in small steps. One change expert has suggested that if a system is trying to change direction, the most change that can be expected at one time is 45 degrees.

The library media specialist has to maintain a careful balance during implementation between provocation and support. The school will not make progress toward the library improvement goals unless pressure is applied, but everyone will be frustrated if support (in professional development, time, encouragement, celebrations of success) is not provided in equal measure.

DRIVING SCHOOL CHANGE

Because the library media program is embedded in the learning and culture of the school, a change in the library media program drives a change in the school as a whole. Inquiry-based learning in the library will lead to increased inquiry learning in the classroom. If students are actively engaged in authentic learning experiences in the library media center, they will expect to have those experiences at other times.

Essential to any change process is a broad consensus on the vision and a clear definition of goals. Using a rubric based on national guidelines for school library media programs to drive school change can help schools move toward a culture that is focused on high standards of learning for all students and teachers. With that focus, school library media programs can help improve student achievement.

Behind every change process is the person driving the change. What cannot be captured by a rubric or any description of a change process is the most important element of library media program design—the library media specialist. When the library media specialist is focused on touching the life of each student in positive and essential ways, then the library media program will reflect that emphasis in every activity, resource purchase, and lesson plan. Library media specialists who respond to the needs of Jerry, Michael, and LaShanda in their attitudes and actions have learned the essential "rule" and aim of library media program design: to create an environment in which each student is challenged to succeed and is nurtured in that effort.

NOTES

1. The three scenarios are re-creations of experiences described to me by two very effective school library media specialists in Chattanooga, Tennessee: Jo Ann Everett of Lakeside Elementary and Nancy Davidson of the Chattanooga School for the Liberal Arts.
2. The principles of effective library media programs that form the target indicators of the rubric are adapted, with permission, from *Information Power: Building Partnerships for Learning* (AASL and AECT 1998). Copyright © 1998 American Library Association and Association for Educational Communications and Technology.
3. The "Rubric for the Assessment of the School Library Media Program" was created in February 1996 by a group of Colorado librarians working with the Colorado State Library. The group included Eugene Hainer, Colorado State Library; Kay Evatz and Marcie Haloin, Adams 12 School District; Jody Gehrig and Yvonne Jost, Denver Public Schools; Deb Kirk, Weld County School District #6; Billie Wolter and Christette Soderberg, Jefferson County Public Schools; Judy MacDonald and Marcene Amand, Poudre Valley Public Schools.

REFERENCE

American Association of School Librarians and Association for Educational Communications and Technology. 1998. *Information Power: Building Partnerships for Learning*. Chicago: American Library Association.

Figure 11.1. School library media program design

LMS = Library Media Specialist
LMC = Library Media Center
LMP = Library Media Program

Learning and Teaching

Target Indicators	Basic	Proficient	Exemplary
1. Is essential to learning and teaching in the school. Functions as integral aspect of curriculum to promote students' achievement of learning goals.	• The LMP supports the curriculum as it has been decided by the teachers. • Occasionally, assignments are designed to allow students to pursue learning through library resources.	• The LMP provides essential support to all areas of the curriculum. • Some units are designed collaboratively by teachers and the LMS to provide in-depth and meaningful learning experiences through independent investigations in the library.	• The LMP is a catalyst for intellectual work in all areas of the curriculum. • LMC resources and information literacy processes are integral to the instruction in the school. • Assignments are designed by teachers and the LMS to involve authentic learning tasks in which students are expected to learn in depth, to follow an inquiry process, to engage in intellectual conversation and shared learning, to construct their own meaning, and to connect their learning to the world beyond school.
2. Integrates information literacy standards into content learning.	• Lessons on the use of library materials are taught in the context of classroom content. However, the definition of "library skills" is still the traditional locational skills, or how to find information. • Information literacy skills are sometimes still considered	• Teachers and the LMS assume joint responsibility for information literacy skills, which extend beyond location to analysis, evaluation, and use of information. • Information literacy skills are incorporated into most units.	• Teachers and the LMS assume joint responsibility for information literacy skills and they are incorporated into every appropriate unit. • Under the LMS's leadership, the definition of information literacy has expanded to include process,

(continued on next page)

Figure 11.1. School library media program design (continued)

LMS = Library Media Specialist
LMC = Library Media Center
LMP = Library Media Program

Learning and Teaching

Target Indicators	Basic	Proficient	Exemplary
	nonessential to content learning.		or learning-how-to-learn, skills (inquiry, synthesis, and expression). • The teaching of process skills has become essential to content learning.
3. Models and promotes collaborative planning and curriculum development.	• Teachers and the LMS occasionally meet to plan some lessons involving use of LMC resources. • The LMS does not contribute to teacher planning other than advice about lessons taught in the library and library resources that can be used. • For some library units, the LMS is informed of the teacher's plans and needs only at the last minute.	• The LMS connects teachers throughout the building and helps build a coordinated instructional program through curriculum mapping. • Teachers and the LMS often meet to plan units of instruction. • The collaboratively planned units are built around use of LMC resources and information literacy processes.	• Curriculum revolves around high intellectual standards for student achievement. The LMS facilitates the regular updating of curriculum maps and their analysis based on the school's high standards. The LMS serves as a catalyst for curriculum development. • The LMS and teachers regularly meet, both formally and informally, to plan curriculum, instructional units, learning strategies, and activities.
4. Models and promotes creative, collaborative, and effective teaching.	• The LMS and teachers coordinate their teaching so that what is taught in the library complements what is taught in the classroom.	• The LMS and teachers plan their teaching together (team teaching): some skills are taught in the classroom, others in the library.	• The LMS and classroom teacher function as a collaborative teaching team.

The LMS and teachers have some mutual understanding of the principles of instructional design; however, the design often results in didactic delivery of information by the LMS and teachers. The instructional units are often structured to lead to limited content that can be delivered to all the students in the same way.	• The teaching is generally facilitative rather than didactic. The teacher or LMS may prescribe the strategies, research questions, or assessment products to be used.	• The teaching is facilitative and creative; students are engaged and both supported and provoked as they do the work of learning. Both reflection and authentic assessment are built into the teaching design.
5. Provides access to a full range of information resources, which provide a fundamental component to learning. • Resources beyond the textbook that are available for student learning are generally limited to a basic library print collection and some electronic access. • The collection matches the curriculum to some extent.	• Resources available through the library target an average student-ability level and a range of interests. • Students have access to some information on almost all areas of the curriculum, although in-depth information is limited.	• Students' learning is supported and challenged by the resources available both within and beyond the library. • Students have access to a wide range of resources that address all areas of the curriculum, varying interests and abilities, and diverse points of view.
6. Engages students in reading, viewing, and listening for understanding and enjoyment. • The LMP supports reading in an isolated way, offering occasional reading events. Viewing and listening skills are not incorporated into the program. • Few attempts are made to integrate a reading focus with the rest of the school.	• Reading, viewing, and listening are promoted continuously through the library media program, with careful attention given to integrating with classroom activities and motivating students to read, view, and listen on their own. • Reading promotion focuses on intrinsic value of reading, not extrinsic rewards.	• The LMP establishes a school-wide culture of learning through reading, viewing, and listening. All students are expected to read, view, and listen in order to discover meaning, to learn, and to find personal pleasure. • Students value those skills for their intrinsic rewards. • The school has become a reading community.

(continued on next page)

Figure 11.1. School library media program design (continued)

Learning and Teaching

LMS = Library Media Specialist
LMC = Library Media Center
LMP = Library Media Program

Target Indicators	Basic	Proficient	Exemplary
		• Most teachers and students use the library for reading, viewing, and listening materials for both academic and personal interests.	
7. Supports students who have diverse learning abilities, styles, and needs.	• Students are encouraged to use information in various formats to discover their own preferences. • Students are taught a few different strategies for steps in the inquiry process (e.g., graphic organizers and linear outlines).	• Students are comfortable accessing and using information in multiple formats. • Students are able to find materials that answer their personal and academic questions, at reading levels that are appropriate. • Students are beginning to learn various strategies for organizing and presenting their ideas (e.g., visual, verbal, demonstration).	• Students use their own learning styles, abilities, and needs to solve complex information problems and present their solutions in various formats (e.g., charts, posters, formal papers, models, videos, Web pages). • They are supported by a collection that is well balanced in terms of level of difficulty, format, and subject matter. • Teaching strategies in the LMC incorporate attention to learning styles and abilities.
8. Fosters individual and collaborative inquiry.	• Learning is based around main ideas in the curriculum, rather than a series of minute objectives. • Most of students' information comes from the textbook.	• Learning is based around main ideas or themes in the curriculum, and students often have the opportunity to pursue subjects in greater depth through independent or collaborative investigation, using the textbook and	• Under broad curriculum guidelines, students are generally self-directive. Given the assignments, students determine what they need to know and assume responsibility for learning it.

	Students occasionally have the opportunity to pursue learning on their own. • Group inquiry tends to be individuals working independently, compiling their work into a group product, rather than sharing and true collaboration.	multiple resources beyond it, both within and outside of the school. • Students are learning how to learn while they are learning content.	Students are active and independent learners, using a wide range of resources with responsibility and thoughtfulness. • Each student is able to assume responsibility either individually or as a member of a collaborative group. • Students are developing sophisticated inquiry, synthesis, and expression skills and are learning in-depth concepts in the content areas.
9. Integrates the use of technology for learning.	• The library offers some access to computers and other technological equipment (e.g., videodisc, CD-ROM, multimedia stations, scanners). Students use the technology to enhance their comprehension of content. • The LMS is moderately skilled in the use of various technologies for learning.	• LMC technology is used regularly throughout the day. Many students use the various programs and equipment for learning experiences in all classes that involve comprehension, application, and analysis skills. • The LMS is well skilled in the use of technology for learning and provides appropriate staff development.	• A wide range of technology is available through the LMC. The technology is up-to-date and integral to teaching and learning in all areas of the curriculum. The technological influence extends throughout the instructional program and provides students with opportunities to develop their application, analysis, synthesis, and evaluation abilities. • Administrative support for the use of technology is strong. • The LMS is exceptionally skilled in the use of technology and is constantly developing new ways to help students use technology for learning. The LMS provides staff development on integrating

(continued on next page)

Figure 11.1. School library media program design (continued)

LMS = Library Media Specialist
LMC = Library Media Center
LMP = Library Media Program

Learning and Teaching

Target Indicators	Basic	Proficient	Exemplary
10. Provides essential link to larger learning community.	• The library offers limited electronic access to the outside world, although personal networks facilitate sharing of materials and expertise from outside agencies. • Some library/classroom assignments address real-world issues.	• Students often connect to the outside world in their learning activities. • The library has some electronic access, although it is not seamless for the student. • Students and teachers recognize the importance of some real-world skills (critical thinking, communication, group process, knowing how to learn).	technology into the curriculum and the instructional design process. • Partnerships, both electronic and personal, with other libraries, cultural institutions, technology consortia, and other agencies link to the larger learning community. • Students often make connections to the real world in their learning through the library. • Students have learned the work skills of creative and critical thinking, flexibility, working in a team, knowing how to learn, and communication.

Figure 11.1. School library media program design (continued)

Information Access and Delivery

Target Indicators	Basic	Proficient	Exemplary
1. Provides intellectual access to information and ideas.	• Although the LMP is focused on what happens in the library, much of the activity is coordinated with classroom learning. • The rigid curriculum of "library skills" has been broken into smaller and more useful segments that are coordinated with what the students are learning at the time (e.g., studying atlases when students are working on a continent project).	• The LMP is focused on learning. • Library units are designed to enhance classroom learning, and they incorporate the teaching of information literacy skills that are specifically related to the research process (e.g., questioning, evaluating, selecting). • Thinking, expressing, and study skills are also considered part of information literacy skills, but are not comprehensively incorporated into library units. • Library opportunities tend to occur in discrete units rather than being suffused throughout the curriculum.	• The LMP is focused on learning and all decisions are made in that context. • The LMS is a teacher whose curriculum encompasses information literacy and the content curriculum of the school. • The entire school maintains a broad definition of information literacy, so that it includes thinking, organizing, questioning, evaluating, concluding, communicating, presenting, and reflecting as a part of the inquiry process. • Equity of intellectual access is maintained through incorporation of information literacy skills and integration of library opportunities throughout the curriculum.
2. Provides physical access to information and resources.	• The dedicated library space is arranged for whole-class use, but can easily be rearranged for special activities. • Some access to information in electronic, audio, and video formats is provided, although hardware is limited.	• The dedicated library space is large with areas for large groups, small groups, and individuals. • At least two large groups of students can work on different projects in the LMC at the same time.	• The dedicated library space is flexible and large enough to meet students' changing learning needs. • Several different student groups (both large and small) often use the center simultaneously.

(continued on next page)

Figure 11.1. School library media program design (continued)

Information Access and Delivery

LMS = Library Media Specialist
LMC = Library Media Center
LMP = Library Media Program

Target Indicators	Basic	Proficient	Exemplary
		• Access to a variety of information sources is made available through adequate hardware and fixtures.	• Access to resources both within and beyond the library is ensured by the arrangement and accessibility of the furniture, resources, and technology, which are flexible enough to accommodate wide and diverse use.
3. Provides a climate conducive to learning.	• Students feel welcome in the library, but go only when prompted by the classroom teacher or required by the schedule. • Students find it difficult to focus on learning while in the library.	• The library is warm and inviting. • Students actively seek opportunities to go to the library to research or read. They are able to work fairly productively in the library environment. • The library is student-centered. Students can find niches in the library that fit their needs.	• The library is one of the warmest and most inviting places in the school. All students are drawn to the library to discover the treasures of learning inside. • The environment stimulates and supports productive and focused learning. • Students and staff feel welcome to ask questions and seek answers in the LMC.
4. Requires flexible and equitable access.	• Students and teachers have flexible access at least half of every day, but the flex time is built into a rigid schedule that carries through the whole year. • Only those students who have finished their work can go during	• Flexible access is provided during all hours that the school is in session; however, many teachers still bring their class to the LMC only as a whole group. • Flexible time is used by individual students and whole classes	• Access to the library and its resources is fully flexible and available both during and beyond the school day. The LMC provides access for the entire learning community, including parents.

flexible time unless the whole class goes together to work on a project.
- Teachers who use the flexible access times are supportive. The administration provides nominal support for flexible access.

5. Provides collections that support the curriculum and fulfill diverse learning needs.

- The collection is fairly up-to-date and has been developed according to the district-approved selection policy. The LMS has a general idea about the existing collection, although no collection map has been done.
- The collection usually provides the resources required by the curriculum, although the quantity will accommodate only two or three students working on the same topic.
- Electronic and multimedia materials are available on a limited basis.

working on research projects.
- The schedule is generally accepted by the faculty and strongly supported by the school and central office administrators.

- The up-to-date collection has been built following the selection policy and a map of the strengths of the existing collection as they relate to the curriculum.
- The LMC provides a fairly diverse collection of books as well as a variety of other resources.
- It meets most curricular, learning-style, and personal needs of the students. The collection is large enough to accommodate several students working on the same topic at the same time.
- Interlibrary loan, electronic databases, and Internet are available, but used only occasionally.

- All students get to use the library often. The library is fully utilized by individuals, small groups, and whole classes working on projects designed collaboratively by classroom teachers and the LMS.
- Staff members are strongly supportive of the flexible access. Open and flexible access is enthusiastically supported by both school and central office administrators.

- The collection is up-to-date, diverse, and particularly responsive to the curricular, learning-style, and personal needs of the students. The collection is large enough to accommodate comprehensive research by several classes at once.
- The collection has been developed according to the district selection policy and a map of the existing collection and future collection goals based on the curriculum.
- The collection represents a balance of print, multimedia, and electronic resources.
- Access to information is regularly enhanced with interlibrary loan, electronic databases, and the Internet.

(continued on next page)

Figure 11.1. School library media program design (continued)

Information Access and Delivery

LMS = Library Media Specialist
LMC = Library Media Center
LMP = Library Media Program

Target Indicators	Basic	Proficient	Exemplary
6. Is founded on a commitment to the right of intellectual freedom.	• The LMS is fully committed to the freedom of each student to have access to information.	• The LMS and school staff understand the concept of intellectual freedom and are fully committed to its implementation through LMP policies and practices.	• The entire school community understands and supports intellectual freedom for all students. • No policies or decisions are implemented by the school or district that conflict with the right of intellectual freedom.
7. Reflects legal guidelines and professional ethics in information policies, procedures, and practices.	• Some written policies about copyright, intellectual freedom, confidentiality, and acceptable use exist; however, their implementation is irregular and the community is not generally aware of the underlying issues.	• Written policies on information issues (copyright, intellectual freedom, confidentiality, acceptable use) have been developed and approved by the school or district. • The LMS has taken responsibility for implementing those policies, but the community both inside and outside of the school has not really grappled with the underlying issues and accepted the policies as its own responsibility.	• Written school and district policies addressing legal and ethical issues such as copyright, intellectual freedom, confidentiality, and acceptable (responsible) use of resources are developed in collaboration with the school community. • These policies are carefully followed in procedures and practices in the library and throughout the school. District board policy includes these issues as well as procedures for their implementation. • The school community engages in ongoing conversation about information issues.

Figure 11.1. School library media program design (continued)

Program Administration

LMS = Library Media Specialist
LMC = Library Media Center
LMP = Library Media Program

Target Indicators	Basic	Proficient	Exemplary
1. Supports mission, goals, and continuous improvement of school.	• The LMS is aware of the school's mission and goals and takes those into account in designing the LMP.	• The LMS serves on the decision-making council of the school and helps formulate school goals. • The LMS designs the LMP to fulfill those goals.	• The LMS serves on the decision-making council of the school and helps formulate school goals and long-range plans that are directed at school-district goals and school improvement. The LMP is integral to those plans. • The LMS provokes and supports school improvement efforts by providing opportunities for professional development, access to professional materials, and facilitation of professional conversation.
2. Requires a minimum of one full-time, certified/licensed LMS supported by qualified staff.	• The LMC is staffed with at least one full-time LMS who has at least a half-time flexible schedule. A full-time paraprofessional provides nonprofessional services.	• The LMC is staffed with at least one full-time LMS with a flexible schedule, as well as two paraprofessionals.	• The LMC is staffed with at least one full-time LMS for every 500 students. The number of paraprofessionals varies with the school population and the level of services, but the minimum is one paraprofessional for each 500 students.

(continued on next page)

Figure 11.1. School library media program design (continued)

Program Administration

LMS = Library Media Specialist
LMC = Library Media Center
LMP = Library Media Program

Target Indicators	Basic	Proficient	Exemplary
3. Requires a level of professional and support staffing based on a school's instructional programs, services, facilities, size, and numbers of students and teachers.	• With a full-time LMS and full-time paraprofessional, services offered include collection development, circulation of materials, some collaborative development of units with classroom teachers, and some teaching of location skills to students in the context of content-based units.	• Services offered by the paraprofessionals include regular maintenance of the collection; circulation of materials; maintenance of special reading programs; preparation of bibliographies and special collections; help with technology; and general assistance to teachers, readers, and researchers. • Professional services if the LMS has a flexible schedule include collection development, regular and ongoing development of collaborative units by teachers and the LMS, the teaching of information literacy skills in the context of those units, and an emphasis on reading for understanding and pleasure.	• Additional paraprofessionals provide services for valuable additions such as computer lab access, production facilities, extended hours, special programs, and community outreach. • A team of professionals provides comprehensive integration of the library media program with the curriculum and appropriate staff development to teachers. The planned units of instruction involve in-depth learning and the teaching of sophisticated information literacy skills.
4. Requires ongoing administrative support.	• The building administrator and central office offer verbal support to the school community about the library program. • There is some understanding that the library should serve as	• The building administrator and central office actively encourage the integration of library and classroom learning and of the teaching of information literacy skills with content units.	• The building administrator and central office (which includes a district library administrator in multischool districts) have built the integration of library and

		classroom learning into the structure and operation of the school and school system.
the hub of resource-based teaching and active learning.	• A schoolwide emphasis is placed on developing students as independent investigators who use a variety of library and community resources.	• The building administrator ensures that professional development is provided to help strengthen this inquiry- and resource-based approach to teaching.
• The LMS meets occasionally with the school administrator.	• The LMS meets regularly with the school administrator.	• The LMS and LM district administrator meet regularly with school and district administrators.
5. Utilizes comprehensive and collaborative program planning.	• Broad-based involvement from the school community in a media/technology committee helps to develop the mission statement, goals, and objectives for the LMC program, all of which reinforce the school plan.	• Broad-based involvement from the school community (including parents, students, community members, teachers, administrators) helps to develop the mission statement, goals, and objectives for the LMC program.
• Occasionally, the school community is involved in LMC program planning through a media/technology committee.	• A short-range plan for the LMC program and resources is developed each year.	• The school community actively seeks ways in which it can help the LMC more fully achieve the vision of being a learning center for the school.
• Strategic planning and goal setting are infrequent, usually when there is a crisis or a need for fundraising.		• Based on reflective practice and current research, a long-range, strategic plan for the program, resources, and facility is developed and revisited every year. This plan is congruent with and instrumental to the school plan and accreditation process.

(continued on next page)

Figure 11.1. School library media program design (continued)

LMS = Library Media Specialist
LMC = Library Media Center
LMP = Library Media Program

Program Administration Target Indicators	Basic	Proficient	Exemplary
6. Incorporates ongoing assessment of program and student achievement.	• Assessment of the LMP is conducted sporadically and is based on input criteria, such as the number of books added, the number of classes taught, circulation statistics, the number of units designed. • No attempt is made to judge the effect of those efforts on student learning. • No attempt is made to judge the effectiveness of the purchase and management of resources.	• Assessment of the LMP is conducted on a fairly regular basis, with some attention to traditional criteria (e.g., circulation statistics, number of resources, number of classes), but also with some attempt to assess the quality of learning that occurred during library activities. • The LMS and teachers evaluate the effectiveness of library units. • The purchase and management of resources are expected to provide good value for the dollars expended.	• Ongoing assessment of the LMP is based on established goals and criteria for success. Success for the library media program is largely based on student achievement of content standards and the Information Literacy Standards for Student Learning (content and process together). • Although informal assessment occurs on a daily basis, more formal assessment is conducted at least yearly using a locally approved rubric and reflective conversation. • The purchase and management of resources are expected to ensure the best value for the dollars expended.
7. Requires sufficient funding.	• The library program is funded at a level that allows maintenance of personnel and addition of new materials in order to keep the collection up-to-date.	• The LMS has the opportunity to propose a budget for resources, professional development, capital outlay, and personnel, with justifications that are linked to	• A collaboratively developed long-range plan for ongoing and new programs in the library is incorporated into the school budget. The plan includes resources, profes-

- Requests by the LMS for special items are funded whenever possible.

- the collaboratively developed library goals.
- Teacher involvement in mapping the collection provides teacher buy-in to collection development funding.
- Budget decisions are based on thorough discussion of proposed budget and justifications.
- Grant and fundraising opportunities are sought for special resources.

- sional development, capital outlay, and personnel needs and justifications.
- The budget is sufficient to facilitate student achievement. Support for collection development funding is broad-based because teachers have developed a collection map. Additional funding is provided for special programs.
- Grants, school fundraising, and business partnerships provide additional funding for special resources and services (e.g., evening hours, parent materials).

8. Incorporates ongoing staff development for LMS, teachers, administrators, and other members of the learning community.

- The LMS provides professional resources for use by the faculty.
- The LMS provides individual assistance to teachers in using technology and designing instruction.
- The LMS occasionally attends professional development opportunities for personal growth.

- The LMS takes responsibility for professional development of teachers and library staff in the use of technological resources for learning and the development of units around principles of active learning.
- The LMS regularly attends professional development opportunities and shares with the rest of the school.

- The LMS takes responsibility for making professional development opportunities available to teachers and library staff on a wide range of issues, including use of technological resources for learning, assessment, curriculum development, instructional design, learning theory, and information literacy.
- The LMS actively pursues professional development opportunities and makes appropriate changes in the LMP. The LMS shares both informally and formally with the school staff and audiences beyond.

(continued on next page)

Figure 11.1. School library media program design (continued)

LMS = Library Media Specialist
LMC = Library Media Center
LMP = Library Media Program

Program Administration

Target Indicators	Basic	Proficient	Exemplary
9. Communicates the mission, goals, functions, and impact of the library media program.	• The library media program has an important function within the school and the LMS communicates that function clearly to the school community. • The LMS does not, however, go beyond communication to advocate for the effectiveness of the LMP.	• The LMS communicates about the effectiveness of the LMP to the school and the community at large. • When offered the opportunity, the LMS will advocate to administrators and school board members.	• The LMS provides ongoing communication about the effectiveness of the LMP to the school and the community at large. • The LMS takes every opportunity to advocate for the program to administrators, parents, school board members, legislators, and other decision makers.
10. Operates effectively through careful management of human, financial, and physical resources.	• Clearly established procedures for human, financial, and physical resources maintain a smooth, efficient operation of the library media program as an independent entity within the school. • Limited use is made of technology (e.g., word processing, spreadsheets) for library operations. • Instructional activities are expected to fit within the established procedures, with emphasis on efficiency.	• Most operating procedures have been established to enhance student learning. • The LMS uses technology for some library operations and library management of resources. • Some procedures, however, are residuals from the time when the focus was on running the library smoothly rather than enhancing learning (e.g., limiting book checkout because of worry about time required for reshelving). • Policies and procedures are occasionally reviewed.	• The LMS establishes operating procedures that use the human, financial, and physical resources most effectively to enhance student learning. • Library operations and resource management are completely automated. • The procedures are consistently followed and yet are flexible enough to be adapted to changing needs. • All procedures and policies clearly relate to the goals and objectives of the program and are regularly reviewed and revised.

Figure 11.2. Template for school library media program design

LMS = Library Media Specialist
LMC = Library Media Center
LMP = Library Media Program

Learning and Teaching

Target Indicators	Basic	Proficient	Exemplary
1. Is essential to learning and teaching in the school. Functions as integral aspect of curriculum to promote students' achievement of learning goals.			
2. Integrates information literacy standards into content learning.			
3. Models and promotes collaborative planning and curriculum development.			
4. Models and promotes creative, collaborative, and effective teaching.			
5. Provides access to a full range of information resources, which provide a fundamental component to learning.			

(continued on next page)

Figure 11.2. Template for school library media program design (continued)

LMS = Library Media Specialist
LMC = Library Media Center
LMP = Library Media Program

Learning and Teaching

Target Indicators	Basic	Proficient	Exemplary
6. Engages students in reading, viewing, and listening for understanding and enjoyment.			
7. Supports students who have diverse learning abilities, styles, and needs.			
8. Fosters individual and collaborative inquiry.			
9. Integrates the use of technology for learning.			
10. Provides essential link to larger learning community.			

Figure 11.2. Template for school library media program design (continued)

Information Access and Delivery

LMS = Library Media Specialist
LMC = Library Media Center
LMP = Library Media Program

Target Indicators	Basic	Proficient	Exemplary
1. Provides intellectual access to information and ideas.			
2. Provides physical access to information and resources.			
3. Provides a climate conducive to learning.			

(continued on next page)

Figure 11.2. Template for school library media program design (continued)

LMS = Library Media Specialist
LMC = Library Media Center
LMP = Library Media Program

Information Access and Delivery

Target Indicators	Basic	Proficient	Exemplary
4. Requires flexible and equitable access.			
5. Provides collections that support the curriculum and fulfill diverse learning needs.			
6. Is founded on a commitment to the right of intellectual freedom.			
7. Reflects legal guidelines and professional ethics in information policies, procedures, and practices.			

Figure 11.2. Template for school library media program design (continued)

LMS = Library Media Specialist
LMC = Library Media Center
LMP = Library Media Program

Program Administration			
Target Indicators	Basic	Proficient	Exemplary
1. Supports mission, goals, and continuous improvement of school.			
2. Requires a minimum of one full-time, certified/licensed LMS supported by qualified staff.			
3. Requires a level of professional and support staffing based on a school's instructional programs, services, facilities, size, and numbers of students and teachers.			
4. Requires ongoing administrative support.			
5. Utilizes comprehensive and collaborative program planning.			

(continued on next page)

Figure 11.2. Template for school library media program design (continued)

LMS = Library Media Specialist
LMC = Library Media Center
LMP = Library Media Program

Program Administration

Target Indicators	Basic	Proficient	Exemplary
6. Incorporates ongoing assessment of program and student achievement.			
7. Requires sufficient funding.			
8. Incorporates ongoing staff development for LMS, teachers, administrators, and other members of the learning community.			
9. Communicates the mission, goals, functions, and impact of the library media program.			
10. Operates effectively through careful management of human, financial, and physical resources.			

Part V
Connecting to the Community

12

A Community of Learning
for the Information Age

Dianne Oberg

THE INFORMATION AGE AND SCHOOLS

Our young people live, grow, and learn within the information-rich environment of the information age. This environment requires that individuals deal with an immense amount of information as they make many critical judgments related to their personal lives, their work, and their role as citizens (Kuhlthau 1990). Young people have the benefit of access to large quantities of information from worldwide sources. This abundance of information is not without its downside, however. Like adults in information-rich environments, young people need sophisticated information skills to find and apply the reliable and usable information they need. Like adults, students can suffer from information overload that results in frustration, disappointment, and anger (Akin 1998). Can schools, as they are structured now, take a strong role in ensuring that our young people are competent and confident citizens in the information age?

Our schools, structured for an earlier industrial age, in general are not well-suited for helping young people to develop the sophisticated information skills needed for the information age. School learning continues in many instances to be centered around textbook information, around students' learning prescribed content, and around the testing and measuring of student learning for grading purposes. School learning for the information age must be centered around developing information skills, around students' learning to use information for creative and innovative thinking, problem solving, and decision making. School structure for the information age must be based on a commitment to ensuring that all students achieve high levels of learning.

If our schools are going to carry out the important work of helping students become competent and confident citizens of their world, today and in the future, many schools will need to reconceptualize and restructure themselves. An important part of education for an information age is learning how to learn within the complex world of information. As educators, we can do a better job of helping students to live in this world of information if we work together with others within and beyond our schools. As educators, we need to understand the world in which students live outside of school, to help them make the connections between what they learn in school and its application outside the school. That means that we must understand the world of their homes and families as well as the world of the information media. The resources of the school alone are inadequate, even in the wealthiest places, to provide the learning environments that students need without calling on resources beyond the school. As educators, we can and should take the lead in building communities of learning.

The ideas considered here have been drawn from widely dispersed literatures. In addition to the literature related to building communities of learning, articles related to informational and other literacies, to educational change, and to home, school, and community partnerships have been particularly useful in expanding perspectives on this topic.

Some fundamental and important ideas underlie the concept of communities of learning. First, three spheres of influence directly affect student learning and development: the school, the family, and the community. Second, these spheres of influence can be drawn together or pushed apart, but student success in school is more likely when these spheres overlap. That is, when there is frequent interaction among these spheres of influence, "more students are more likely to receive common messages from various people about the importance of school, of working hard, of thinking creatively, of helping one another, and of staying in school" (Epstein 1995, 702). Students are at the center of the spheres of influence and, although no one can learn for them, students who feel cared for and encouraged are more likely to be motivated to do their best as learners. Communities of learning are student-centered, but they also result in many benefits for the adult members of the communities—educators, parents, and members of society as a whole.

A COMMUNITY OF LEARNING

The concept of a *community of learning* challenges traditional views of the role of the school in society. Building a community of learning "requires forsaking the metaphor of school-as-organization for school-as-community" (Sergiovanni 1994, 143). It means creating a vision of a school as a center for teaching and learning for adults as well as for young people, a place where improvement comes through inquiry and problem solving, and a place where there is a commitment to caring about and serving others. "[A]s we learn together and as we inquire together, we create the ties that enable us to become a learning community" (Sergiovanni 1994, 167).

A *community* is "an inherently cooperative, cohesive, and self-reflective group entity whose members work on a regular, face-to-face basis toward common goals while respecting a variety of perspectives, values, and life styles" (Graves 1992, 64). A community of learning involves students, parents, teachers, principals, and other educators such as library media specialists. A community of learning also can involve other citizens who are concerned about the education of society's young people. In a community of learning, everyone belongs and is respected. Over time, through regular interaction, a community of learning develops a sense of solidarity and unity which is balanced by an ability to self-examine and revise its functioning. The members of a community of learning work together toward developing common values that guide the life within the community. A common value that guides the life of a community of learning is the belief that all young people can learn at high levels.

School as a Community of Learning

A school that is working to re-create itself as a community of learning is not closed to the external world. It reaches out to gain new ideas and to form partnerships with others. It looks for opportunities to work with others, in the educational system and in the world of work (Fullan 1993). Partnerships are sought that are consistent with the school's vision and that support collaborative working relationships. The members of the community of learning recognize that they are involved in difficult and complex work and that the support of others (such as leaders at the district and state or provincial level) can facilitate their work at the local school level. They recognize that the active leadership of the superintendent and the school trustees and the presence of strong policies and guidelines can support the work of building a community of learning. The ultimate goal of this work is improving student learning.

A school that is a community of learning in this information age will be characterized by interactivity, self-initiated learning, a changing role for teachers, a central role for library media and technology specialists, continuous evaluation, and a changed environment (Hancock 1997). Students will communicate with other students and with their teachers about their learning tasks. Students will also interact with businesspeople, professionals, volunteers, and parents, enhancing their curriculum studies with information from beyond the school. Students will initiate their own learning, asking their own questions rather than waiting for teachers to ask the questions.

Teachers will still ask questions, but they will be doing so to arouse curiosity or to move students forward in their thinking, rather than to have students demonstrate their retention of predetermined curriculum content. Teachers will work together to plan exciting learning opportunities for students; teachers will also learn with and from each other. Library media and technology specialists will work with teachers and with students, using their knowledge of resources and of the process of learning from information to enhance teaching and learning.

Evaluation of progress will be ongoing and carried out by all members of the community of learning. Everyone in the community will be engaged in critical reflection to improve teaching and learning, from the evaluation of information sources to the assessment of how the school is organized for teaching and learning. A school that is a community of learning in this information age will look and feel very different from the traditional school, from the methods used to the ways in which decisions are made.

Creating a Community of Learning Within and Beyond the School

A community of learning is developed, maintained, and enhanced through collaborative work—through the process of developing a culture of collaboration within the school and of connections beyond the school. Collaborative work helps to contribute to the development of shared goals, positive relationships, and ongoing learning—all characteristics of effective schools, of schools that encourage and support student learning and achievement. Principals, library media specialists, teachers, students, and parents, as members of a community of learning, are important participants in developing opportunities for student learning. Other members of society interested in improving student learning can and should be members of a community of learning as well.

The educators have both motivation and opportunity for collaboration within a community of learning. For teachers and all other educators, collaboration brings benefits in terms of professional growth and in terms of improved learning for their students. Library media specialists realize that it is impossible to meet the goals of learning for all our young people without collaboration. For principals, collaboration contributes to the development of effective schools.

Parents and students have strong motivation for participating in the learning community, but their opportunity is much more limited than that of the educator groups. Parents want to be involved in the community of learning because they value education and care about their children's future. This is true even of parents with low literacy levels (see, for example, Merrifield, Bingman, Hemphill, and Bennett de Marrais 1997). Educational research tells us that "[t]he closer the parent is to the education of the child, the greater the impact on child development and educational achievement" (Fullan 1991, 227); however, educators do not always support or know how to support an active role for parents in the community of learning. Students also want to be active participants in the community of learning, but often are regarded as passive receivers of knowledge rather than as active shapers of their own learning. Students are an untapped potential source of information about how to move our schools toward the concept of the community of learning.

The other members of society interested in improving student learning will vary from place to place. The ones most interested in connections with schools at this time appear to be businesspeople, whose connections are seen by them and by the schools primarily as ones of financial advantage. Businesspeople and other members of society have much more to offer schools if their connections are seen in terms of the vital interest that every society has in educating its young people effectively for life, work, and citizenship.

The primary goal of the school as a community of learning is to ensure high levels of learning for all students. Various factors shape the collaborative work that is necessary for building a community of learning. There is much research on the role of teachers, library media specialists, and principals in developing collaborative school cultures. There is much less research on the role of parents and students and on the role of other society members in developing collaborative school cultures and in developing connections between the school and society.

Obstacles to Building a Community of Learning

Culture of the School

The most formidable obstacle to building a community of learning can be the very culture of the school, that is, the way in which the school and the society it serves organize and think about teaching and learning. Many teachers, library media specialists, and principals in our schools today have been trained to teach in isolation, and they have internalized the rules and values of the industrial-age school. That model of schooling emphasizes the classroom as the center of learning and the teacher as an independent and self-reliant professional (Oberg 1991). Few educators have had any introduction to the skills of collaboration or to the concept of a community of learning in their own education for work in schools. Many educators feel uneasy about any activity that might be seen as interfering with another's domain within the school, or with the role of parents in relation to their children.

Parents have also often experienced the same traditional school culture, in their own schooling as well as in that of their children. Parents often hold beliefs about the role of the home and the school that make them uneasy about making demands on the school and about interfering in the life of the school. Members of society without children in school or without other direct school connections are rarely considered as potential members of the school community. Students are rarely given much opportunity to play a role in shaping their own learning environment, even that of the classroom and its activities.

Lack of Time

Time is another formidable obstacle to the development of a community of learning. Many teachers have heavy workloads and are reluctant to invest time in changes that may soon be replaced by yet another change—especially when each change seems to make little or no difference in the basic system of teaching and learning. Principals have little time to reflect on different ways to organize school life, especially in school systems where they have a dual role as managers as well as instructional leaders. Many library media specialists, especially in elementary schools, have dual roles as well: part-time in the library media center and part-time as classroom teachers, assigned to teaching a class of students or to providing preparation time for other teachers.

Beliefs about the Role of Students

Another obstacle to building a community of learning is the beliefs of adults (and of the students themselves) about the role of students in their learning. All of us in education know that students are rarely consulted in relation to any aspect of their schooling. As a consequence, it should not be surprising to find, from research beginning in the 1970s (Fullan 1991), that the majority of students in elementary and secondary schools think that teachers do not understand their point of view and that principals and other administrators do not listen to their concerns. The majority of elementary and secondary students say that teachers do not ask for their ideas in deciding what and how to teach, and a substantial minority say that most of their classes are boring.

Studies of high school classrooms reveal that only a few students regularly participate in class discussions or ask questions, and only the college- and university-bound students appear to be interested in discussing the curriculum. The majority of high school students feel that their classmates do not understand their point of view. Most high school students have only a few close friends and, for students not planning to go to college or university, interaction with close friends provides their only satisfaction with school. The adults engaged in building a community of learning will have to find ways to engage students meaningfully in a process from which they have so far been excluded.

Noninvolvement of Parents

Similar challenges will have to be addressed in working to include parents as members of a community of learning. Parents are usually not consulted about or involved in school change or in curriculum change. Our efforts in education to work with parents, to involve them in their children's schools, have generally been centered on teachers helping parents to support their children in school learning (for example, through home reading programs or parents-in-the-school volunteer programs). These efforts may have, in some instances, tended to cast teachers in the role of the "expert giving advice" and the parents in the role of "nonexpert needing advice." Rarely do we in education think about how parents define learning and how they want the schools to educate their children. Where programs of parental involvement have reached only a few parents, and/or where parents come to the school mainly when their children are in trouble for academic or discipline reasons, layers of distrust and disillusionment will challenge change.

External Demands

A fifth obstacle is the plethora of external demands and pressures upon schools. Within society, there are multiple views of the goals and desirable future directions of schooling. For example, the business sector has called for improving schools by placing more emphasis on employability and skills for the workplace; others in society call for "cultural literacy" and a return to an emphasis on the "classic works" of Western culture. Within education, there are frequent initiatives for school reform and for curriculum revision. These conflicting demands and pressures upon the school have created another obstacle to the building of a community of learning.

BUILDING A COMMUNITY OF LEARNING

Building a community of learning requires a quantum leap, a paradigm shift of major proportions. It involves both individual learning and organizational change. To create a community of learning, the members of the community must work together to decide what they want to achieve in student learning and how they can best achieve it. They must commit to learning together, to teaching each other, and to changing any aspects of the school-as-an-organization that limit growth and improvement. There are always many pressures and dilemmas facing members of a community of learning, but their commitment to shared values strengthens their capacity to meet the challenges and to continue building their community of learning. "Successful community building depends in large measure on each individual school defining for itself its own life and creating for itself its own practice of schooling" (Sergiovanni 1994, xv).

A community of learning in this information age must be built upon a constructivist view of learning and teaching: an understanding that students learn by actively constructing, rather than acquiring, knowledge; and that the purpose of instruction is to support this construction of knowledge, rather than the communication of information. This view often challenges many of the beliefs and practices of the people who are trying to build a community of learning. However, unless all of the current beliefs and practices of school learning are subjected to close scrutiny, it is unlikely that the changes needed to build a community of learning can be made. All participants in this endeavor have roles to play in analyzing current beliefs and practices and in devising innovative ways to change those beliefs and practices.

In the following discussion, the particular challenges and contributions of various members of the community of learning are highlighted, but all members have a responsibility for contributing in multiple ways. The principal, for example, has a key leadership role, but that does not preclude others taking leadership roles; in fact, others need to take leadership roles to ensure that the best possible work is accomplished.

The Principal

Research and practice emphasize that the principal is the key factor in development of the collaborative school culture necessary for a community of learning. The principal gives support for collaboration and for those working to build collaboration. The principal shows support for collaboration by clearly demonstrating personal commitment to it and by using the management role of the school leader to enable it. The principal makes it clear that all teachers, parents, and students are expected to be involved in collaborative activities and that their contributions are essential for success. The principal uses active leadership to provide opportunities for members of the learning community to work and learn together, starting with the collaborative development of a community vision that clearly describes what students are to learn and how they are to show what they have learned.

The Teachers

Classroom teachers contribute to the building of a community of learning by analyzing their own classroom practices and by committing to a collaborative effort to improve student learning. Their efforts need to be schoolwide rather than classroom-centered. For many teachers, this represents a major shift: from taking responsibility for the learning of the students in one's own classroom to taking responsibility for all of the students in the school. As teachers participate in communities of learning, the cooperative and collaborative work facilitates teachers' professional growth and changes the nature of teaching and learning in the school. However, in the short term, teachers must have a strong sense of self-efficacy, of their own ability to help students learn, if they are to be able to risk the changes that a schoolwide approach may entail. The culture of a community of learning supports teachers' continuous improvement and facilitates behaviors that would be impossibly risky in schools organized in traditional ways.

The Students

Students are crucial participants in communities of learning. One of their major roles is to act as effective communication links between the school and their families. Beyond enabling the more traditional communication, by taking school memos and reports home to their parents, students discuss at home what they are learning at school and participate in parent/teacher interviews. In traditional schools, students are rarely consulted about any aspect of the learning program. In a community of learning, students are encouraged within the limits of their developmental levels to express their views about the content and process of their education, and their views are taken seriously by the other members of the community of learning. Within classrooms and across the school as well, students are asked to talk and write about things to accomplish, things to change, and things that they would like others to support them in doing.

The Parents

Parents also are critical members of the community of learning. However, unless appropriate programs for involvement are developed, parental interaction with schools tends to be less frequent and more negative in less affluent communities than in more affluent ones, and it tends to decline at the higher grade levels. Parental involvement can encompass many aspects of home, school, and community activities: parenting, communicating, volunteering, learning at home, decision making, and collaborating with the community (Epstein 1995). Not all parents will contribute in the same ways to the community of learning, but the community recognizes that each type of involvement is important and that none is more important than the other. Each type of involvement leads to different outcomes and benefits for the adults as well as the students in the community.

The Library Media Specialists

The expertise of library media specialists in information literacy, in collaboration, and in program design and implementation can provide a valuable contribution to the creation of a community of learning. For example, library media specialists may begin their work in a school by analyzing the different philosophical bases or "platforms" of teachers, because those differences complicate the task of collaboration. They often initiate an explicit sharing and examination of these differing platforms. With that knowledge and with experience in collaboration, library media specialists work with teachers not only to develop learning activities for students, but also to bring about some changes in traditional organization and thinking about teaching and learning, in order to develop schoolwide approaches that lead to a community of learning.

LIBRARY MEDIA SPECIALISTS AND THE DEVELOPMENT OF THE COMMUNITY OF LEARNING

What can library media specialists do to develop, support, and maintain communities of learning? The size and complexity of the work is daunting—even more so if collaboration and connections with the outside community are new to the school—and it takes time and effort to learn to go about this work.

Working with Principals

Library media specialists are very aware that the principal has a key role in the development of an effective program of learning. From the research in school library media program implementation, library media specialists know that principals develop their understandings of information literacy programs through their interactions with library media specialists. Successful library media specialists are careful to develop their principals' understanding of the program and of the specific ways in which their principals can offer support to the program and to them (Oberg 1996).

Library media specialists know that they need to be direct in their communication with their principals and active in gaining their principals' support. Library media specialists who understand the culture of their school are able to engage in conversation with their principal; by engaging in such interaction, they work with the principal to initiate some changes in the school culture and help create a stronger culture of change. Knowledge and experience of the educational change process can be utilized in helping principals to appreciate the benefits of working to build communities of learning.

Working with Teachers

From research and practice in the school library media field, library media specialists know that teachers who have experience working with library media specialists are more positive about collaborative work. These teachers say that library media specialists should be more invitational and more active in showing the benefits of collaboration and in getting others involved in collaboration (Sweeney 1996). Again, library media specialists can use this knowledge in helping teachers to see the benefits of working to develop consistent schoolwide approaches to learning.

Library media specialists also know that a new practice may represent a smaller change in one school than in another. Take, for example, beginning to implement a research model, such as The Big6™ or Focus on Research, that is based on a constructivist view of learning. When library research projects are routinely carried out using a constructivist and collaborative approach, using a model of the research process may be seen simply as an improvement of practice. When lecture and textbook are the regular teaching strategies used by teachers in classrooms, working to use a model of the research process may represent challenges to traditions such as teacher autonomy and the classroom teacher's control of the learning environment.

Similarly, efforts to design meaningful learning projects that involve students in authentic, difficult, and current real-world problems will be met with more support by some teachers than others. Even in effective schools that are working to build communities of learning, teachers are not all at the same stage in their thinking about teaching and learning. Library media specialists must consider the needs of the individual teachers in the school and, informally but systematically, discuss with the teachers how they feel about these approaches to student learning and how they might use these approaches in their teaching.

School library media specialists, in their "insider/outsider" role, have much to bring to instructional planning, including improved quality of resources, enhanced cooperation and communication within and among teaching teams, and increased focus of instruction on learners' needs (Van Deusen 1996).

Working with Students

The key element in successful learning environments is student engagement. The factors that have been identified in research related to student engagement in elementary schools include: challenging, interesting work; higher-order inquiry; a learning-centered environment; focused curriculum; and maximum learning-related communication between teachers and students and among students (Mortimore, Sammons, Stoll, Lewis and Ecob 1988). Similar factors have been identified in the research related to student retention and dropout in high schools. Schools that have been successful in keeping students, including low-achieving students, in school provide programs characterized by relevance, affiliation, support, expectation, and influence (Firestone and Rosenblum 1988).

Factors identified from the research on effective schools include descriptors of "best practice" in information literacy programs. In working with students, library media specialists need to use strategies that lead to increased student interest in learning and to higher levels of student achievement. In exemplary information literacy programs, students work on learning activities that extend and deepen their knowledge of curriculum topics. Curriculum topic areas are related to the students' interests and to the world outside of school. The specific topics for investigation are selected by students from the ideas and questions that have emerged from their studies of curriculum topics. In developing focuses for their investigations, the students talk to their families and to others outside the school, as well as to their classmates and teachers.

Throughout their investigations, students reflect on the information they have found and their changing understanding of their topic and the learning process. They are challenged to create new knowledge, to bring a personal perspective to their learning, and to share their learning with an authentic audience. They assess their learning: about their topic, about the learning process, and about themselves as learners. They are encouraged to see the connections between their investigations and the investigations that go on in the wider world of work and community. Their teachers discuss the students' assessments with them and use those discussions to develop future teaching and learning activities.

Working with Parents

Parents can play a vital partnership role with the school, but the school must be careful to use respectful and varied approaches to parental involvement. Library media specialists can begin with a reflective look at the school's programs of literacy, including information literacy, from the perspective of students and their families. Library media specialists need to acknowledge the existence of information literacy forms and values beyond schools and libraries, and they need to respect these forms and values (Wiegand 1998). Library media specialists and other educators need to know that "educational practices are not the only literacy practices; rather they are a particular set of practices which may complement and enhance the practices of home and community, but which are also capable of violating and devaluing them" (Barton and Hamilton 1998, 282). For example, on the one hand, reading promotion programs developed by library media specialists do not always take into account that many working-class parents value reading for information more highly than reading for pleasure. On the other hand, library media specialists may not realize how important the library is to children as a place where their choices about what to read and how to use space are allowed (Dressman 1997).

If we consciously learn about and consider parents' (and children's) perspectives on learning, we can build those perspectives into our school programs. We can use that knowledge as a basis for discussion and investigation of learning issues with students and their parents. Numerous studies have shown that parents want more communication with and involvement in the schools, but few schools involve parents in their children's learning in a systematic and focused way. Although *teachers* say they want more contact, many believe that parents are unavailable or uninterested; although *parents* say they want more contact, many find that teachers are unwilling to give them specific direction so they can help their children at home. Parents are often unsure how to improve the situation and schools sometimes feel that what efforts they make in this direction are or will be met with hostility or indifference. Library media specialists, using the experience gained from their "insider-outsider" position within schools, can work as advocates for greater understanding of parents' perspectives on learning.

Working with the Community

Library media specialists are accustomed to working with many individuals outside the school who are potential members of a community of learning. They have special relationships with other librarians and information providers as advocates for intellectual freedom and the right of everyone, including children, to have access to information. Through their relationships with the "business of information" through vendors and publishers, they are uniquely placed to act as intermediaries between the producers of information and the users of information. Library media specialists also are aware that support from district and state or provincial-level leaders is important for the development and maintenance of learning programs.

The interest of library media specialists in designing meaningful learning activities for students also draws them to work with others outside the school. They understand that students need to be able to see the relevance of the work they do in school to their lives outside of school. They encourage teachers to develop learning activities that involve students in addressing concepts, problems, or issues that they will encounter in life beyond the classroom and that engage students in sharing their new knowledge with an audience beyond the teacher, the classroom, and the school building.

FROM STUDENT LEARNING IN AN INFORMATION AGE TO COMMUNITIES OF LEARNING IN AN INFORMATION AGE

Whole-School Approach

The work of building communities of learning requires time, hard work, and the challenging task of reconceptualizing and redefining ways in which schools and society think about teaching and learning. Individual schools will begin this work in different ways, but there are examples that schools can follow in this endeavor. For example, Epstein (1995), in her work on school/home/community partnerships, suggested an action-team approach that could be readily adapted for building a community of learning. The action team is made up of classroom teachers, an administrator, students, parents, members of the school's support staff, members of the school's specialist staff, and members of the community at large. The action team takes responsibility for assessing current practices, for identifying options for action, for implementing selected activities, for evaluating progress and recommending next steps, and for continuing to improve and coordinate the action plan. The process of learning and working together develops the underlying pattern for successful communities of learning—educators understand the families of their students, families understand their children's schools, and communities understand and assist the schools, families, and students.

Implications for the Library Media Program

The shift in focus from student learning to communities of learning has implications for the library and for the library media specialist. The library that serves a community of learning has a clientele broader than teachers and students; it also serves parents, administrators, and community members. Members of the community of learning will struggle to improve instructional practices, to learn how to work together, and to challenge their beliefs about teaching and learning. They will need access to a range of information resources broader than that needed just to support the school curriculum. In addition, as more real-life learning and more student-initiated learning enter the school curriculum (see, for example, Bush 1998), the students and the educators who facilitate their learning will also need more diverse information and information sources.

Library media specialists working as members of communities of learning will spend more time out of the library working with others in and beyond the school. They will spend more time engaged in defining learning programs as well as in supporting learning programs. They will work with students and with other members of the community of learning as teachers, coaches, and facilitators. They must reach out to participate within the wide network of information providers in our society to assist learners to access the information they need.

Library media specialists also have critical roles to play as supporters of change and growth within communities of learning. They have experienced in their own field the transformation of the definition of exemplary practice, and they understand the complexity of implementing a new program vision. They understand the need for careful analysis of present practice and the need to plan the implementation process carefully, with conscious attention to the school's previous implementation history. Without this analysis and planning, library media specialists know that initial efforts can flounder, even after an ambitious and enthusiastic start, and that this may mean a retreat from change efforts and a return to traditional practices. They know that the implementation process must be guided by a recognition of the critical importance of the principal, teachers, students, and parents in the change process and a sensitivity to where individuals and groups are in relation to the new vision. The library media specialist has much to contribute to ensuring that the implementation process for a new vision of teaching and learning establishes a culture within the school that facilitates continuing change and enhances continuous improvement.

Taking the time to develop a thorough understanding of the learning community within which changes are to be implemented has great potential benefit over time for all participants. Thinking carefully about the nature of the changes that collaborative work entails; about the culture of the school; and about the collaborative roles of the principal, teachers, students, parents, and other members of the community will help library media specialists contribute to the building of a community of learning. By encouraging and supporting collaborative work, library media specialists will participate in building their school's capacity for change. Caring adults work together in a community of learning to create the best possible learning environment for students—but also for themselves as learners and for the teachers, principals, parents, and others with whom they work.

REFERENCES

Akin, Lynn. 1998. "Information Overload and Children: A Survey of Texas Elementary School Students." *SLMQ Online*. Available at <http://www.ala.org/aasl/SLMQ/overload.html>.

Barton, David, and Mary Hamilton. 1998. *Local Literacies: Reading and Writing in One Community*. New York: Routledge.

Bush, Gail. 1998. "Be True to Your School: Real-Life Learning through the Library Media Center." *Knowledge Quest* 26, no. 3: 28–31.

Dressman, Mark. 1997. *Literacy in the Library: Negotiating the Spaces Between Order and Desire*. Westport, Conn.: Bergin & Garvey.

Epstein, Joyce. 1995. "School/Family/Community Partnerships: Caring for the Children We Share." *Phi Delta Kappan* 76, no. 9: 701–12.

Firestone, William A., and Sheila Rosenblum. 1988. "Building Commitment in Urban High Schools." *Educational Evaluation and Policy Analysis* 10, no. 4: 285–99.

Fullan, Michael. 1991. *The New Meaning of Educational Change*. 2d ed. New York: Teachers College Press.

———. 1993. *Change Forces: Probing the Depths of Educational Reform*. London: Falmer.

Graves, Liana Nan. 1992. "Cooperative Learning Communities: Context for a New Vision of Education and Society." *Journal of Education* 174, no. 2: 57–79.

Hancock, Vicki. 1997. "Creating the Information Age School." *Educational Leadership* 55, no. 3: 60–63.

Kuhlthau, Carol C. 1990. "Bringing Up an Information Literate Generation: Dynamic Roles for School and Public Libraries." In *Information Literacy: Learning How to Learn 6–12*. Proceedings of the 28th Annual Symposium of the Graduate Alumni and Faculty of the Rutgers School of Communication, Information and Library Studies, 6 April.

Merrifield, Juliet, Mary Beth Bingman, David Hemphill, and Kathleen P. Bennett de Marrais. 1997. *Life at the Margins: Literacy, Language, and Technology in Everyday Life*. New York: Teachers College Press.

Mortimore, P., P. Sammons, L. Stoll, D. Lewis, and R. Ecob. 1988. *School Matters: The Junior Years*. Somerset, UK: Open Books.

Oberg, D. 1991. "The School Library Program and the Culture of the School." *Emergency Librarian* 18, no. 1: 9–16.

———. 1996. "Principal Support: What Does It Mean to Teacher-Librarians?" In *Sustaining the Vision: A Collection of Articles and Papers on Research in School Librarianship*, ed. L. A. Clyde, 221–30. Castle Rock, Colo.: Hi Willow Research & Publishing.

Sergiovanni, Thomas J. 1994. *Building Community in Schools*. San Francisco: Jossey-Bass.

Sweeney, Lorine. 1996. "Collegial Experiences: Teachers and Teacher-Librarians Working Together." *Teacher-Librarian Today* 2, no. 1: 23–27.

Van Deusen, Jean Donham. 1996. "The School Library Media Specialist as a Member of the Teaching Team: 'Insider' and 'Outsider.'" *Journal of Curriculum & Supervision* 11, no. 3: 229–48.

Wiegand, Wayne. 1998. "Mom and Me: A Difference in Information Values." *American Libraries* 29, no. 7: 56–58.

Part VI
Connecting to Research

13

Student Learning: Linking Research and Practice

A. James Jones and Carrie Gardner

INTRODUCTION

Schools everywhere are trying to reinvent themselves with an increasing emphasis on students' learning to high standards. This process has been aided by the rapid evolution of technology and online information services (i.e., the Internet). Schools and school library media centers now may have low-cost access to resources once available only at academic or large public libraries. New technologies commonly now reach beyond the walls of the school library media center into classrooms and homes of students and staff. Students can and do interact with information in ways and places that were not possible only a few years ago. Technology has provoked a growing change from passive to active learning.

This age of information has brought with it challenges to the industrial-age model of education. Educators are shifting their focus to higher standards for student learning. Practicing teachers and administrators, however, often

Table 13.1. Learning Environment Comparison

Traditional Learning Environment	New Learning Environment
Teacher instruction ⟶	Student-centered learning
Instruction (lecture) ⟶	Multimedia approaches
Information delivery ⟶	Information exchange
Passive learning ⟶	Engaged/Inquiry-based learning
Isolated work ⟶	Collaborative work

misunderstand the major implication of this move to standards: a difference in the quality of learning we expect from our students. Traditional learning environments evolve as we set higher expectations and take advantage of the continuously increasing number of learning resources. Some of the changes and shifts are shown in Table 13.1. Today's school library media specialist must understand these changes, advocate the importance of high standards for student learning, and purchase resources that reinforce the shifting paradigm.

FOCUS ON LEARNING

In recent years, an increasing consensus on learning and information/technology literacy has emerged from research. First, a consistent theme that has developed is a strong reaction against traditional models of learning. Teacher-centered instruction is changing to student-centered learning; isolated work to collaborative work; information delivery to information exchange; and passive learning to active/exploratory/inquiry-based learning. Second, a very strong consensus is forming from research on the importance of engaged, meaningful learning and collaboration involving challenging, authentic tasks. This contemporary learning theory, promoted by cognitive psychologists, defines learning as active building of knowledge through interaction with information and experiences. Authentic learning experiences demand that students interact with and use information from varied sources to solve problems and construct new knowledge. Third, recent research on learning is influencing, and being influenced by, our understanding of technology and our abilities to use information as a strategic resource (Jones et al. 1994, 7).

Although quality learning can take many forms, the learning theory that this research describes has been labeled constructivism. In the constructivist approach, the learner "constructs" his or her own meaning through active engagement with information and real-world experiences. A constructivist classroom/library model as described in educational literature would have students working with and organizing information, exploring new information resources, participating in learning activities, and monitoring their own progress. Teachers would collaboratively help the students focus on depth of understanding, and would assume a supportive, reflective, or provocative role while students construct meaning for themselves and engage in critical thinking and problem solving (Iran-Nejad 1995, 18). Constructivist theory and practice provide significant opportunities for the school library media specialist to collaborate with faculty and administration and, as a result, serve as a leader to promote this practice.

The quality of the school library media program is directly linked to the overall quality of the education offered at the school. School libraries must be a part of and not separate from the total school's evolution toward students' learning to high standards. Therefore, to be a collaborative part of the overall quality education of the school, the library media specialist needs to understand, collaboratively promote, and have resources available to support student learning. The latest national guidelines document for school library media programs, *Information Power: Building Partnerships for Learning,* clearly identifies the aspect of learning and teaching as one of the three key areas on which library media specialists should focus their efforts (AASL and AECT 1998).

AASL Task Force on Learning Through the Library

Much of what is presented in this chapter is based on the work of the American Association of School Librarians' Learning Through the Library Task Force. This two-year initiative was established in 1996 to promote the important role of school library media specialists as partners in student learning. The AASL Learning Through the Library Task Force was charged with identifying and disseminating information on successful practices and quality research about school library media programs that focus on improving student learning and achievement. The references in this chapter identify a broad range of resources to help professionals understand learning theory and practice.

Organization of Chapter

The annotated bibliography presented in this chapter is organized around a learning cycle containing three simple concepts that facilitate student learning (see figure 13.1).

- Standards: How content and performance standards drive the instructional process.
- Instructional Strategies: How instruction is delivered and learning should occur.
- Assessment: How achievement of content and performance standards is measured.

Resources cited in this chapter are anchored in vision, philosophy, and practices as described in *Information Power:*

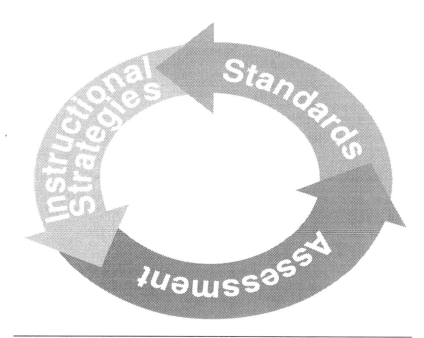

Figure 13.1. Learning cycle: high standards

Building Partnerships for Learning (AASL and AECT 1998). The chapter is divided into five main sections that provide both print and, in many cases, electronic resources:

> Section 1: Understanding students and learning in an electronic age
>
> Section 2: Supporting standards, especially literacy
>
> Section 3: Building instructional strategies—leadership and collaboration
>
> Section 4: Assessing student learning
>
> Section 5: Developing the school library media program for an electronic age.

The amount of educational literature available on these topics can be overwhelming. These resources have been selected as core references for a professional collection to build understanding within the local learning community and support student learning through the library.

SECTION 1: STUDENTS AND LEARNING IN AN ELECTRONIC AGE

Today's students live and learn in a world that has been radically altered by the rapid increase of information in a variety of forms. The information explosion is creating a generation of children surrounded by technologies that provide countless opportunities for students to learn and play. These technologies and online resources have dramatically altered the information-seeking and processing skills students need to complete their studies. Reports from major employers discuss the technology and information-processing skills employees need now and in the future to be successful on the job—in particular, the ability to synthesize a large amount of information into a manageable quantity to meet a specific information need. Without a doubt, students must be able to navigate in the electronic information age in order to live productive lives in the twenty-first century.

Information Power (AASL and AECT 1998) stated that students need to become full members of the *learning community*, which is defined as the global web of individuals and organizations who are interconnected in a lifelong quest to understand and meet constantly changing needs.

The Children We Serve

Benson, Peter L., and Carl D. Glickman. *All Kids Are Our Kids: What Communities Must Do to Raise Caring and Responsible Children and Adolescents.* **San Francisco: Jossey-Bass, 1997.**

Benson prescribes methods by which we can give serious attention to the social strife of our nation's children, including teen-committed homicides; alcohol, tobacco, and drug use; school dropout; pregnancy and sexual promiscuity; and poverty. The author details powerful ways to address the needs of our youth by emphasizing human developmental assets and imperatives, language, and culture. He also examines the need for unification of communities around youths, presenting his perspective and interpretation of what it means when we say, "It takes a village to raise a child."

Tapscott, Don. *Growing Up Digital.* **New York: McGraw-Hill, 1997.**

This book highlights the advancement from the industrial to the information age, reviewing how computers have become an integral part of our society and how child development greatly hinges on the use of computers and technology. Tapscott presents chapters on the role technology will inevitably play in children's education, work, and play. One section presents a view of the current educational crisis and the role of technology and access to information.

Technology and Information—Emerging Trends

Negroponte, Nicholas. *Being Digital.* **New York: Vintage Books, 1995.**

Being Digital discusses the implications of moving further into the information age and, in particular, the digital age. The author helps the reader comprehend the technological changes that our society and the world are experiencing. He discusses aspects of many technology changes and their impact on society and learning in the future. This book presents a framework for understanding how and how fast the information world will change in the very near future. It is an excellent resource to support the need for universal information access and explain the challenges that society will face with the massive amount of low-cost information available to everyone.

Postman, Neil. *The End of Education*. New York: Alfred A. Knopf, 1995.

This book focuses on the current crisis in education that has allowed pedagogical philosophy and practice to become far too mechanical. Postman begins with a synopsis of the bases and purposes for schooling in the earlier part of this century. He then turns to contemporary issues, such as economic utility, consumerism, technology, and separatism, that confront and hinder education today. He finishes with prescriptions for reinstilling true purpose in schools.

Postman, Neil. *Technopoly*. New York: Vintage Books, 1993.

This book's subtitle, "The Surrender of Culture to Technology," illustrates the nature of the book. The author reveals how, when, and why technology became dangerous. He further warns that society's highly positive view of technology's benefits can ultimately have disastrous implications on learning and society. He reviews major technology innovations and their impact on society. This book helps everyone put the perceived value of technology into a realistic context.

Shenk, David. *Data Smog*. San Francisco: HarperEdge, 1997.

The author addresses the growing problem of having too much information available and in demand, citing the law of diminishing returns as an indicator of this dilemma. The book is divided into four sections. The first section reviews the evolution of the availability of information from scarce to overloading, and the resultant effect on our existence and our ability to absorb so much data at once. Section 2 examines the social and political implications triggered by this "information revolution." The third part "outlines the new power dynamics that arise out of the information chaos" and examines why many see such development as being beneficial rather than detrimental. The final section prescribes methods in which we can fight the growing difficulties brought on by the information revolution. This work provides a different perspective on the impact information may have on our students, families, teachers, and staff. It cautions us all to respect information. His first law of data smog is something we all must ponder: Information, once rare and cherished like caviar, is now plentiful and taken for granted like potatoes.

SECTION 2: STANDARDS—CONTENT AND PERFORMANCE

Overview of Standards

One of the educational movements of this decade has been the development of national standards. Teachers and administrators in schools across the country are adopting these standards and establishing age-appropriate benchmarks by which student achievement can be measured.

AASL and the Association for Educational Communications and Technology (AECT) spent three years developing new standards for information literacy and guidelines for school library media programs. School library media specialists everywhere must view and use these standards and guidelines, not in isolation, but as part of the total educational program for the child. The library media specialist now has the opportunity and the responsibility to connect faculty and staff to resources dealing with all standards. This opportunity for advocacy should be a deliberate, sustained effort to gain understanding of and support for the standards movement and the role the school library program plays. The publication of library program standards integrates the school library media program into the content-standard movement.

Fogarty, Robin. *Best Practices for the Learner-Centered Classroom: A Collection of Articles.* **Palatine, Ill.: IRI/Skylight Publishing, 1995. (ERIC Document Reproduction Service No. ED 395 709.)**

Topics in the following major categories are covered:

1. Integrated curriculum—discusses holistic approaches that emphasize thematic instruction and collaborative teaching.
2. Thoughtful instruction—elaborates on critical thinking, problem solving, and multiple intelligences.
3. Active learning—focuses on interactive intervention techniques for both high school and college-level instruction.
4. Reflective transfer—describes metacognitive approaches to learning and strategies for teaching for transfer and assessing student transfer.
5. Authentic assessment—highlights learning logs and portfolios, as well as ways to use Howard Gardner's theory of multiple intelligences as a tool for assessment.

Kendall, John S., and Robert J. Marzano. *Content Knowledge: A Compendium of Standards and Benchmarks for K-12 Education.* **Aurora, Colo.: Mid-Continent Regional Educational Laboratory, 1996.**

This work presents national subject-area standards that have been developed and compiled by a wide range of organizations. This work is done in both print and CD-

ROM versions. It attempts to pull a variety of standards into one document and create a common format. Unless standards and benchmarks are presented in an equivalent and useable format, decisions regarding curriculum or assessment can become problematic. This work helps to provide that common format and can serve as a very helpful tool to schools trying to develop and/or agree upon standards. Using this work in tandem with *Information Power* may facilitate collaborative interaction between teacher and library media specialist.

Rothman, Robert. "How to Make the Link Between Standards, Assessment, and Real Student Achievement." In *New American Schools*. Arlington, Va.: NAS, 1997.

This article helps the reader understand content and performance standards and how they should be achieved. Rothman emphasizes the need for schools to develop a sound standards-and-assessment system. He first argues that solid standards and assessment greatly enhance student learning. He distinguishes between content and performance standards and explains how the two work together and how they can be used as learning tools. The author further argues for the implementation of districtwide standards and assessments for the purposes of enhancing student achievement and creating an atmosphere that is more conducive to both teaching and learning. Finally, the article presents four key challenges to and solutions for implementing effective standards-and-assessment systems, and details five positive examples from New American Schools, one of the five original national school-reform initiatives.

Schmoker, Mike. *Results: The Key to Continuous School Improvement*. Alexandria, Va.: ASCD, 1996.

The purpose of this book is to elaborate on the simple conditions that lead to results; to briefly discuss the theory behind the conditions; and to demonstrate, using examples from schools, how anyone in virtually any school setting can begin to replicate these conditions successfully. Results equate to students' learning to higher standards. A focus throughout is on principles and practices that are simple and supported by research. An emphasis on results is central to school improvements that undeniably affect the lives of children, what they learn, and what they potentially can learn. Concentrating on results does not negate the importance of processes. This work helps the teacher know that processes only exist to obtain results. Much of what is presented is derived from the total quality management (TQM) movement. The author reinforces the need to obtain quality data and to use the data for programmatic decisions.

Tucker, Marc S., and Judy B. Codding. *Standards for Our Schools*. San Francisco: Jossey-Bass, 1998.

The authors seek an alternative to today's mainstream mindset and practices that have indicated an abandonment of the public school. Their prescription for better schools is creating high standards, accurately measuring them, and ultimately reaching them. This book outlines how to achieve those ends. It combines theory and proven practice. The chapters highlight setting high standards, teaching to those standards, and the implications of such standards at all levels of K-12 education. This work may provide a conceptual framework that supports *Information Power: Building Partnerships for Learning* (1998), in that it discusses the standards movement and helps the reader understand that student learning to high standards is one of the most promising alternatives for improving today's schools.

Tyack, David B., and Larry Cuban. *Tinkering Toward Utopia: A Century of Public School Reform*. Cambridge, Mass.: Harvard University Press, 1995.

The authors explore some basic questions about the nature of educational reform. Why have Americans come to believe that schooling has regressed? Have educational reforms occurred in cycles, and if so, why? The authors suggest that reformers today need to focus on ways to help teachers improve instruction from the inside out, instead of decreeing change by remote control; and that reformers must keep in mind the democratic purposes that guide public education. This work will help set educational reform into a context that is easily understood by all.

Web Tips

Visit <http://www.mcrel.org> to find current articles dealing with developing a standards-driven curriculum. These online articles answer many questions raised by educators about standards-based learning—in particular, what standards are and how they can be used to improve learning.

Visit <http://putwest.boces.org/Standards.html> to find standards state by state. This site reinforces the concept that standards are conceptually nothing new, but have received new emphasis over the last decade through various state initiatives and passage of the Goals 2000: Educate America Act. This site also provides links to the sites of groups and organizations that deal with standards.

Visit <http://www.ncee.org> to learn more about designing learning environments to facilitate development of standards for our schools. Originally called NCEE's National Alliance for Restructuring Education (NARE), but renamed America's Choice, this site offers a comprehensive, research-based design for schools and districts committed to standards-based education.

Literacy Standards—Developing Capable Readers

The library media program must support and advocate reading across the curriculum as part of the fabric of every school. Literacy can and should be the cornerstone upon which to build collaboration with classroom teachers. School library media specialists must be the reading advocates for all. Technology certainly should not cause reading levels and student interest in reading to decrease, but instead should enhance student reading levels and student interest in reading. School library media specialists will not be supporting learning to high standards unless they ensure that students are literate as well as connected.

A common theme in the resources presented here is the need for adults, whether family or teachers, to model actions that show that reading is a valued activity. These actions may include reading aloud to children, having reading material in home and classroom, visiting libraries, and letting children see an adult read a variety of materials.

At School

Allen, Jobeth, Marilynn Cary, and Lisa Delgado. *Exploring Blue Highways: Literacy Reform, School Change, and the Creation of Learning Communities.* **New York: Teachers College Press, 1995.**

This book records critical aspects of a literacy project undertaken in two Georgia elementary schools where the action-research team worked primarily with disadvantaged children. It provides insight into how a group of teachers used literacy to establish learning standards, which helped promote school (learning) changes. Different chapters written by the various team members describe the intervention and assessment strategies used and the importance of home-school connections. The sense of an evolving learning community is captured in these reflective chapters.

Allington, R. L., and S. A. Walmsley, eds. *No Quick Fix: Rethinking Literacy Programs in America's Elementary Schools*. **New York: Teachers College Press, 1995.**

In response to growing demands for educational reform, this book addresses strategies to improve literacy instruction for all children, particularly those considered at-risk. The writers are critical of traditional approaches that have proven to be ineffective and present case studies of programs that have produced substantive improvements in student reading and writing performances. Contributors include Carol A. Lyons, Lesley Mandel Morrow, Jane A. Stallings, Robert J. Tierney, and Linda F. Winfield.

Krashen, Stephen D. *The Power of Reading: Insights from the Research*. **Englewood, Colo.: Libraries Unlimited, 1993.**

Supported by research, the author makes a case for Free Voluntary Reading (FVR) as a powerful means of promoting reading and writing literacy in youngsters. Krashen summarizes research on various aspects of FVR from the early 1900s to the present and suggests ways FVR may be implemented. His conclusions have critical implications for library media specialists as providers of print-rich environments. He also explores related issues, including the limits of FVR, when direct instruction is most effective, and the effects of television viewing on literacy. This is a definitive work that will help any library media specialist gain support for developing reading programs in the school.

Miller, M. L. "The Implications for Libraries of Research on the Reading of Children." *IFLA Journal* 19 (1993): 155–61.

This article provides a summary of surveys conducted in the United States. These surveys point to the importance of the adult role model in the family and of easy access to books in the home, school, and public library, as well as to the role of the school in encouraging reading promotion for leisure and instructional purposes. Miller also indicates that librarians need to define access much more "broadly and aggressively" to include all forms of information.

Ross, S. M., and L. J. Smith. "Restructuring Elementary Schools to Help At-Risk Students Become Effective Readers: Present Strategies and Future Directions of 'Success for All.'" *School Library Media Quarterly* 24 (1995): 34–41.

This article summarizes the progress of Success for All (SFA), a K–3 preventive and intensive intervention program for students at risk of failing to learn to read. Robert Slavin and his associates at Johns Hopkins University developed the comprehensive schoolwide program in 1987. Ross and Smith describe SFA's major features and discuss their implications for library media specialists and other members of the instructional team. A basic assumption is that education itself should be restructured to help students master reading strategies. The program supports active learning, curriculum integration, reading guidance, links between reading and higher-order thinking skills, and authentic assessment of student performance.

At Home

Briggs, N. M. "The Relationship Between Adult Participation in a Family Literacy Program and the Reading Attitudes, Behaviors and Home Environment of Adult and Child Family Members." Ph.D. diss., Indiana University of Pennsylvania, 1994. Abstract in *Dissertation Abstracts International* 55 (1995): 3740.

The investigator studied the relationship between parent participation in two different family literacy programs and any changes that occurred in the reading attitudes, behaviors, and home environment of adult and child family members. Both programs met weekly for fourteen sessions. One program focused on a series of workshops dealing with different types of literature; the other introduced mixed-genre literature built around themes. Pre- and post-test questionnaires were administered to parents, children, and teachers. No meaningful difference in attitudes or behaviors resulted from the genre-based workshops; however, participants were positively influenced by the theme-based workshops.

Ellis, M. G. "The Effects of a Parent-Child Reading Program on Reading Ability and Self-Perceptions of Reading Ability in Struggling Young Readers." Ph.D. diss., University of Maryland-College Park, 1995. Abstract in *Dissertation Abstracts International* 57 (1996): 1013.

This study investigated the effects of a twelve-week parent-and-child reading intervention on the reading ability and self-perceptions of reading ability in second- and third-grade students. The experimental group of twenty parents used such techniques as relaxed reading, paired reading, discussion questions, and praise and encouragement with their children. Students were administered a basic reading inventory and a self-concept-as-a-reader scale before and after the intervention period. Children in the program showed significantly greater improvement in reading as measured by the number of errors made on graded passages. However, they did not perform significantly better in terms of the number of errors made on graded word lists or graded comprehension questions, or in self-perceptions of reading ability.

Hale, C., and E. Windecker. *Influence of Parent-Child Interaction during Reading on Preschoolers' Cognitive Abilities.* **ERIC Document Reproduction Service No. ED 360 083, 1992.**

The authors report on a study of the relationship between parent behavior during reading situations and preschool children's cognitive development. They videotaped the interactions among children and administered a battery of tests that measured intelligence, creativity, perceived self-competence, and language skills. Results revealed significant relationships between the quantity of reading interactions and vocabulary development. Children's creativity was also related to quality of interactions, and their perceived self-competence was related to both the quantity and quality of reading interactions.

Morrow, L. M., D. H. Tracey, and C. M. Maxwell, eds. *A Survey of Family Literacy in the United States.* **Newark, Del.: International Reading Association, 1995.**

Intended as a resource guide for policy makers, teachers, and parents, this book traces the historical development of family literacy and provides an overview of the field in the United States. It discusses more than a hundred sources on the topic and identifies specific programs and initiatives. This work helps the library media specialist understand the literacy problem in the United States.

SECTION 3: INSTRUCTIONAL STRATEGIES

Three basic ideas—collaboration, leadership, and technology—underlie the vision of library media programs presented in *Information Power: Building Partnerships for Learning* (1998). These ideas present opportunities for library media specialists to expand their areas of influence to the classroom and schoolwide as they work on curriculum development for the benefit of the student body. The library media specialist can help focus the curriculum and develop an understanding among key faculty and staff of the need to convert the power of technology and information resources into improved learning opportunities. Very often this will require that the teachers and school library media specialists change their instructional strategies to a more student-focused method. Student learning must remain the central theme and the raison d'être of all actions the school library media specialist takes.

Leadership

American Association of School Librarians and Association for Educational Communications and Technology. *Information Power: Building Partnerships for Learning*. **Chicago: American Library Association, 1998.**
This work builds upon a long history of guidelines published by the American Library Association to foster improvement in school library media programs. This work presents AASL/AECT guidelines for developing

library media programs that focus on student achievement. It creates, for the first time, a nationally recognized set of standards for information skills and demonstrates clear linkages with standards in other curriculum areas. In addition, this work emphasizes the importance of the teaching and learning role of the library media specialist. Leadership, collaboration, and standards are three key terms that are the focus of this work. This is the authoritative work to define the role of the school library program and the library media specialist in relationship to student learning.

Cole, Robert W., ed. *Educating Everybody's Children: Diverse Teaching Strategies for Diverse Learners.* Alexandria, Va.: ASCD, 1995.

This book focuses on what research and practice say about improving achievement for all learners. It provides an overview of research and practice dealing with a high-performance model for student learning: content, expectations, and support. Topics covered in this work include setting standards and appropriate assessments, developing supporting instructional practices, and developing desired student outcomes. It also includes discussions on organization of the school and the learning environment. If America is to educate all of its children to higher standards, then Americans must be willing to embrace a major paradigm shift in our beliefs about how students learn. Currently, students are required to adapt to the prevalent teaching practices and instructional materials used in schools. This model produces many up-front deficits for children from diverse cultures. This book offers discussion of and some practical approaches to offering opportunities for schools and learning to include all cultures.

This book is particularly helpful for teachers seeking to develop an understanding of barriers to high standards for all students. Intervention strategies are described for a variety of core skills.

Loertscher, David V. *Reinvent Your School's Library in the Age of Technology: A Guide for Principals and Superintendents*. **San Jose, Calif.: Hi Willow Research & Publishing, 1998.**

The need to reconceptualize school libraries has never been greater. Technology has provided both opportunities and challenges. Questions have been raised as to the need for the school library when so much information is available on the Internet. This work is designed as a short course for administrators who want to maximize the impact of all information technologies (print to electronic). The book contains many forms and worksheets, which can be reproduced. It is divided into five sections: collaboration, reading, learning through technology, information literacy, and information infrastructure.

Maurer, Matthew M., and George Steven Davidson. *Leadership in Instructional Technology*. **Englewood Cliffs, N.J.: Prentice Hall, 1997.**

This book intends to aid teachers, administrators, school board members, and parents as they expand strategies for teaching and learning environments that are rich in technology. The first of this book's three sections deals with foundations in leadership and instructional technology, from building a leadership community to working with software. The second addresses instructional applications for various educational disciplines and media. The final portion discusses how to further the development of the leadership community once it is established, using a variety of strategies from conducting staff development to funding technology projects.

Picciano, Anthony G. *Educational Leadership and Planning for Technology.* **Englewood Cliffs, N.J.: Prentice Hall, 1997.**

As stated in the preface, the intent of this book is to "provide educators with both the theoretical and the practical considerations for planning and implementing technology, particularly computer applications, in schools." The author divides the book into four sections: basic concepts and foundations, applications, planning and implementation, and a look into the future. Questions, activities, and case studies pertaining to the subject matter accompany every chapter of this book.

Collaboration—Integrating the Curricula

Beane, James A. "Curriculum Integration and the Disciplines of Knowledge." *Phi Delta Kappan* **(1995): 616–22.**

The author provides insight into the theory and practice of curriculum integration. The discussion transcends subject-area and disciplinary identifications without abandoning them. The goal is integrative activities that use knowledge without regard for subject or disciplines. Twenty-six references are provided.

Erickson, H. Lynn. *Stirring the Head, Heart, and Soul: Redefining Curriculum and Instruction.* **Thousand Oaks, Calif.: Corwin Press, 1998. (ERIC Document Reproduction Services No. ED 379804, 1995.)**

This book examines the current trends in K-12 curriculum and instruction. It shows how the trends interrelate and provides a higher-order, comprehensive model for curriculum reform. The model is based on critical, content-based concepts. It provides a sound explanation of the change process and illustrates dilemmas encountered in school-based management and curricular planning. It also examines how societal trends shape the definition of student outcomes. The author provides a clear definition and demonstrates the value of an interdisciplinary, integrated curriculum and suggests opportunities for teachers to work on integrated curriculum design. The work contains a glossary and extensive bibliography of references.

Fogarty, Robin, ed. *Integrating the Curricula: A Collection.* **Palatine, Ill.: IRI/Skylight Publishing, 1993. (ERIC Document Reproduction Services No. ED 334677.)**

This work is designed to help readers understand the challenge of developing interdisciplinary curriculum. It seeks to use this interdisciplinary curriculum development as a tool for educational reform. The work is a collection of articles written by nationally recognized authorities on curriculum development. Articles include comparison of traditional versus the integrated curriculum, teacher development, and student perceptions of an integrated unit.

Miller, Kathleen A. *Curriculum: To Integrate or Not to Integrate.* **Ohio: Opinion Paper. (ERIC Document Reproduction Services No. ED 384591, 1995.)**

The author asserts that teachers who use cooperative, integrated methods will produce students more competent in solving problems, communicating, and working cooperatively with others. Benefits of integrated curriculum include: (1) reaching students with different learning styles; (2) developing critical and divergent thinking skills; and (3) improving teaching skills in areas such as reading in a subject context. This work reinforces the importance of resource-based learning and development of information literacy skills in students.

SECTION 4: ASSESSMENT

For too long, we have relied on a limited range of acceptable assessment measures for student learning. Primarily we have used paper-and-pencil-type tests and standardized tests that focus on content knowledge. No matter how valid the test scores are, they are often inadequate to provide the complete data necessary to assess the full range of student learning.

Another common assessment measure found in American schools is a report that requires the regurgitation of information found in print resources, with little or no synthesis or evaluation of the found information. When teaching methods are changed to focus on student-centered work, but require the production of only a written report, it defeats the purpose of teaching the students how to navigate through the online information world. With the widespread availability of software that can easily manipulate text, video clips, and full-color images, student assignments and their assessments must link process skills with information presentation. Truly assessing student learning requires a new look at assessment techniques, which may include problem-solving observations, portfolios, extended projects, logs and journals, multimedia presentations, and other products.

Assessment is the critical component in determining if student learning is occurring, and must be a cornerstone in developing any curriculum. Assessment should be ongoing, continuously measuring student performance throughout the learning cycle. The following works help create a paradigm for enhanced student learning.

General

Archbald, Doug A., and Fred M. Newmann. *Beyond Standardized Testing: Assessing Authentic Achievement in the Secondary School.* **Reston, Va.: NAASP, 1988.**

The authors present an analysis of authentic assessment and limitations of standardized testing. The first of four chapters consists of definition criteria for authentic achievement. Chapter 2 presents alternatives for assessing authentic achievement. The balance of the work deals with measuring schoolwide success using more than just exit outcomes and with implementing authentic assessment to make it an effective part of student evaluation. An appendix presents the uses and limitations of standardized tests.

Baron, Mark A., and Floyd Boschee. *Authentic Assessment: The Key to Unlocking Student Success.* **Lancaster, Pa.: Technomic Publishing, 1995.**

Authentic assessment means measuring student performance based on tasks that are relevant and used in real life. Authentic assessment methods include, but are not limited to, portfolios, reports, and reflective journals. The authors do not advocate doing away with all traditional tests, however. The book clearly explains that the key to unlocking students' success is finding superior ways to evaluate their ability to use academic skills. In short, are students really learning? This book combines theory and practice. It helps school administrators and teachers restructure curriculum to focus on learning.

Bird, L. B. *Assessment: Continuous Learning.* **ERIC Document Reproduction Service No. ED 390811, 1995.**

Part of a series of monographs on the art of teaching, this item focuses on the role of assessment. Specific chapters deal with the purpose of assessment in the learning cycle and describe specific tools for each stage of the "kid-watching" process. Portfolio development is one of the techniques discussed to help students engage in self-reflection.

Costa, Arthur L., and Bena Kallick, eds. *Assessment in the Learning Organization: Shifting the Paradigm.* **Alexandria, Va.: ASCD, 1995.**

This work is a collection of writings by outstanding educators who have taken up the challenge of improving assessment in schools across the country. They approach their task from a relatively new perspective, one informed by Peter Senge's concept of the "learning organization" and by the late W. Edwards Deming's concept of total quality management through continuous improvement of processes. This work can and does apply to student work as well as to assessments of the learning community in which the student works. In the chapter dealing with collaboration, leadership, and technology, *Information Power* (1998) refers to the importance of placing the student at the center of a learning community.

Educators in Connecticut's Pomperaug Regional School District 15. *A Teacher's Guide to Performance-Based Learning and Assessment.* **Alexandria, Va.: ASCD, 1996.**

The educators and administrators of this Connecticut school district convey how performance-based learning and assessment can be implemented at all grade levels and among all disciplines. The book defines perfor-mance-based learning and assessment, specifically addressing rubrics, benchmarks, and portfolios. The book also presents strategies to implement this form of assessment most effectively and describes the impact on student, teacher, parent, and school district.

Kuhlthau, Carol, ed. *Assessment and the School Library Media Center*. Englewood, Colo.: Libraries Unlimited, 1994.

This compilation of articles addresses the issue of assessment of library media services from different per-spectives. It begins with an article on the history of test-ing and assessment in American education and presents other pieces that discuss the development of measures of effectiveness, the expansion of evaluation to address the critical thinking curriculum, and defini-tions and descriptions of alternative and authentic assessment.

Lance, K. C., L. Welborn, and C. Hamilton-Pennell. *The Impact of School Library Media Centers on Academic Achievement*. Castle Rock, Colo.: Hi Willow Research & Publishing, 1997.

This publication details the research methodology as well as major findings of a Colorado public school study conducted in 1988–1989. In contrast to previous research, this investigation used schools rather than students as the unit of analysis and service output as well as resource input. The results underscored the importance of library media expenditures (staff and collections) in promoting academic achievement. They also verified the importance of the library media spe-cialist's instructional role.

Wiggins, Grant. *Educative Assessment: Designing Assessments to Inform and Improve Student Performance.* **San Francisco: Jossey-Bass, 1998.**

This is a defining work on linking student achievement and assessment techniques. The book presents a rationale for learning-centered assessment in our schools and an overview of the tools, techniques, and issues that educators should consider as they design and use assessments focused on learner needs. It argues strongly for a different kind of student assessment from the one most schools now use. It does not just explain theory, but clearly shows what a new assessment system would look like and how it should satisfy learner needs rather than simply offering efficiency and expediency. The work presents standards and criteria we can use to judge the value and effectiveness of this or any other assessment system. The simple principle that is consistent throughout the book is that assessment should be deliberately designed to improve and educate student performance, not merely to audit it as most school tests currently do. This work is the single most significant reference for any school seeking to develop quality assessments of student work.

Web Tips

Visit <http://www.ericae.net/main.htm> to find the ERIC Clearinghouse on Assessment and Evaluation. This site contains numerous links such as Assessment, Evaluation, Statistics, and Educational Research, included under the following subheadings: Test Locator; Assessment & Evaluation on the Internet; Search and explore all assessment & evaluation sites; ERIC & the American Educational Research Association; a variety of listservs; an online assessment library; recent ERIC briefing papers

(Digests); a How-to series; "Voluntary" National Tests; and a series of articles on assessment and testing found in nationally recognized newspapers and magazines.

Visit <http://cresst96.cse.ucla.edu/> to find information and research pertaining to measurement and evaluation. Available on this site are a key-word-searchable index for assessment topics, professional research reports, access to a broad database on assessment, sample assessments, discussion forums, and access to a variety of listservs dealing with assessment.

Portfolios

Portfolios are significant assessment tools. They are selective and purposeful collections of student work used to measure progress toward attainment of standards. They provide information to students, parents, teachers, and members of the community about what students have learned (content standards) and/or are able to do (performance standards). Portfolios provide for evaluation of the efficiency of learning goals, the effectiveness of learning strategies, and the clarity of knowledge presentation. Portfolio evaluation can provide feedback on several processes in the educational cycle simultaneously.

Johnson, Nancy Jean, and Leonie Marie Rose. *Portfolios: Clarifying, Constructing, and Enhancing.* Lancaster, Pa.: Technomic Publishing, 1997.

This book provides a comprehensive overview of portfolios, including a review of assessment, design of different types of portfolios, discussion of the role of teachers, and the merging of assessment and instruction. There is a special emphasis throughout the book on how to involve school staff in creating a climate for standards-based learning and instruction. The authors examine many complex topics dealing with assessment, including grading portfolios, managing staff resistance to change, and managing the "nuts and bolts" of portfolios.

SECTION 5: ROLE OF THE LIBRARY MEDIA PROGRAM IN THE ELECTRONIC AGE

The growth of technology has made a significant impact on the way we learn. Library media specialists must not only be proficient in the use of new technologies that support learning, they must be able to instruct teachers and students in how these technologies can be used to gather and interact with information.

In many school situations, library media specialists were the first to embrace technology and incorporate it in an educational program. Because of this, many school library media specialists find themselves in the position of being the "one in the building who can fix the technology" when it ceases to function. This has caused library media specialists to spend what should be student-contact time under desks and in front of servers diagnosing and fixing technology problems when, in fact, their time is better used teaching students and faculty how to locate, evaluate, and use the information the technology delivers.

Technology and Copyright

Bielefield, Arlene, and Lawrence Cheeseman. *Technology and Copyright Law.* **New York: Neal-Schuman, 1997.**

This work presents an in-depth look at copyright laws and their application. The book is divided into three sections. The first examines the history of copyright law, including the intent of the law, how the law was created, and its possible future. Section 2 prescribes the best ways for libraries and schools to adhere to copyright laws, through making smart decisions about fair use, archival exemptions, and licensing agreements. The final portion contains actual guidelines to copyright laws. Frequently asked questions appear, as do texts and reviews of copyright laws and agreements.

Library Media Program and the Curriculum—Making a Connection

Haycock, K. *What Works: Research About Teaching and Learning Through the School's Library Resource Center*. Vancouver, B.C.: Rockland Press, 1992.

This bibliographic volume highlights doctoral research from the 1960s through the early 1990s dealing with the instructional effectiveness of school library media centers. Research findings are clustered around topics, including information literacy, programs, staffing, learning resources, administration and management, and school and district leadership. The author cites his sources of information on doctoral dissertations.

McGregor, J. H. "Process or Product: Constructing or Reproducing Knowledge." *School Libraries Worldwide* 1 (1995): 28–40.

The article discusses how one-on-one interaction between library media specialists, teachers, and students can turn research projects into meaningful experiences that challenge students to construct knowledge with regard to information problem solving. These conversations enable the adult facilitators to discern gaps in student understanding. The author urges teachers and library media specialists to consider interventions that provide the "right balance of dialogue and noninterference" to help students strengthen their skills in one or more of the following "learning strands": content knowledge, life skills (e.g., reading comprehension), information searching and use, and production (e.g., creating a videotape).

Stripling, Barbara K. "Quality in School Library Media Programs: Focus on Learning." *Library Trends* **44 (1996): 631–56.**

The author surveys instruction in school library media centers from its early focus on source location and retrieval to its current emphasis on an information-search-process approach to information searching and use. She also comments on the developing roles of the school library media specialist as change agent and catalyst for curriculum reform. This article was selected as one of the ALA Library Instruction Round Table's Top Twenty Articles for 1996.

Vandergrift, K. E. *Power Teaching: A Primary Role of the School Library Media Specialist.* **Chicago: American Library Association, 1994.**

The author examines the expanded teaching role of the library media specialist and discusses the selection and uses of print and nonprint media resources in the context of instruction and learning. She integrates a summary of computer and telecommunications technologies and presents examples of instructional interventions and curricular units that emphasize active engagement of the cognitive and affective domains of student intelligence.

Yesner, Bernice L., and Hilda L. Jay. *Operating and Evaluating School Library Media Programs: A Handbook for Administrators and Librarians.* **New York: Neal-Schuman, 1998.**

The authors provide a very helpful document that covers a broad range of useful topics: program administration, collection management, instructional elements, technology, and dealing with staff. The focus is on student learning. The authors cover a topic by providing both positive and negative elements and possible solutions to practical problems that the practicing library media specialist may face. The work provides a variety of discussion bullets for the school administrator. Several sections in the book deal with program evaluation from various perspectives, such as those of other teachers, administrators, and students. This work can be a practical guide to facilitate collaboration between administrative staff and the library media specialist.

NEXT STEPS

Building a library media program for future needs of our schools and students requires continuous learning by administrators, teachers, and library media specialists. Once resources in this core collection have been fully utilized, educators may choose to access additional resources through the Learning Through the Library Web page on the AASL home page at <http://www.ala.org/aasl>. These resources, which include both print and electronic formats, will help the reader link to new research about learning and apply effective strategies in information literacy, assessment, standards, technology, literacy, and collaborative planning and teaching.

REFERENCES

American Association of School Librarians and Association for Educational Communications and Technology. 1998. *Information Power: Building Partnerships for Learning.* Chicago: American Library Association.

Iran-Nejad, Asghar. 1995. "Constructivism as Substitute for Memorization in Learning: Meaning Is Created by Learner." *Education* 116, no. 1: 16–31.

Jones, Beau Fly, et al. 1994. *Designing Learning and Technology for Educational Reform.* Oak Brook, Ill.: NCREL.

Index

AASL. *See* American
   Association of School
   Librarians
Ability, 16, 165, 302
Acceptable use policy (AUP),
   87, 93
Accountability, professional,
   178, 179
Accountable talk, 175–76
Accuracy, 86, 92
Achievement, 165, 221
Active learning, 29–30, 33, 35,
   163, 316, 328
   change to, 327
   information literacy for, 145
Activities, authentic, 30, 49–50,
   181, 328. *See also*
   Research projects/
   assignments
Administrators, 155–56, 159,
   269–70, 303, 310–11
   LMS work with, 313–14, 320
AECT. *See* Association for
   Educational
   Communications and
   Technology
"America Dreams" unit,
   199–201

American Association of School
   Librarians (AASL), 25, 56,
   67, 143
collaboration workshop,
   157–58
information literacy
   standards, 102, 111–12,
   164, 169, 211, 335
Learning Through the
   Library Task Force, 330
American Library Association
   Presidential Committee on
   Information Literacy, 55,
   59, 79–80
American Memory, 196, 197,
   198
Analysis, 15, 41, 43, 113. *See
   also* Information
Application, 41
Aptitude, 165
Assessment, 109–10, 206–27,
   235–36, 330. *See also*
   Evaluation
accomplishment recognition
   via, 221
authentic, 10, 265
formative, 212, 213
individualizing, 38

of information literacy
skills/abilities, 70
instruction improvement via,
220–21
opportunities for, 211
performance improvement
via, 212, 213–20
performance-based, 97, 207
of personality type, 39
program improvement via,
221–24
of public education, 139–40
purposes of, 211–212, 226
references re, 351–54
of research process, 109–11
summative, 212, 221
of teaching, 178, 179
Assessment tools, techniques,
and methods, 29, 164, 350
strategies, 212, 213, 220,
226–27
Assignments. *See* Research
projects/assignments
Association for Educational
Communications and
Technology (AECT), 25,
67
information literacy
standards, 102, 111–12,
164, 169, 211, 335
AUP. *See* Acceptable use policy
Authenticity, 207–8
Authority, 92, 156, 157

Bandura, Albert, 28
Barron, Daniel, 155
Behavior, changing, 28, 29
Behaviorist view of learning,
26–29, 33, 40, 57
Benchmarks, 97, 112, 168, 244
Bergen, Timothy, 155
Berkowitz, Robert, 60, 61, 103

Bias, 86, 87, 187, 202
Big6 Skills– Information
Problem-Solving
Approach to Library
and Information Skills
Instruction, 60–61, 103,
314
Bloom, Benjamin S., 41–42
Brainstorming, 168
Brainstorms and Blueprints, 58
Brand, Glenn A., 114
Brown, Ian, 98
Browsing, 98
Bruner, Jerome, 32, 33
Budgeting, 248–49. *See also*
Funding
Busywork, 49

CAI. *See* Computer-assisted
instruction
Calculating, 8
California School Library
Association, 66
Carvin, Andy, 117–18
Catalogs, 85, 94
CD-ROMs, 4, 86, 91–92
Center for Democracy and
Technology, 87
Center on Organization and
Restructuring in Schools,
148
Change
accommodating technology
use, 95
commitment to, 12–13, 111
implementing, 13, 151
mechanisms for, 250–51
need for, 155
resistance to, 75, 149–50,
157
size of, 314–15
speed of, 272

time needed for, 307
vision for, 270, 271, 273
Charting, 18, 19, 222, 224
Charts, 18, 92
Checklists, 218–20
Children. *See* Students
Choosing, 17–18, 19
Citizenship, preparation
    for, 8, 300
Coaching, 7, 46–47, 173
    by LMS, 174, 320
Cognitive development, 30–31,
    188–89
Cognitive growth, 32
Cognitive psychology, 25, 29, 34,
    328–29
Cognitive structure, 32
Cognitive style, 38
Collaboration, 26, 133–34, 155,
    159, 328
    barriers to, 145–52, 159
    in collection development,
        236, 238, 240–41,
        245–47
    for community of learning,
        304, 305–6, 310–19
    constructivist view of, 329
    definitions, 134–36
    environment for, 155–57
    implementing, 151–52, 154,
        157–58
    improving learning via,
        142–45, 156–57, 182
    for inquiry learning, 11, 12
    interpersonal relations in,
        153–54, 159
    library media program and,
        139–41
    LMS role in, 136, 137–38
    ongoing, 97
    participation in, 158
    in planning, 264

references re, 348–50
    by students, 16, 19, 107
    teacher–LMS, 10, 11, 204,
        252
    in teaching, 264
    techniques for, 174
    time for, 147–49, 272
Collaborative access environ-
    ment, 240–50, 258
Collection (library), 232–33,
    237, 253–54. *See also*
    Library media center;
    Resources
    collaborative access environ-
        ment, 240–50, 257
    constructivist, 238–40
    traditional, 236–38, 264
Communities of learning, 30,
    300–306, 332
    action team, 319
    building, 301, 309–13
    LMS role in, 313–21
    obstacles to, 306–9
Community, 300, 301, 302
    of learners, 239, 241–42, 254
    LMS work with, 318–19
    school connections to, 302–3,
        305, 320
    technology and, 8
Completeness, 92
Composing, 18, 19
Comprehension, 41
Computer as Learning Partner
    project, 117
Computer-assisted instruction
    (CAI), 4
Computers, 84. *See also*
    Technology
Conditioning, 27–28
Conferencing, 218, 222
Consensus building, 133. *See
    also* Collaboration

Constructivism, 29–30, 233–34, 244, 329
learning models, 107
Constructivist view of learning, 26, 29–33, 34, 310, 314, 329
use in teaching, 57, 103, 118, 329
Consultation, 16
Content. *See* Subject content
Continuing, 17, 19
Convergent thinking, 43
Conversing, 16–17, 19. *See also* Talking
Cooperation, 134, 135. *See also* Collaboration
Cooperative learning, 30, 35–36, 49
Coordination, 135–36. *See also* Collaboration
Copyright, 356–57
Creative thinking, 43
Critical thinking, 42–43, 47, 329
Curiosity, 44, 183, 263
Currency, 92
Curriculum. *See also* Subject content
information access/use as part of, 26
information literacy integration with, 61, 67, 75–76, 186–87, 265
resource-based, 54
standards-driven, 339
student-designed, 54
Curriculum integration, 209–10, 348–50
Curriculum mapping, 244
Curriculum standards, 10

Data, 86, 95, 104. *See also* Information; Resources

Davis, Hilarie Bryce, 108
Decision making, 43, 56, 299
Design, 104
Dewey, John, 30, 33
Dialogue. *See* Talking
Difficulty level, 40
Discipline, 27
Discovery learning, 34–35, 57
Distance Education Clearinghouse, 90
Distance learning, 90
Distressing ignorance, 69–70
Divergent thinking, 43, 47
Documents, primary-source, 196–201
Donlan, Leni, 199
Drawings, 18
Dresang, Eliza T., 99

Education, 6, 10. *See also* Learning; Teaching
assessments of, 139–40
Educational psychology, 27
Effort-based learning, 165–68
Eisenberg, Michael B., 60, 102, 103
Electronic Frontier Foundation, 88
Electronic Privacy Information Center, 88
Ennis, Robert, 42
Epstein, Joyce, 319
Essential Skills for Information Literacy (WLMA), 64, 74
Ethical issues, 88, 257
Evaluation, 41–42, 43, 113. *See also* Assessment
of collection, 237
continuous, 97, 303–4
critical, 71, 104
forms for, 105
of Internet sources, 105–6

of products, 187
of project, 72–73
of research process, 105, 110
of teaching, 178, 179
Experts
student access to, 89, 118
support by, 40, 177
Exploration, 14–15, 17, 18, 101

Facts, 15. *See also* Data;
Information
distinguishing, 104, 187
Fair use, 88
Family, 301, 311. *See also*
Parents
Federal Family Educational
Rights and Privacy Act, 88
Ferenz, Kathleen, 199–201
Focus on Research, 314
Formulation, 14, 18
*From Library Skills to
Information Literacy*
(California), 66, 74
Funding, 12, 75, 140, 249
changes and, 150
use of, 243

Gardner, Howard, 37–38
Glynn, Shawn, 45
Grading, 165, 221, 300
Graphic organizers, 172, 210
Graphics, 98, 99
Graphs, 18
Griffiths, Jos,-Marie, 231, 245
Group work, 105, 168

Heisel, Odile, 87
Higher-order thinking, 42, 47,
142, 166, 207

ICONnect, 250–51
ILS. *See* Institute for Learning
Sciences

INFOhio DIALOGUE Model
for Information Literacy
(Ohio), 64–65, 69
Information. *See also* Data;
Resources
accessibility of, 4, 113
accessing, 46, 55, 56, 70, 71,
85
amount and nature of, 232
analyzing, 113
changing, 7, 105
customizing, 116
evaluating, 14, 55, 71–72, 87,
113, 210–11
extending, 16, 17, 19
filtering, 86, 116–17
formats, 88–94, 102, 113
gathering, 14
Internet organization of, 97
locating, 9, 14, 56, 70–71
managing, 7, 299, 300
meaningful use of, 6
need for, 69
non-linear, 98, 99
organizing, 6, 14, 71, 104
preselection of, 6–7
presentation of. See
Production/presentation
skills
processes, 208–9, 224–25
references re, 333–34
sources of, 8, 86, 92
using, 10, 11, 14, 55, 72, 171
Information literacy, xviii, 3, 14,
54–55
assessment and, 224, 226, 227
competence in, 11
definitions of, 6, 11, 15,
55–57, 67
developing, 101–2
documents re, 78–82
elements of, 102–3

information on Web re,
80–81
integrating into curriculum,
61, 67, 75–76, 186–87,
265
as learning foundation, 142
need for, 14, 208
of teachers, 114
research application to, 25
teaching, 141, 143–45
Information literacy skills, 25
integrating into classroom,
136
need for, 201, 264
scope and sequence for, 96,
111, 112
teaching, 203–4
tracking, 70, 187–88
use in research projects,
186–95
Information literacy skills
models, 54, 59–69, 73–76
common components of,
69–73, 74
comparison, 62–63
history, 57–59
use, 73–75
Information literacy standards,
67–69, 78, 143–44
AASL/AECT, 102, 111–12,
164, 169, 211, 335
Information overload, 7, 107,
116, 299
*Information Power: Building
Partnerships for Learning*,
25, 55, 74, 164, 330
on collaboration, 133, 138,
232
as framework, 75, 247, 264,
265, 345
information literacy standards, 67–69, 78

*Information Power: Guidelines
for School Library Media
Programs*, 59, 137–38
Information processing, 33
Information professionals,
231–32
Information skills, 11, 95, 332
integrating into curriculum,
155
integrating with technology
and content, 102
search process, 14–15
teaching, 104–5
*Information Skills for an
Information Society*, 58
"Information Skills Rating
Scale," 111
Initiation, 14
Innovation, 4, 8, 13. *See also*
Change
Inquiry approach, 8, 11–19
Inquiry(-based) learning, 34–35,
57, 106–11, 328. *See also*
Research
in library media center, 273
primary source documents
for, 198, 235
skills, 171–72, 186
teaching for, 111–16
Institute for Learning Sciences
(ILS), 101
Instructional design, 142–53
Instructional teams, 10, 19
Intellectual property, 88, 92
Intelligence, 38
academic, 233
learnable, 176
multiple, 37–38
socializing, 176
Interaction, 301, 303
with LMS, 110
student–others, 303

student–student, 35, 208
teacher–student, 208
International Society for
    Technology in Education,
    142
Internet, 85, 93–94, 242. *See also*
    World Wide Web
    competencies for, 104
    ethical issues re, 88, 257
    evaluating sources on, 105–6
    filtering access to, 87, 93
    managing, 116–17
    organization of information,
        97, 98
    purpose of use, 93
    safety and privacy on, 87–88,
        104
    school connection to, 4
    use in learning, 103
Interpretation, 6, 15
I-Search, 44–45
Isolation, 146, 147, 247, 306, 328

Johnson, Doug, 88, 102, 115
Journals and journaling, 18,
    44–45, 109, 220–21
Judging, 47

KIDLINK, 118
Kids Network, 117
KidsConnect, 118
Knowledge, 41, 42. *See also*
    Meaning; Understanding
    constructing, 37, 329
    depth of, 207
    prior, 5, 45
    as process, 233
Knowledge base, 242, 244
Kuhlthau, Carol, 58, 110

Language development and use,
    32, 33

Learner characteristics, 241–42,
    244
Learning
    active. See Active learning
    adults, 301
    architectures, 101
    authentic/meaningful, 37, 265
    brain-based, 36–37, 49
    context of, 242
    cooperative, 30, 35–36, 49
    by discovery, 34–35, 57, 101
    effort-based, 165–68
    emotions in, 36–37
    enabling, 233
    ensuring, 300
    by evaluation of project,
        72–73
    expectations re, 168, 176–77,
        261
    facilitating, 264
    focus on, 238
    future, 143
    as goal, 19
    goals of, 50
    how to learn, 7, 300
    improving, 303
    incidental, 101
    individual, 32
    inquiry approach to. See
        Inquiry approach
    kinds of, 28, 98
    library media program
        benefit to, 159
    lifelong, 14, 57, 207, 359
    mental models and, 45
    observational, 28
    parents' perspective on, 317
    philosophy of, 12–13
    prior, 187–88
    problem-based, 10
    problems, 19
    project-based, 83

by reflection, 101
resource-based, 25, 57, 140
responsibility for, 111
in school libraries, xvii
self-initiated, 303
simulation-based, 101
skills for, 15
social, 32, 234
social aspects of, 35
student-centered, 35, 204, 328
student-directed, 107–8
students' role in, 261
technology and. See Technology
time needed for, 17, 165, 169, 187
tools/techniques to promote, 46–48
Learning cycle, 330, 331
Learning environments, 164, 263, 300, 328
authentic, 10
changes in, 5–6
designing, 339–40
preference, 39
Learning models, 34–37, 107, 237, 328
Learning process, 11, 37–40, 208–9, 214
Learning styles, 5, 38–39
Learning theories, 26–33, 232–33, 329
Libraries, 9–10, 12, 20, 243. See also Library media center
need for, 7
role in instructional program, 13
stereotypes of, 137
Library advisory committee, 270
Library media center. See also Collection

access to, 170
collection-oriented, 57
connection to classroom, 261
evolution of, 140
as learning environment, 164
research application in, 33
resource-rich, 174
responsibilities of, 68
scheduling, 148
Library media program, 198
attitudes toward, 144
as change driver, 273
clientele, 320
collaboration as basis of, 138–41
communities of learning and, 320
design rubric, 265–68, 273, 275–90
designing, xvii, 260–61, 264–73
development process, 269–73
effort-based learning and, 166–68
flexibility in, 263
goals of, 137
guidelines for, 264–66
integration into curriculum, 264, 357–59
learning focus, 159, 264
proactive, 139
quality of, 329
role of, 25, 356
template for status assessment, 270, 291–96
Library media specialist (LMS)
assessment role, 70, 226
as change agent, 245, 246, 247, 271, 272–73, 320–21
as coach, 174, 320

collaborative access environment development, 244–50
in community of learning, 303, 312–19, 320–21
constructivist education role, 329–30
content taught, 182
as expert, 253
expertise, 10, 12, 197–98, 205, 247, 254
as facilitator, 320
former role, 94
as guide, 17, 108
as information consultant, 70
as information literacy expert, 58
information selection and management by, 203
as instructional consultant, 59, 140, 141, 152
as instructional partner, 136–38, 141, 152–53, 159, 163, 178, 204
instructional planning role, 315
as leader, 54, 75, 148, 152, 157, 159, 245–46, 248–49
as learner, 245, 246, 249–50, 359
learning theory application by, 25, 26, 48–51
library media program design by, xvii
as mentor, 163
as partner, 26
personal relationships, 269
professional development, 114
research project role, 186, 197–205

as resource guide, 231–32, 241, 245–47, 253
responsibility for student learning, 147
roles, 7, 8, 11–12, 20, 59, 232, 356
skills assessment and instruction by, 70
as standards advocate, 335–36, 340
as teacher, 50, 70, 113, 163–64, 257, 320
teacher support by, 203–4
technology use and, 96, 203
work with parents, 317–18
work with students, 315–16
Library of Congress, 196
Library skills, 11, 57, 58
Life skills, 207
Listening, 47
Literacy, definitions of, 7
LMS. See Library media specialist
Loertscher, David V., 134
Logic, 43
Logistical problems, 19

Macrorie, Ken, 44
Matrix, 222, 223, 224
McClelland, Kate, 99
McKenzie, Jamie, 95, 101–3, 107, 108, 111, 112, 115
Meaning, 6, 7. See also Understanding
constructing/making, 29, 33, 49, 224, 329
Media, 86
Media literacy, 89
Mental models, 45–46, 209
Mentoring, 97
Metacognition, 44–45, 47, 109
MidLink, 117

Mini-lessons, 107, 109, 167–68, 177, 211
MIT Media Laboratory Epistemology & Learning Group Projects, 118
"Model Academic Standards for Information and Technology Literacy," 111
Model Information Literacy Guidelines (Colorado), 65–66
Modeling, 28–29, 109
   accountable talk, 175
   coaching, 174
   by experts, 177
   information literacy skills, 105
   Internet searches, 93
   reading, 340
   resource use, 247
   technology use, 92
   thinking process, 177–78
Motivation, 39–40, 183, 301
   reward, 28, 29
Murphy, Elizabeth, 107

A Nation at Risk, 139
National Digital Library, 196
National Geographic Kids Network, 117, 118
National Library Power Initiative, 12, 156–57
Negroponte, Nicholas, 4, 5
Neuroscience, 36
Neuwirth, Christine, 99
New Standards Project, 164, 167
Newmann, Fred M., 207
Northwest Regional Educational Laboratory, 112

Observation, 27, 28, 106, 214

Opinion, 104
Oppenheimer, Todd, 5
Owston, Ronald, 83

Papert, Seymour, 4–5, 119
Pappas, Marjorie, 61
Paraphrasing, 16, 17, 19
Parents, 109, 305, 306, 308–9, 312, 317–18
Partnerships, 242–43, 245, 302–3, 319
Pathways to Knowledge– (Follett), 61, 64, 69
Paul, Richard, 42–43
Pavlov, 27
Perception, alteration of, 100
Performance, 213–17, 214
Piaget, Jean, 30–31, 33, 45
Pictures, 92
Pitts, Judy M., 58
Plagiarism, 88, 104, 114
Planning, 303
   collaboration in, 49, 50, 148
   teachers' ways of, 152–53
   time for, 97
Portfolios, 221, 355–56
Position Statement on Information Literacy, 56, 78–79
Power sharing, 247, 257
Practice, 100, 111
Presentation. *See* Production/ presentation skills
"Principles of Learning," 164
Printing, 92, 95
Privacy, 87–88, 146
Privacy Rights Clearinghouse, 88
Problem-based learning, 10
Problem solving, 43, 182, 208
   for learning, 30, 329
   models, 103–4, 107

skills, 56, 142
Process, awareness of, 209, 226, 234
Process approaches, 10
Production/presentation skills, 14, 175, 187, 189, 192–94, 350
Professional development, 114, 244. *See also* Staff development
Proficiency levels, 68, 164, 169, 265–66
Profit, 4
Progress Report on Information Literacy, 56
Projects, 101–2, 118. *See also* Research project/ assignments

Questioning, 47–48, 49, 103, 108
Questionnaires, 222, 223

RAND Microworlds, 117
Ray, Karen, 135
Reading, 8, 44, 99, 317, 340
    as foundation for learning, 262
    goals, 167
    references re, 340–48
    strategies, 15
Reasoning, 43
Recalling, 17, 19
Reflection, 109, 110, 168, 172, 269
    critical, 304
    time for, 201
Reflective thinking, 30
Reinforcement, 28
Relevance, 181, 183, 318
Research. *See also* Inquiry approach
    availability of, 331

bibliography, 332–59
    on education/learning, 25, 249–50, 314, 329
    implementing, 25, 140, 314
    meaningful, 103, 182, 224, 227, 315
    organizing, 104
    primary sources for, 196–98
    skills, 186. See also Inquiry(-based) learning
    by teachers, 97
Research Cycle (McKenzie), 107
Research guides/pathfinders, 187, 188, 189, 190–92
Research process, 13, 16–19, 58, 92, 107–11, 269
    choice of, 183, 186
    evaluating, 105, 110
    initiating, 69
    monitoring, 202
    planning guide for, 184–85
    topic lists, 186
Research projects/assignments, 13, 171–75, 224
    component importance, 194–95
    designing, 171, 181–95, 227, 315
    evaluating, 72–73
    initial, 108–9
    interactive, 118
    interdisciplinary/thematic, 201
    kinds of, 101–2
    planning, 214
    primary sources for, 198–201
    purposes, 182–83
Resnick, Lauren B., 164, 165
Resource-based learning, 25, 57, 140

Resources, 14–15. *See also* Data;
    Information
    access to, 10, 85–86, 187,
        197–98, 231, 247, 327
    authority and accuracy of, 86
    availability of, 5, 6
    balancing, 200
    for collaboration, 158
    comparing, 92
    competition for, 140
    cost of use, 94
    equipment needed to access,
        94
    formats, 70, 236, 237, 250
    for inquiry learning, 34, 35
    matching to learners, 244,
        245, 247–48, 254–55
    multiple, 264
    need for, 232, 320
    organization of, 104
    portability of, 94
    reviewed, 86–87
    scope/depth, 187
    selecting, 10, 255, 256
    types of, 232, 245
    use of, 10, 70
Restructuring. *See* School
    restructuring
Revision, 165, 168, 170, 172–73
Reward, 28, 29, 40
Rigor, academic, 170–75
Role playing, 109
Routman, Regie, 247
Rubrics, 108, 111
    as assessment tools, 212,
        213–17
    for library media program
        development, 265–68,
        275–90
    obtaining, 111
    sample, 215, 217
    for staff development, 115–16

for student technology use,
    97
use, 169, 214, 215

Scheduling, 91
    for collaboration/planning,
        147–49, 157
    flexible, 12, 148, 157
    practice time, 100
School library media
    specialists. *See* Library
    media specialist
School restructuring, 3, 9–11,
    19, 300, 304
    elements of, 155
    libraries, 12
Schools, 300, 301
    changes needed for
        technology use, 95–97
    connections with outside,
        302–3, 305, 312
    culture of, 156, 157, 263, 264,
        306–7
    external demands on, 309
    implementing inquiry
        learning, 111–16
    role, 301–2, 304
    traditional, 306
Scientific method, 29
Scriven, Michael, 43
Scrutiny, 15
Search Process Model, 58
Self-assessment, 211, 222, 226,
    235
Self-awareness, 43
Self, sense of, 8
Sensory preference, 39
Setzer, Valdemar W., 84
Skinner, B. F., 28
Software, 90–91
Sources, documenting, 104
Staff development, 97, 113–16,
    158

Standards, 327–28, 335–36
 analyzing, 265
 for educational technology,
  142
 effect on instruction, 330
 equal, 169
 information literacy. See
  Information literacy
  standards
 literacy, 340
 national, 26, 142, 143
 performance/accomplish-
  ment, 164, 165–66, 167
 practical application of, 68
 references, 336–39
 rubrics re, 169
 state, 25, 339
Standards-based education, 10
*Standards for School Library
 Programs*, 58
Stoll, Clifford, 5
Strategies
 for assessment, 212, 213, 220,
  226–27
 for change implementation,
  151
 for collaboration, 154
 cross-media use, 100
 for evaluation, 72–73
 for Internet searches, 106
 metacognitive, 44, 47
 observing, 114
 for reading, 15
 suggesting, 209
 for teaching. See Teaching
  strategies/techniques
 for understanding, 16
Stripling, Barbara K., 58
Student achievement, xvii
Student-centered learning, 35,
 204, 328
Student-directed learning, 107–8

Students, 261
 commitment to activity, 183
 engagement, 315–16
 information literacy abilities,
  16
 as knowledge producers, 173
 as participants, 142, 145, 305,
  306–8, 311–12
 references re, 332–33
Subject content, 102, 170
 accuracy of, 86
 competence in, 11
 in research projects, 182, 183,
  186
 technology's changes to, 119
Success, 176–77, 213
Summarizing, 16, 17, 19
Support/scaffolding
 by experts, 40, 177
 for information literacy skills,
  105
 for inquiry learning, 108, 111
 to reach standards, 166, 168,
  169–70, 173
Synthesis, 41

Talking, 32, 33
 accountable, 175–76
 to students, 47, 50–51
 substantive, 208, 224
 teacher–LMS, 244
Teacher
 as coach, 7, 46–47, 173
 in community of learning,
  311, 314–15
 constructivist role, 329
 as facilitator, 7, 57
 as guide, 17, 30, 34, 108
 interaction with parents,
  317–18
 resource decision-making by,
  243

role of, 233–34, 303
Teacher training, 114–16, 119,
150. *See also* Staff
development
Teaching. *See also* Education;
Learning
appropriate developmental
level for, 31
case-based, 101
changing, 7, 144–45, 149–51,
198
context of, 242
evaluating, 178, 179
improving, 220–21
individualizing, 38
information literacy, 141,
143–45
inquiry approach, 8, 11–19
for inquiry learning, 111–16
norms, 146–47
of process, 209
purpose of, 310
remedial, 70
research-based, 140–41
standards-based, 176
transmission approach, 9
using varied learning styles,
39
Teaching strategies/techniques,
25, 101, 233, 234, 330
inquiry, 111
references re, 345–47
Technical support, 97
Technology, 4, 8, 116
access to, 84–85, 119
changes to learning from, 3,
119, 327
cost, 119
as enhancement, 5
equipment needs, 94–95
integration with curriculum,
101, 251–52

learning to use, 84, 85, 90–91
LMS as serviceperson, 356
for production/presentation
of projects, 193–94
references re, 333–34
teacher knowledge of, 116
tools for working with,
116–17
tools of, 90–91
use in education/learning,
4–5, 83–84, 95–97,
117–18, 329
Telephones, 89
Templates, 108, 109
Tepe, Ann, 61
Testing, standardized, 27, 29, 33,
233. *See also* Assessment;
Evaluation
Textbooks, 6
Thinking, 59
analytical, 202
before using information, 72
creative, 43
critical, 42–43, 47, 329
higher-order, 42, 47, 142, 166,
207
improving, 42–43, 44
increasing sophistication in,
189
lower-order, 210
opportunities for, 262
out loud, 177–78
reflective, 30
style, 39
time needed for, 48
Thinking skills, 40–46, 49, 170,
171–72
order for, 41–42
Time, use of, 110
Transmission approach, 9
Trotter, Andrew, 88
Tucker, Marc, 164

Understanding. *See also*
    Knowledge; Meaning
    building on previous, 31, 32
    constructing, 7, 9, 10, 29, 57
    strategies for, 16

Valenza, Joyce Kasman, 109
Vygotsky, Lev, 31–32, 33, 45

Washington Library Media
    Association (WLMA), 58,
    64
Wehlage, Gary G., 207
Winer, Michael, 135
Wittrock, Merlin C., 146
WLMA. *See* Washington Library
    Media Association

Workplace, 8, 14
World Wide Web, 72, 83, 93. *See
    also* Internet
    library media access via, 203
    materials available on,
        196–98
    research references on,
        339–40, 354–55
Wright, Doug, 112
Writing, 8
    during research process, 18
    researching, 187
    tools for, 99–100

Zone of proximal development,
    31–32, 40, 44